Secrets In Naples

SYLVIA VALEVICIUS

DEDICATION

To Families

To those who are born into theirs, as well
as people who create their own.

May they all enjoy loving and caring for one another.

PRAISE
for
SYLVIA VALEVICIUS and
her PREVIOUS BOOKS

MEMOIR OF HOPE & RESILIENCE

"A Masterclass in Courage and Fortitude" – Amazon USA: Dr. Catana Tully

"A Tour de Force" - Amazon UK: Gerald Wiener

"LOVED IT!" – Amazon Germany: Chirasambwa.: "This is the best and most uplifting contemporary autobiography I have read this year, strongly recommended."

"A five-star book I read for five straight hours." Oakville Public Library: Joanne Panizza

From: **Judge, 27th Annual Writer's Digest Self-Published Book Awards**

"The author writes well and conveys the force of her own individuality. The narrative is gripping...the thoughts are intelligent. The pictures are wonderful, and the writer has talent."

Evaluation: 5 in four areas (outstanding); 4 in two areas

MONOLOGUES FOR YOUTH

"Great writing, fascinating adolescent stories – I could hear the confusion, the pain, the hope, as these teenagers told their stories... stunning work of fiction." 5 stars ~Vicki Addesso, Amazon, USA.

TO THE READER

The Story Behind the Story

Inspiration comes anytime from anywhere.

Some years back, as a newbie to town, I spotted a house facing the lake that proverbially stopped me in my tracks. I stared at it. Took a photo. Then, I mentally installed a fictitious family into this big yellow house.

I had no idea this house was already *famous*! Excited to write, I shared the picture with my librarian. She said: "It's Plum Johnson's house. She wrote a book about growing up there and won a Canadian award." When I closed my dropped jaw, I learned Plum's memoir was titled: *They Left Us Everything*.

Later, I met Plum when she came to town as a speaker for the Historical Society. I told her my fictitious family now lives in her former home. She delighted me with best wishes for my novel and signed her wonderful memoir. Gracious on her part, it was a lovely experience for me.

Now- other coincidences: I made my preferred choices and months later, names, connections suddenly popped up in the news, TV shows, etc. Deep into my plot, I chose to keep them, but pride in *originality* plummeted. Yet, my consolation stemmed from the *Book of Ecclesiastes*: "there is nothing new under the sun." My wobbly pride pushed aside, I continued my work mollified. Thus, both inspiration and coincidence organically connected and allowed me peace and joy in my writing project.

I *may* write the next version of this novel. However, allow me to *inspire* you, the reader, to write and continue the story as you feel it...just for fun!

Cheers,
Sylvia

PROLOGUE

Simon's white shirttails barely cover his exposed lap.

Spinning, his head lolls back onto the sofa.

Guilt grows wild in his queasy gut.

His cheeks burn more from shame than friction.

He needs to flee, yet his body is heavy, immobile.

Why can't he get up?

He did not expect this reaction, action, reaction.

Didn't see it coming.

Disloyal to his dead wife, too.

A sacred vow, broken.

Yet another secret.

Sucker punched. Maybe even drugged.

By a woman...

PART ONE

Naples, Ontario, 2015

Chapter 1

"It's not your groundskeeper I'm concerned with…"

WHAT THE DEVIL were his parents *thinking* to stick him with such a monogram? S.I.N.

It didn't bother *Simon Ignatius Nesbitt* at all. Not a bit.

Some folks achieve greatness, others struggle for a livelihood. Some regular people survive day-to-day, happy, sad. They argue with their families and do their best at jobs for which they're unsuited, but what the hell – that's life.

Simon believed himself to be a good guy, and he owned his flaws. How Simon differed from the crowd was due to his kindness. He understood life held struggles. In school he studied Joseph Conrad's novel, *Heart of Darkness,* which exposed an abusive world of evil - power and corruption run wild. Simon detested cruelty, deemed such malice should never touch his soul regardless of his weird initials: S.I.N.

In fact, Simon laughed when people raised an eyebrow at his monogram. With playful humility, he boasted how the government of Canada chose *his* initials as their acronym for various programs. SIN – a unique *social insurance number* issued to each permanent citizen. While 'nobody's fool', Simon enjoyed a joke, even when his initials startled others. He concluded he was special enough. I *am* SIN.

Simon loved his middle name, *Ignatius*. His mom's younger sibling, Brother Ignatius, spent his adult life as a contemplative monk in the *Monastery of Gethsemane* in Kentucky. Simon took pride in this significant religious component of his ancestry. Brother Ignatius joined when the famous writer and Trappist monk, Thomas Merton, lived on the monastery's grounds - in a cabin. The monks took lifelong vows of silence, obedience, and poverty. However, due to his prolific writings, Thomas Merton earned the privilege of travel, and made in-roads to join the spirituality of Buddhism with Christianity.

Brother Ignatius felt honoured to serve at the funeral after the *body* of Thomas Merton arrived at the monastery. An accidental electrocution during a conference trip to Thailand returned Merton to his Creator. Job well-done.

Simon's own sense of duty stemmed from his birth advantage - an *only child* born into inherited wealth. Like the modern royal family in Great Britain, one acted in a spirit of generosity from unearned privilege.

Rarely one to overindulge his children, Simon taught them his ethics, to respect others regardless of their circumstance. He knew sixteen-year-old Fiona could succeed on this path, but he worried for her twin, Darius. A sweet son, big and soft like his shadow, Charity, the Labrador Retriever, lived in a bubble of unpredictability. Thus, Simon's life and mood often seemed in a heightened state of implied unrest. Suspended.

SATURDAY, AUGUST 22, 2015

"Hey, Dad, get a look at this," green-eyed Fiona tugged at her chestnut braid and tapped it against her flushed cheek. She urged, "Come and see what I found!" She sucked in her breath and swiped her finger across the tablet. More images populated the screen. Rural Scottish cottages bordered by wind-swept beaches of the vast North Sea beckoned her attention.

"One second, Fi." Simon wiped his hands on a red gingham tea towel, slid on his readers. He leaned into his daughter's shoulder, supported his elbow on the gleaming brown granite island of their kitchen.

A relaxed Saturday breakfast with his teenagers mellowed Simon's earlier agitation from some *intrusive* phone call. He ignored it -would deal with it later. Nothing was more important than this moment.

He loved cooking with flair on the unrushed mornings. Crisping the bacon, flipping cheese omelets, and slicing the melon into zigzag shapes for his two heart-stealers while he sipped on a hot coffee, his *proverbial* cup filled to the brim. He had to remember to thank his young and energetic housekeeper, Ms. Wallace – well, Marjorie, to Simon, and now to the kids too since they were older - for the fancy kitchen tool she added to their collection. A *live-in*, Marjorie usually took Saturdays off to board the GO train to visit her sister, Hazel, in Toronto.

Simon's conversation with the kids during the meal developed into plans for a well-overdue family holiday. Now, everyone had special thoughts on which to ruminate.

Even Darius got involved. After lowering his plate into the dishwasher, he flopped his full belly onto the undulating chaise in the Great Room and slipped on his headphones. Seconds later, an ivory, floor-covering stirred into motion, and with quiet dignity followed him. Charity rearranged herself, and then stretched out on the warm hardwood, nose on paws, alongside her young master.

"Do you think we could visit some of the places you went with Mom?" asked Fiona.

"You bet, Princess." Simon replied, kissing her forehead, which stirred the puppy Prudence, curled in Fiona's lap, to peek with renewed curiosity.

After the miniature Dachshund arrived in their lives a year ago, she and Fiona became practically inseparable. Pru's auburn silky ears and tiny, short-fur body matched Fiona's brilliant hair color, although Pru's hair was straight, while Fiona's mostly fell into a mass of loose, copper corkscrews.

"Do a *Trip-Advisor* check for us, Fi, and see what comes up on these places. I'm going downstairs for a swim."

"After eating, Daddy?"

"Just a couple of laps, honey. You know, I need to think..."

"Not going outside?" said Fiona, as she and Prudence, both wide-eyed, looked up at Simon.

"Carlos is trying some new, gentle chemicals there this morning."

"Well, there's an oxymoron if I ever heard one, Dad – '*gentle chemicals.* Hah!"

"Hah, yourself. You're right, Fi. If Dare wakes, let him know where I am sweetie. You can find me in my office later. I've a couple of calls to make before we go out."

4

"I'll probably go to my room and riff out a new song I'm working on. I'll put a 'post-it' on Charity's collar – Darey will find that. See ya, later, Pops."

"Okay, doll."

Simon gave his daughter's shoulder a squeeze, left the kids and their pets in sweet harmony, and headed down to the indoor pool.

The lower level of this spacious home re-designed as a spa contained a teakwood dressing area, plus decay-free bamboo seating, surrounded by greenery-shoots of various heights. Simon knew he made the right call to install an indoor pool; he could continue swimming exercises even in winter without leaving the family.

The east sun streamed through the high windows, not yet fogged. Simon looked out, noticed his groundskeeper busying himself with a yellow wheelbarrow amidst splaying green and ivory ground-hugging hostas. A wall of tall, pink peonies, like slim ballerinas in their tutus waiting to dance, swayed with the gentle breeze. These garden beauties did justice to their purpose, planted in honour of Peggy. They were always her favourite.

Simon slipped into the pool, pushed off from the edge, and cut through the refreshing water with a glide, moving his lean torso into a front crawl. His long arms took a good reach as he swam with strength, grace, and intention. At the other end, he somersaulted back, dipping his face down and up, switching to a side stroke, then turned over and floated on his back.

With each stroke, Simon's thoughts turned to Peggy. Peggy, darling Peggy. Six years gone. How she suffered. Not from the pain, as much as from the knowledge she'd be leaving us, especially her children. What mother could accept the thought of disappearing from the lives of her beloved eleven-year-olds?

Peggy died not at home, but at the *Ian Brooks Hospice* in their town of Naples. Simon established a financial fund for breast cancer research, and each year he and the kids participated in charity walks, runs, rides, even road-hockey-to-conquer-cancer marathons. Simon knew Fiona had to be tested soon for the inherited gene BRCA2 which carried an eighty percent chance of susceptibility to this cancer. He would steel his nerves for this procedure and bring some calm strength to his dear girl.

But now he wanted to float in peace remembering the summer of *July 1990*. He and Peggy acquired tickets to the *Three Tenors* in Rome, Italy, from his father, Quinn, who *made things happen*. A fabulous twenty-second birthday present for opera student Peggy, that Saturday, July eighth.

Both in their early twenties and newly engaged, they were thrilled to attend the FIFA (international soccer) World Cup. That evening the opera greats performed a fabulous show. On an outdoor stage under a full moon, the concert vibrated in the ancient red-brick ruins of the Baths of Caracalla. How they sang, those tenors! The two Spaniards, Jose Carreras and Placido Domingo, appearing for the first time together with Luciano Pavarotti, their Italian host. With an orchestra of almost two hundred musicians, and led by the renowned conductor Zubin Mehta, the tenors delivered such a spirited rendition of what had become a 'World Cup Anthem', Puccini's *Nessun Dorma*. And true to the song lyrics, nobody slept that night; Italy lost, but everyone still partied!

Simon's heart ached at these thoughts of his life with Peggy; his tears of sorrow blended with the water as he flipped over and continued more strokes, several consisting of butterfly moves to energize him. He had his kids. He would be forever grateful to Peggy, and always see Darius gets what he needs. Fiona was his little kick-ass girl. They would stick together, the three of them. Now, time to relinquish the reverie and exit the pool.

After a quick shower, Simon towelled his body, rubbed his head, and checked his stubble in the mirror. He turned his face, those high cheekbones, from side to side as he inspected the growth covering his cleft chin. He decided to keep it. No shaving. The kids called this a *cool* look. They didn't want a geeky dad. Simon also noticed an increased freckle count on his face and forearms. His olive skin offered a natural tanned look all year. Down to some good luck, he supposed. Still, he applied a thin layer of sunscreen as an example for the kids. No sissy thing to be cancer aware. This century of reduced ozone layers exposed a more dangerous sun.

Simon pulled on grey track-pants and a plain white tee shirt, from the supply of casuals Marjorie stacked in the cabinetry. He looked to the garden again and noticed Carlos had let Kent out.

Kent! The most mischievous black and white Border Collie anybody could be so privileged to call family. *Kent Alfred Nesbitt* - his dignified name bestowed by the kids - constantly sought trouble, a hope to sniff out a deer or a racoon. Often, he pretended to keep strangers at bay, as the ever-vigilant, proud guard dog. In fact, with no sheep available to herd, out of plain boredom, Kent grew a bit on the lazy side. The beloved rascal developed into a playful little schemer.

Except where it counted.

Kent was Simon's healer, no doubt about it. Kent brought forth belly laughter and acted as the family's chief endorphin releaser, serotonin creator, those happiness hormones needed to stave off moments of unwelcome sadness. Well-aware of his own sensitivities, Simon also felt those of others'. Kent held this empathy too. His pink panting tongue, hopeful bright eyes, and pricked shaggy ears mostly spoke joy.

A few ceramic steps up, and a hallway to the right, Simon reached his home office. A fine burgundy and navy wool Persian carpet graced the dark hardwood. He turned on his Sonos music system, and allowed a gentle, low volume of Chris Botti's trumpet, together with the accompaniment of Yo-Yo Ma's cello, stream into the room.

He sat on his brown leather swivel chair, at the grand mahogany executive desk with a glass topping and took in the view of the lake ahead. A solitary white sail bobbed in the distance. Should be more, he mused. People probably sleeping in – plenty of sailors in the afternoons. Outside his window, the summer snow-globes of hydrangeas gaily dressed the walkway bordering the house.

Simon glanced with tenderness at his framed photo of Peggy, the two-year-old twins on her lap, all three heads of ginger waves – their curly-haired family, his own too, albeit tighter, darker. Small wonder people now pinned Darius as a doppel-ganger for a young prince Harry.

Earlier, Simon had ignored the voice mail from the Naples Police Second Division requesting a call-back. Relaxed when he had prepared breakfast for the kids, he thought perhaps another donation appeal, and felt no immediacy. Precious family time together, and with Margie away at Hazel's, he aimed to excel as the man in charge.

Now he pressed the dials on the desk phone and swirled his chair to face the floor-to-ceiling black bookcase. Along with music, his books were another source of comfort.

Simon's father gifted him a collection of classics eight years ago, for his fortieth birthday, August 17, 2007. Such wonderful books, each a treasure; leather embossed covers, gold-edged pages, every volume with a silk ribbon bookmark sewn into the spine. These tomes acted as a showpiece, but Simon valued their real purpose. They were to be explored, not just function as facades of wealth. So, when Simon pressed them open, he stroked the pages gently, then did what in his father's view would be unforgiveable: he wrote in them, just in pencil. These books came alive for him.

His father never looked nor knew. For Simon, this was no desecration, but more akin to making love to an exciting woman – so much to touch and honour at the same time. And this collection belonged to him. The books offered knowledge of history, joy of art, and the intricacies of human nature with plots and poetry from the modern, caustic rage of Dylan Thomas to the love discourses and arguments of seventeenth century poet, John Donne. The set included many of the greats from Tolstoy, Shakespeare, to the Americans such as Hawthorne, and the inimitable William Faulkner. Of that one, Simon was never quite sure, understanding the dialects, but realized he wrote with empathy for the Black folks and other outcasts of that era. The problems of the American South.

Finally, an answer:

"District Two Division, staff Sergeant Bliss, speaking."

"Inspector Bram Brandt, please."

"One moment."

Simon waited patiently, still focused on his book collection.

"Inspector Brandt, speaking."

"Nesbitt here. Returning your call."

Simon listened, intrigued, while Inspector Brandt politely questioned him.

Was he the owner of *Nesbitt Holdings*?

"President and C.E.O. How can I help you, Inspector?" Simon's manner, equally civil, the timbre of his voice, rich and relaxed.

"Do you have a Filipe Delgado working for you?"

Simon left his chair, walked in front of his desk, leaned back. His gaze took in a side wall piece, a Golden Pheasant perched on a tree branch, exotic tail extended, a Chinese watercolour. Part of the company's art collection.

"*Nesbitt Holdings* employs many people, Inspector. However, the gentleman you mention is not on our payroll. May I ask why you are inquiring?"

"He told us he works for you – or rather your company, *Nesbitt Holdings*."

"Is he in some legal trouble?" Simon now paced, east to west in front of the office window. The lake slapped soft waves against the sand pebbles. A struggling windsurfer took advantage of the breeze.

"Do you at least *recognize* this name, Mr. Nesbitt?"

"Actually, I do, Inspector. Filipe is the nephew of my groundskeeper, Carlos Delgado."

"You mean the guy who played for the *Blue Jays*?"

"No, no, Inspector." Amused by this misunderstanding, Simon hid his smile from his tone.

"I said my *groundskeeper*, not the baseball player. Occasionally people make this mistake - to Carlos' delight. Same name.

"But I 'm concerned police are calling me about his relative. Would you kindly elaborate? Do you think Carlos is involved in something he shouldn't be? Because that would be a huge mistake. He's been working for me for ten years, an honest fellow, a family man, and Filipe has been staying with Carlos and his wife Albina..." Simon trailed off.

"It's not your groundskeeper I'm concerned with," the inspector said. "This nephew we picked up for speeding, found him to be intoxicated, and furthermore, we found controlled substances in his possession. In addition, Mr. Nesbitt, he lacks proper documentation. He is an illegal in Canada. If you are concerned, Mr. Nesbitt, I suggest you help your man retain an immigration lawyer for his nephew, as well as a criminal defence attorney. We are holding Filipe Delgado in custody at *The South*. You will probably want to notify the uncle. Immediately."

Simon's shoulders slumped. Heat rushed through his veins, and his belly knotted. He stared straight ahead, stunned. *Trouble with the law. Shit. Don't need this.*

"Yes, of course, Inspector. Carlos is working in the garden this morning. I'll go now and speak to him. Although, I'm sure he knows nothing about this. He would have *said* something. But what do you mean by *The South*?"

"Sorry, Mr. Nesbitt. That's how we in public enforcement refer to *The Toronto South Detention Centre*. It's fairly new, located in Etobicoke. I can appreciate the institution is not on your radar, Mr. Nesbitt."

"Oh, well, of course, I'm aware of it now that you explain it. Several of my associates are attorneys, Inspector. Just didn't realize the new detention centre already had a label. I thought those degrading monikers ended with the closing of Toronto's *Don Jail*."

Inspector Brandt ignored Simon's comments and continued his business inquiry.

"One more thing, Mr. Nesbitt. The Delgado's live on Jordan Street, in Naples. Correct? And they have a son? How old is he?"

"Eduardo is twenty-two, and a student at *Saunders College*, lives at home. Yes, they are on Jordan Street. But, with all due respect, sir, I will not answer further questions without my lawyer's advice. I appreciate your call. And I can assure you, *Nesbitt Holdings* is not involved in any illegal activities. No doubt frightened of deportation, Filipe must have named my company to give him perceived status. His uncle occasionally brought him by to help out, and this nephew lived as a family visitor."

They ended the conversation just in time.

Darius shuffled into the office, quiet in his moccasins, with Charity at his heels. Simon embraced his son fully, never any shyness with family love. This moment not lost on Simon of sons, drugs, and other possible dangers. He hugged his boy tighter.

"Hey, big guy, nice nap?" Simon held Darius at arm's length, then mussed his hair. A pat to Charity, and an ear tug brought on an extra wag.

"Where we goin', today, Dad?"

"We're going riding, Son."

"Horses?" Darius brightened.

"We did that last weekend. Those horses are expensive. Do I look like I'm made of gold?"

"Well, ah, yeah, Dad... looked down lately? Your arms covered with fuzzy gold hair?"

"That part's true, Dare." Simon chuckled. "Born that way. We're going bike riding, along the lake trails. Get your sister and the two of you arrange your gear. Wear cycle shorts, helmets, and remember the water bottles. I'm just going to have a word with Carlos, and I'll meet you guys in fifteen by the side driveway. Oh, and Darius, just make sure there's fresh water in the dog-bowls. Marjorie's gone till tomorrow. Go."

"Right, Dad, I'm on it." Darius spun around, and he and Charity were off to follow dad's instructions.

Before going outside to see Carlos, Simon pressed a few buttons on his desk phone, once again, and connected to his best friend and attorney.

"Hamish, man!"

"Iggy, what's up?

Hamish, and Simon's other old-time pals called him by various versions of his middle name, such as Iggy, Igster, affectionate nicknames left over from boarding school days.

"Just thinking of you Ig. You guys want to come for a barbecue later?"

"Possibly, thanks, Ham. But I have a problem. Legal. Listen up and advise."

Grateful to connect with Hamish, Simon then blew out a raspberry of relief.

After he laid out his conversation with the inspector to Hamish and a request to do what it takes to protect the Delgado family, Simon stepped outside to inform and console his unsuspecting groundskeeper.

Known for his pride and joy in caring for the Nesbitt property, Carlos loved his gardenwork. In a back wired off area of the yard, Carlos planted vegetables: chard, green lettuce, orange peppers, and zucchini. He created a spice section for parsley, oregano, and onions. He made beds for tomatoes, strawberries, and sour rhubarb stalks.

Now Carlos worked by the pool, adjusting the gracious urns stuffed with red geraniums. They dominated the patio in front of the double-hut cabana. Kent, often Carlos' outdoor companion, sniffed around the back of the huts for a renegade chipmunk. He bounded forward in glee as he caught sight of his real master present.

Simon approached Carlos and revealed the disturbing business about Filipe. Carlos took it personally. His friendly smile, crooked teeth under a bushy moustache, came full stop. His dark eyes, hooded, reflected shock and sorrow. Simon suggested he take the rest of the day off.

"Mr. Simon, you are so good to me. I am ashamed." Carlos dropped his chin to his chest. Kent sped off to make a show of duty and left the men to their conversation.

"Carlos, look at me." Simon placed his hand on the groundskeeper's shoulder. "You have nothing to be ashamed of. You and Albina opened your home to Filipe. His actions are not your fault. He's twenty-eight, isn't he?"

Carlos nodded. Sweating, he pulled a crumbled handkerchief from his pocket. Wiped his brow, his tanned, creased face, but mostly used it to mask his humiliation.

"Hamish will call you later. Tell him everything you know. We'll help you deal with this, Carlos. Both you and Albina have a drink on me. Before you leave, go to the wine cellar, take home a couple of bottles of your favourites. The red will go down nicely, I'm sure, with whatever Albina has stewing for dinner. And feel free to call me after your talk with Hamish. You can return to work Monday. Go man. This will be okay, hear?"

Simon made sure of good eye contact between them. Then he patted Carlos on the back, and said, "Bring the dogs in when you lock up. The kids and I are going cycling."

Chapter 2

"Historical facts of Naples"

W henever he left the country and was asked by officials or fellow travellers where he was born, Simon said *Naples*. Of course, a smiling explanation followed the expected question. No, not the famed Italian seacoast region, but rather in a green and elegant town which curled around the edge of Lake Ontario, Canada.

Naples stretched as a crescent about thirty miles, between the expanding cities of Mississauga and Burlington and a forty-minute drive west of Ontario's capital city, Toronto. Charming Naples boasted grand ancient trees in the south, and delicate saplings in the north, where new homes with young families spread at a startling rate.

A century earlier the land belonged to First Nations Indigenous Mississauga tribe who sold parts to the Crown, and a portion to a Colonel Wendall Calbraith. With his fondness for European places, Calbraith founded the village of Naples. By 1846 the population grew to 1,500. The Colonel and his family launched a shipbuilding enterprise, set up sawmills, and contributed to a thriving port with shipping of wheat and lumber at the mouth of Sixteen Mile Creek, as it opened to Lake Ontario.

By 1962, Naples merged with the surrounding villages of Bronte and Saunders, and in 2015 the now well-established town of Naples claimed approximately 192,000 residents. Places of worship included churches, synagogues, and temples to accommodate various ethnicities and faiths. Demographically, fifty-five percent of citizens were immigrants from parts of the United Kingdom. The rest consisted of Italian, German, French, Polish, Chinese, and East Indian descent.

Naples maintained a reputation as a good town in which to live. Several sports arenas, a performing arts centre, libraries, parks, chic restaurants, and shops. Low crime rate. A pretty and safe place to raise a family. Green, clean, and beautiful.

One of the proud and significant historical facts of Naples of which newer residents seemed unaware is the major role Naples played in sheltering and providing safe refuge to American Black slaves. Those who escaped bondage to flee their cruel circumstances and search for freedom found their way through the now famous *Underground Railroad* to the safety of Naples and Bronte shores.

The Nesbitt family lived in the established south, along the strand of Lake Ontario, their waterfront home at Number One, beginning a street called Hackberry Road. Simon grew up in the same house his father Quinn was raised with three sisters. The estate had been in the family ninety years. After Quinn's father, Seamus, passed on, Quinn's mother, Fleur, allowed renovation. Through metamorphic bliss, Quinn's sisters, Em, Gigi, and Milly, upon reaching legal age, transformed into Emily, Georgina, and Millicent. They chose to sell their shares and move elsewhere with their respective husbands. They accepted nothing but the best: they were, of course, *Nesbitt* girls.

Simon's parents, Quinn, and Virginia enjoyed forty years at Number One Hackberry Road, affectionately *HR* for short.

Grandmother Fleur lived with them a few months of the year, but also kept her Paris apartment. She spent much time travelling to the homes of her daughters in Scotland, Spain, and South Africa. She took her last breath at *HR*.

The senior Nesbitt's held fine gatherings for their friends in the South-East Naples community, including those they met at *The Naples Leisure Club*. But when Quinn and Ginny chose to travel more, they officially turned the property over to Simon and Peggy as a tenth wedding anniversary gift and moved into Twelve Forest Street, a luxury condo at the foot of the Lakeshore Road Bridge with a winding view of the river and marina.

In the Seventies, this prime riverside landsite held a high, multi-tiered night club with waterfront patios not seen for miles around. No longer *Shakey's,* this site was redeveloped into an apricot-brick condominium, also sky high and with black wrought-iron ornate railings enclosing the expansive balconies. Old-style coach-lamps hung on strategic segments of outdoor wall space, affording the illusion of antique dignity. When their intended unit was adjusted to their specifications and deemed available, Quinn and Ginny took the Penthouse - for a cool four million.

Chapter 3

"This wonderful home, our love nest..."

J oyful in their early years of marriage, Simon and
Peggy grew ecstatic with the gift of the Hackberry
Road Estate. Given this opportunity to renovate and redecorate
the house as their new home created dreams they hardly imagined. They gathered clippings from their favorite décor magazines
for inspiration and guidance.

Even essentials like rewiring, updating the pipes and the
heating/air-conditioning system took on a certain glamour. They
learned about plastic tubing touted to be imperviable to rust, less
chance for corrosion than old copper, and would prevent freezing.
California gal Peggy insisted they hire the best service people to
make their home safe and cozy. Her lakeside house would protect
them from Canadian winters.

Simon hired architects from *Nesbitt Holdings* to draw
plans, and their team of contractors to re-structure the massive
frame. The building even had to be raised to accommodate the
downstairs indoor pool and new wine cellar.

Some main floor walls were demolished for an open effect
and rustic ceiling beams added. Workers re-built the main and
back staircases with red oakwood steps; smooth black iron hand-
rails over fine spindles completed a clean and safe look.

In front, the kitchen faced the lakeview verandah. A stained-glass door placed in the centre wall intended for special occasions while the two street-side entrances were kept for every day. A brown granite island floated here which included an apron farm sink. Five copper, back-padded barstools lined one side for comfortable casual meals.

Distressed eggshell cupboards with glass panes were installed to contrast the island. Quartz countertops with marble striations kept the clean look. The lighting, some recessed ceiling pots, and a pair of fine brass pendants, shared ceiling space with a special rack for sparkling water and wine glasses. The double door refrigerator, gas range and a tall pantry matched the soft brown of the island.

Facing north, the kitchen spread itself open wide to a family area where the west walls held high windows. New French doors opened to the gardens and pool cabana area. This *Great Room* flooring combined warm terracotta tiles from the street-side entrance to a spread of smooth oakwood in the larger space.

Also, west of the kitchen through an archway of white plaster was their intimate dining room, framed by insulated windows on two walls which also offered a two-thirds view of both lake and poolside gardens. A new gas-fireplace provided a cozy feel and extra warmth for those winter evenings when howling winds hurled snow in all directions outdoors and candles flickered in their holders on a generous harvest table during dinner.

The second floor contained six bedrooms and four washrooms, two of the latter connected to bedrooms at each end. All were upgraded with porcelain white tiles, sinks, new tubs, and walk-in showers.

And that was just the interior.

The exterior of *HR* received fresh tan shingles which covered the vast slanted A-frame roof. Six wide white pillars supported the verandah graced by a broad balustrade and thinner decorative posts. The verandah became a place to cozy up with the family on a porch swing or a safe venue to hold fifty people for a garden party. Also ideal for a fund-raising cocktail gathering. Twelve concrete steps, with railings at each side, held embedded led lights as a direction to the front carpet of green grass.

The front lawn extended from the stairs about thirty meters, where a wrought-iron fence enclosed the property from the public pathway. This style of fence kept the water view clear. High ancient oaks and maples with their magnificent greenery stood dignified in the grassy area just steps from the shoreline, spread out, not blocking, but enhancing nature's beauty with their bushy leaves and hard, gnarled brown trunks.

Eighteen months later, the new owners were anxious to move in. But there was still more to be done.

Memories from Simon's secondary school days at *Kawartha Lakes Academy*, in Ontario's northland, played a role in their *HR* expansion. Surrounded by nature at KLA, Simon loved the sunsets, so he included a screened *Muskoka* porch to the back of his Naples house, a place to admire the setting sun while sipping on a gin and tonic.

He had the outdoor pool converted to a salt-water system, as well as the new indoor one with proper ventilation and maintenance for both by an established company. New 'his and her' cabanas were built and a fire-pit in the lounge seating area, which their friends and the kids would love.

He and Peggy also decided to turn one of the garages, formerly a coach house, into a two-story modernized nanny apartment. Fitted with secure communication and protective devices it offered an enclosed all-weather breezeway to the main house.

When the time came for more interior design, color, and furniture selection, Peggy sang her arias up to the raised ceilings of those wooden beams with such joy as she moved from room to room, planning, with her notebook and color swatches. Simon's heart ached from so much happiness hearing his lovely Peggy's soprano's voice coupled with her infectious enthusiasm for all things beautiful. They agreed on warmth and fullness as their *style*, as-it-were.

The Great Room siding of red brick, enclosed a natural fireplace, extending to warm dark-oak floorboards, and a red Turkish-patterned wool carpet. A baby-grand piano in gloss black finish would sit close to the ivory French doors for natural light but not directly. Pianos were not meant to be in too much sun. They wanted to combine beauty as well as informal luxury, both classic and traditional.

Couches in chili pepper and cream, stuffed armchairs provided coziness and complemented their chocolate kitchen island, in full view.

The happy couple knew this project was a great expense. However, Simon's parents, had set aside funds for their only child. Grateful that budget was not an issue, still, Simon, and Peggy, did not live with a sense of entitlement. Their innate wisdom: everything in life could disappear in a flash. They appreciated the moment and loved the importance of family. They contributed regularly to charities particularly for women and kids.

After these extensive renovations of the house and property, Simon and Peggy sold their charming townhouse, and moved in with the three-year-old twins. Life was good for several years. Until Peggy discovered the lump that ended her life

In ignorant bliss of their future troubles, after the first few days in the house putting away multiple household items, Simon and Peggy left the twins with the grandparents, and just took some alone time. After a lovely shower, they freshened up and had their 'sit down' together. This was their special moment.

"Darling," murmured Peggy. She nuzzled into Simon's neck and ran a soft finger over his *Adam's* apple. "We shall have such romantic times here." She tossed one capri'd leg over his lap, her bare tangerine-painted toes wiggling, and her bangled wrists resting on his broad shoulders.

"You and me, darling man, will always call this wonderful home our love nest and the nest for our two little birdies to grow – won't we, dearest?"

Simon felt a knot in his throat, a result of restraint. Deep emotion held back to avoid tears. He hoarsely grunted his agreement. He squeezed his precious little wife tighter pulled her into his heart by way of his chest. He stroked her hair, caught a finger in her natural springy curls of auburn gold.

How could a man be this lucky? At times, it was scary.

Chapter 4

"That man has a strange look in his eyes..."

W ith the town's endorsement, Simon commissioned three new park benches to be installed by lakeside paths. Each bench contained an engraved steel plate to honour his beloved late wife and mother-of-two.

Popular in south Naples, memorial benches held soothing reflections such as: 'Follow the sun.' Most faced the open sky above the lake where one could mark the sun's daily trajectory. Eternity lay in that vast sky. To sit and reflect on a lost loved one brought comfort in an often cruel and unpredictable world.

On Peggy's plaque: *Beloved wife and mother - Seraphina Nesbitt: 1967-2009. Always our angel.*

Simon felt blessed his parents lived close by – the only set of grandparents for his twins. With Peggy gone, an extended family held a significant role.

When Peggy was seventeen, she lost her mom, Kristina, to the same form of breast cancer. In earlier times, people delayed checkups. Peggy's dad, Peter Jones, took a trip to Melbourne six months after his wife's death, supposedly to visit relatives, but according to friends and family he went *home* to die. In a massive state of depression, Peter took his own life. Witnesses reported he walked into St. Kilda beach and just kept going.

Peggy's older brother Owen, twenty-five at the time, sheltered her. Fortunately, their mom had left a solid life insurance policy naming Seraphina (Peggy) and Owen as beneficiaries. There was property in Scotland. Peggy was able to continue her music studies in San Diego, and pursued opera. Owen, a quiet man, chose architecture, became a disciple of Frank Lloyd Wright, and moved to the desert landscapes of southwest America in Scottsdale, Arizona to design, build, and meditate.

Their family bike ride proved invigorating. Fiona, with Prudence snuggled in her carrier basket, led in front. Darius followed his sister's moves and Simon, third in the single file, happy to watch his twins ahead, kept a protective eye on them. Like the three riders, Pru relished the breeze from the water as they cycled parallel to the lake's shoreline.

In the interest of safety and comfort, Simon indulged them with high-quality mountain bikes, the thicker tires, easier to navigate bumpy paths, included six-setting gears. All in individual glazed colours – red for Fiona, cobalt blue for Darius, and iridescent green for Simon, himself. *Quality time with my kids,* thought Simon, *creating healthy memories for them.* Nothing felt more important to him than a beautiful moment with his little family.

They headed towards Bronte, the tiny village and marina west of Naples and dismounted at the chip wagon for ice-cream. They sat at the on-site picnic table. Darius went for the order.

Simon spotted a look in the server's eyes he didn't want his kids to pick up. Perhaps the guy was getting off drugs. Often sensitive to nuances missed by others, Simon felt vibes. But Fiona, his insightful girl, recognized similar clues.

"Dad, that man has a strange look in his eyes."

"You noticed too?" asked Simon. "Don't say anything in front of Darius..."

"Hey, Dad, this ice cream is good!" Darius made an awkward climb over the bench to sit by his sister and passed her a cone. "Sure you don't want one, Dad?"

Simon shook his head. "No, thanks, son."

Darius rested his elbows on the stained, wooden table. He took another lick, looked to his father and said, "I think that dude has a problem. Did you guys see the weird look in his eyes?"

Caught off-guard, the moment left Simon and Fiona speechless.

"Probably he's on drugs." Darius offered.

"Let's hope he's in recovery, and that's why he's working," Simon suggested. "Let's give him the benefit of the doubt, shall we?"

"You're right, Dad.," chimed both twins together, as though rehearsed.

Fiona poured a bit of water from a small cannister into a plastic dish for Prudence, and they were good to go after her sipping.

Returning to Hackberry Road all three of them, one by one, in confident fashion wheeled into the side driveway. Surprised, Simon saw Carlos' white landscaping truck still parked in the overflow lot. His intuition hit like a thump to the gut. He heard the dogs barking inside.

At once he gave orders to the kids.

"Something's not right. Park your bikes, guys, and head to the cabana. Put on your swimsuits and hit the pool. Don't come in until I call you. Go, now."

"What are you so worried about, Daddy?" asked Fiona.

"I had sent Carlos home," replied Simon, his mouth dry, "and our dogs sound stressed. Quick, Fiona, give me your mobile."

Fiona cuddled Prudence, took the cell phone from the basket, and passed it to her father.

"Careful, Dad."

"Go kids. Do as I say. I'll just check everything out first. Then I'll call you."

The kids moved it.

Simon pressed the codes and entered the kitchen. At once, he found Kent and Charity parched from barking. He felt their agitation, and their frenzy to let him know something of significance occurred. They ran forwards and back, turned in circles, upset and confused.

The dogs urged Simon to follow them to the wine cellar. They stopped short of the threshold, whimpering. They did not go further.

Simon's emotions exploded at the sight: "Jesus Murphy!" he spat out. "Carlos!"

Spread-eagled on the terrazzo floor, the ladder partly on top of him, Carlos lay in a pool of burgundy liquid, surrounded by shards of glass. Motionless.

Simon reached for the cell phone in his man-pouch and pressed 9-1-1. Nauseated by the pungent tang of grapes, his hands trembled. He noticed blood collected at Carlos' nostril. He couldn't be sure, but his gut said Carlos was dead.

He reported what he saw to the dispatcher and requested an ambulance.

"Please do not touch the deceased or anything else in case Forensics needs to assess further," the dispatcher robotically advised, then verified the address.

Simon stared at Carlos lying on the ground. Bile rose in his gut. *Poor guy, poor guy,* he wept to himself. *Why did he fall from the ladder? Did he have a heart-attack? A stroke?*

Soon he turned his attention to Kent and Charity, checked their paw pads for any glass pieces – thank God they were okay. They would not have approached the chaos but appeared highly stressed at what happened. Simon stroked and calmed them and at the same time received enormous comfort for himself from the love and warmth of these sensitive creatures.

He sat on the floor and pressed his mother's phone icon on the mobile's display.

"Hi Darlin' – how's my beautiful granddaughter this lovely day?"

"It's me, Mom – using Fi's cell."

Ginny's tone changed.

"What's wrong, son? You sound awful," her mother's intuition kicked in.

"We just returned from cycling, and I found Carlos on the floor in the basement – he's had an accident. I think he might be... dead, Mom. I already called *9-1-1.*"

"Oh, dear God, where are the kids? Did they see this?"

"No, Mom, they're out at the pool. I heard the dogs barking when we got home so I didn't let the kids into the house until I checked things. Can you and dad come over? The police and ambulance should be here soon. I need you to stay with the kids.

I'll have to go to Albina. I think the police are here now. I've got to go and shield the kids."

"Of course, honey. We'll be over just as soon as we can. So sorry for you, and for dear Carlos."

Simon hurried. He grabbed his own mobile which he'd left on the kitchen island earlier, and texted Hamish: *Carlos collapsed here. Did you speak to him or Albina about Filipe?*

He headed outside, saw Fiona climb from the pool, wringing her dripping hair. The dogs rushed to greet Darius stretched out on a lawn chair. Prudence snoozed on a neighbouring one.

"Everything, alright?" asked Fiona. She pulled a striped towel from the fence and wrapped it over her shoulders.

Simon couldn't tell them there might be a dead body in the house even if it was their own caretaker. They'd be shaken, especially Darius. He'd be spooked.

"Carlos fell from a ladder in the wine cellar. The ambulance just arrived. You guys stay here, distract Kent and Charity. Leave me to deal with this," Simon ordered.

"Hey, Dad, why are the cops here?" Darius sat up wide-eyed as he noticed a police vehicle next to the ambulance.

"It's just routine." Simon faked a nonchalant tone though the casual demeanour strained his throat. "Grandma and Grandpa are coming over. I'll probably go to see Albina. Take your grandparents for a walk to the pier, order pizza, play scrabble with them. Just wait here 'til the ambulance leaves, and please stay out of the basement for now. There's a bit of broken glass. Is that clear, guys?" Simon's tone was firm. He kept his inner distress to himself.

"And here's your phone back, Fi."

"Thanks, Daddy, no worries. We don't need to go snooping into the wine cellar, trust me." She leaned into her father with a wet hug. Simon needed this more than she realized and held her for a count longer than usual.

Simon led the authorities into the house. After some questioning from the paramedics, he watched them move Carlos' body into the ambulance. When they saw no evidence of foul play, the police gave Simon permission to order a clean-up crew. He had told them no one else was home at the time of the accident. Then he texted his man in charge of maintenance at *Nesbitt Holdings/ Property Division* to come out – ASAP.

Minutes before Quinn and Ginny's taxi appeared, Simon swung open one door of the fridge, reached for a can of beer. He snapped off the ring and poured the amber liquid into a tumbler from the glassware rack. The cold ale slipped down his gullet with a measure of reassurance – a moment's reprieve – before he faced the consequences of having invited his loyal groundskeeper to visit the wine cellar.

Maybe the ladder was weak? How would he explain all this to Carlos' wife and son – and that nasty business of the nephew's actions on top of it?

Simon thought to notify *Corelli-Bauer Funeral,* the mortuary where his Peggy had been laid out. And he should contact Marjorie. But first, he'd wait for the coroner's report. Fortunately, the coroner was another buddy from his school days at *KLA.*

His five years as a boarder gained him the best friends a guy could ever want. James Schroeder – now Doctor Schroeder, chief coroner for Halcyon Region, wherein Naples belonged, would get back to him as soon as he had completed the autopsy.

And through Jim's many visits to the *HR* homestead, he knew Carlos well.

Initially, Simon resented his father for shipping him off to boarding school. He vowed he'd never do that to his kids. Yet, those five years were the most fulfilling of his life – until, of course, he met Peggy and they had their twin babies.

Simon reasoned, as far as parents go, he took after his mother. They shared a spirit. He inherited her soul. Quinn, although cordial when it mattered, could be a cold, son-of-a-bitch. Where Ginny exemplified kindness, Quinn appeared strict, less compassionate than his wife and son. He seemed to lack the tenderness of heart which Ginny and Simon shared. Yet, Simon mused, overall this made for a good balance in the family.

They would arrive soon and be supportive in this crisis. Simon counted his blessings and finished his beer.

Chapter 5

"I wouldn't mind if you could please come back..."

V irginia's sophisticated *Armani* perfume preceded her into a room. Initially meeting her, people paused as though they chanced upon a celebrity. Nevertheless, despite her wealth, and trademark silk scarf, Virginia exuded warmth and cheer. She dismissed formalities, introduced herself as Ginny and put folks at ease. She also held a special sensitivity for the vulnerable.

Being a Kentucky State, American, by birth, Ginny was a great fan of the altruistic Mrs. Roosevelt, a woman to be emulated for her sense of duty. As her heroine would do, Ginny, too, felt called to share her humanity with others.

When Ginny was still a girl, Mrs. Roosevelt's notoriety in civic affairs and good deeds paralleled, even reportedly eclipsed those of her much-admired popular husband, Franklin Delano, the President of the United States.

With strong role-models, Virginia Divera Hill Nesbitt threw herself into active participation, and promoted a plethora of charities. When she and Quinn were not travelling, Ginny limited her playtime at *The Naples Leisure Club*. The hours spent there she turned into recruitment opportunities to gain members for charitable organizations. A solid fund-raiser, Ginny enjoyed her life's choices. And those who knew Ginny as a Canadian for years, claimed she never lost her Kentucky accent.

Upstairs to change, Simon glanced through his bedroom window. As he buttoned a fresh shirt, warmth spread over his chest and melted his heart. A welcome release of tension. His folks already poolside, hugged their grandchildren. He sighed, blinked in gratitude, then looked to watch his family at the patio table, smiling, planning activities for their next few hours. The pups seemed relaxed, tails wagging, eager for a walk.

He'd had a fast shower. Dressed in beige trousers and a crisp, white short-sleeved shirt. Kept it simple. He took a brush to his tight, auburn hair and slapped moisturizer on his face.

By the back door, Simon slipped into his soft loafers with the tassels, and out he went with car keys and sunglasses in hand.

Simon saw to the family. He kissed his mom and Fiona, shook hands with his father, and fist-bumped Darius, as an indicator he would now take care of business.

"Have a good time. I'm going to see Albina and Ed. Not to worry. I'll text you guys."

"We love you, Daddy," from Fiona.

"Good luck, Son," from Quinn.

"Love you Darlin'," from Ginny.

"Yeah, Dad. Catch ya later. Hope it goes okay!" Darius shouted as he draped his arms about Charity's neck in a snuggling embrace.

With tail beating, Kent ran towards Simon and circled him for a quick pat.

Simon backed his silver Mercedes out of the driveway and turned up Hackberry Road, headed north where he turned left to cross the Dante Drive bridge, on route to Jordan Avenue and the home of the Delgado's.

He drove slowly. It wasn't far, and he needed to think. He also needed to consult with Hamish.

Although he wished the drive to Albina's were longer, he realized she wasn't *exactly* expecting him, either. A quick judgement-call, Simon turned off his route. He drove to Lakeshore Road, headed west. He stalled for time.

A soothing ride for a while on a leafy street to nowhere in particular. The massive white oaks with their green leaves reached across from both sides of the narrow road to create a canopy in the sky. Made him think of those military weddings where young couples dash beneath raised swords. Something simple but spectacular. He needed beautiful, emotional thoughts now.

Despite this imagery, Simon choked from claustrophobia; it took effort to swallow his own saliva. He sweat through his shirt, dreaded this mission to speak to Carlos' family.

He focused on the leather of his car's seat. The softest grey hide, therapeutic – something he believed intentional in the workmanship, something he appreciated. He enjoyed quality without ostentation. He preferred the noiseless elegance of his possessions. Yet, he took nothing for granted. He knew how privileged a life he led as a direct beneficiary of inherited family wealth. For him, it wasn't a call for attention as much as the personal satisfaction which he sought from life. Comfort, peace, and security for his family.

And love. Simon sought love. A truth he firmly repressed after losing Peggy.

He used this time to call Hamish, and then Marjorie, and planned a follow-up to Schroeder to check on the autopsy for Carlos.

He reached Hamish's voice mail, but Marjorie's sister picked up the home phone in her downtown Toronto condo. Simon stayed clear of Marjorie's cell on her day off.

"Why hello, Mr. Nesbitt," purred Hazel when she heard Simon's voice. She didn't have to, and he didn't expect it, but Marjorie's half-sister Hazel Wallace enjoyed demonstrating a certain playful deference to her sister's handsome, wealthy employer. Be polite to the rich and gorgeous, she reckoned, never know what happens in life, when one might need to call in a favour from someone influential. Although Hazel already had a life partner whom she deeply loved, she was okay there. But she kept herself open to tips for future business investments in this mad world.

"Hey there, Hazel," Simon responded, with an effort to simulate a more upbeat voice than his mood indicated. "How are you girls doing? Plans for anything special?" Simon inquired trying hard to sound chill.

"Well, we went to St. Lawrence market by subway, and brought back loads of fresh vegetables, and salmon – hey, I'm sure you want to talk to Margie and not me – shall I get her?" Hazel asked.

"That would be great, thanks, Hazel – nice chatting with you." Simon waited and then...

"Simon? Why are you calling me?

Marjorie cut to the chase. He had insisted she address him by his first name ages ago, and as his employee, she appreciated his egalitarian attitude.

Could something have happened to the kids? Simon never bothered her on her free days without good reason.

Now he cut to the chase too.

"I've had a helluva day so far. Cops called me to say Carlos' nephew Filipe is in custody for speeding, drugs, and being an illegal in the country." He heard Marjorie gasp. But he continued. "It gets worse," he said.

"Carlos had a serious fall in the wine cellar when the kids and I were out cycling. I found him unconscious when we got back. The ambulance removed him already. Marjorie, he took it badly when I told him Filipe was in trouble. Maybe he had a heart attack or something when we were gone," Simon told her, as he, himself, tried to find some sense in this.

He pulled his vehicle into a lot overlooking the lake, saw little kids on a nearby playground squealing with delight on their way down hard, yellow plastic slides, cheered on by happy mommies. The sight squeezed his heart. He remembered when his two were that age, and how Peggy enjoyed catching them at the bottom.

"Maybe he took a Valium and got dizzy, Marjorie, I don't know. I'm on my way to Albina's to tell the poor woman – just driving around first trying to sort out my thoughts," Simon exhaled audibly.

"And the kids?" asked Marjorie, more from a perfunctory need to stall *her* thoughts. Knowing Simon, they'd be fine. She swallowed some bile and her stomach somersaulted. Only she knew why.

"Mom and Dad came over. Nobody really knows anything yet. When the paramedics took Carlos, they made no definite pronouncements, but I think he was gone. I expect Dr. Schroeder, er, Jim, will be contacting me. I wouldn't mind if you could please come back later today. Bring Hazel if you want – take a cab – charge it to the company, of course. Around five? That okay?" asked Simon. He needed her strength at home.

"You know, Simon – I'll be there for you guys. Sure, I'll check with Haze if she can join me. She's got this week off. She *could* use a change of scenery, and nowhere more peaceful, well, *usually*, than your place." They both realized Hazel worked with intense dedication in her position as a nurse at *Sick Kids* -the children's hospital in Toronto.

With her own allegiance to her employer, Marjorie put on her 'I've got this!' confident voice Simon came to rely on for the last six years.

"So, what will happen to Filipe?" Marjorie asked.

"Don't know, yet. I've got Hamish on it."

"Well, I know it will be a tough day, Simon. Hang in there. We'll see you soon, then, and we will bring the fresh fish. Okay?"

"So good of you, Marjorie. I appreciate how you are so reliable and dedicated to our family. We'll see you later, and thanks so much. I mean it, Margie. Bye now." He disconnected the call after he heard her say, "You got it."

His mind returned to the warm, sweet spot where he could renew himself: Peggy.

Peggy. Now permanently idealized in his thoughts. The beautiful, laughing red-head Scottish American girl, from San Diego, who he met in a pub in Galway. She described herself as a student of opera. Her soprano voice seemed larger than her tiny body would allow. She had been travelling through Ireland after visiting her maternal grandparents in Glasgow, Scotland.

Fate had brought them together that evening. Their seren-dipitous encounter took on a meaning to which only the roman-tics of the world would subscribe - a definite case of, 'love at first sight' for them both. He, too, was doing that proverbial post-aca-demic tour of Europe which many young folks take to gain some *living* knowledge and adventure. Occasionally, the travel included a tracing of the history of their relatives.

Simon loved Paris, home of his grandmother, Fleur La Chance, and Peggy loved Milano, home of art, beauty, and opera. They threw their lot in together and journeyed the rest of the way into each other's lives, as well as throughout the geographical locations which lured them and filled them with joy to be alive. They even went to Naples, Italy, and toured Mount Vesuvius, mingled with the Neapolitans in the streets enjoying the best pizzas, explored vaulted catacombs, and marveled at the frescoes from the second century.

About to turn the car around and finally deliver the news to his groundskeeper's wife, Simon received a call from Hamish.

"Iggy, she hasn't heard from him – Albina" he uttered. "I kept it short."

"I'm on my way there now, Ham," said Simon. "Is there anything I can tell her about Filipe?"

"Well, I spoke to Judge Harding, and he's looking at six months in the slammer, then deportation, unless they want a trial."

"Hell, no! No trial. Take the deal. And Carlos is probably dead. It's been quite a shock, Ham."

"Yeah, man. I got your text. What the devil happened?"

"Like I said in my text – he collapsed when I was out with the kids – fell off the ladder in the wine cellar. After I gave him that shit about Filipe, he was pretty upset. I told him to take the rest of the day off and grab himself some bottles and go home. The poor guy was on the floor unconscious when we got back."

"Jesus. Hate to sound trite, but when it rains, it bloody-well pours! Good luck with telling her, Iggy." said Hamish.

"Yeah, thanks, man – catch you later. There's Schroeder calling through, now. Probably with the autopsy - I'll get back soon."

And Simon rang off to answer the call from his friend, the region's pathologist.

Chapter 6

"Do boys ever grow up?"

Quinn Nesbitt projected himself as a proud man and didn't care who knew it. To him, humility and success did not belong in the same sentence. Life was about associations. The former combination remained foreign and as ineffective as mixing mother's milk with rich Kentucky bourbon.

Now *there* was a drink Quinn learned to appreciate - smooth bourbon - from his frequent visits with his father to Louisville as they attended the world-class Kentucky Derby at Churchill Downs. Merely a youth, Quinn grew more sophisticated each trip.

The senior Nesbitt, Seamus, employed a breeder and they raced at least two sleek, long-necked Thoroughbreds a year. The stakes were high, and the purse paid off. Their best winners were *Lady Fleur* and *Chance Girl*, named in honour of Quinn's French mother. Naturally, these mares were destined for success.

One beautiful spring Saturday in May, Quinn, age twenty, met the lively sixteen-year-old Southern belle – *Miss* Virginia Hill – at the Derby. She was a picture: a wide-brim straw hat tied with mauve ribbons under her heart-shaped chin, silky cheeks, lustrous white teeth and laughing brown eyes with lashes demanding his attention for fun-filled promises. The way she carried her young curvy figure, with grace and confidence, Quinn wanted that saucy filly for himself.

Avid horsemen, their fathers became acquainted; thus, the Nesbitt's were frequent guests to the Hill Estate, an extensive property situated on the rolling greens of rural Louisville.

In his apprenticeship of worldly experience, Quinn also acquired a taste for the pricey Cohiba Cuban cigars before they were deemed contraband in the United States. Later, Seamus would purchase them in Canada and smuggle them to Virginia's father, Abraham Alexander Hill.

During those times, both exciting and relaxed visits to Kentucky in the 1950s, Quinn and Ginny, as Virginia was known to family, fell in love. They married in grand style in 1963. His three sisters – Emily, Georgina, and Millicent - stood as brides-maids in long white gloves and fuchsia taffeta gowns alongside Ginny's five best girlfriends in attendance on the manicured flowered gardens of the Hill property with the mist from the mountains as their scenic backdrop.

Quinn grew to be known as a man's man. His second-ary education took place close to home at the private Appleton College, in Naples. Although a day student, Quinn chummed with several of the global boarders which increased his knowledge of the world at large. Quinn chose business electives at AC and continued in that stream at the University of Western Ontario.

Seamus provided Quinn with a vintage, two-story house to share with other students during his university years in London, Ontario. The energetic young male tenants slid down the banis-ter at least once daily, leaving both the seats of their pants and the wide railing shiny and polished. These rituals frequently occurred with boisterous Tarzan jungle calls, to which Ginny was occasionally a witness.

Do boys ever grow up? thought Ginny as she came for holidays. Ginny visited the dashing young Quinn often during these days of courtship. She took the train up to Naples and stayed with the Nesbitt's.

She loved Naples' history of the *Underground Railroad*, the clever communication method and safe 'stations' used to hide American Black slaves on their route to gain freedom in Canada. Growing up in Louisville, she heard of Naples from the domestic staff. What a coincidence the Nesbitt's were from a Canadian town she knew something about. She knew little about the rest of Canada.

Seamus showed Ginny some of the businesses of *Nesbitt Holdings* in Naples, places where he was a proud investor.

Although Seamus' Welsh father made the family fortune through shipbuilding in Scotland, his mother had a passion for design, and frequently attended fashion shows in Paris. On one occasion, Seamus came along where he met Fleur, a tall, dark-haired fashion model, an art student at the Sorbonne. The following year, Seamus took up art classes in the same university, and the Nesbitt family expanded with the marriage of these two art lovers.

Seamus took Ginny to the *Old Masters Collections Gallery* just off *Naples Square,* and Fleur took her to *Carmella Elegance for Women,* situated on Lakeshore Road where the fine shops stood. Particularly fond of the *Donatello Men's Wear* shop, Seamus suggested Ginny choose a little something for Quinn. He also gave her one of the family cars for weekend trips to Quinn's, Western University, in London, Ontario.

Quinn achieved graduate status of the new MBA program at UWO, a bit of a surprise considering all the drinking which took place in the *CHANCE HOUSE* with his roommates and their lovelies visiting at all hours. The late Fifties, a wild time for quality boozing if you weren't a Beatnik and could afford the finest. Quinn could, by way of his indulgent parents. Being an only son in a family-of-girls paid off for him.

Quinn as a dad, also wanted to keep his only son close to home. When it came time, he sent Simon only a few hours away to the *Kawartha Lakes Academy* (KLA). Fresh air from the Kawartha Lakes, the campus grounds held scattered rustic cottages as residences for the students and forested pathways led towards the main school buildings.

KLA boasted a full outdoor curriculum which included swimming, kayaking, and equestrian instruction. A special place, the school where even Prince Alexander of England had been an exchange student, albeit a few years before Simon's time.

Pleased that Simon made several close friends, Quinn held some queer thoughts of a few of them, which, in his wisdom, he kept to himself. Although he often appeared cold, even dismissive, Quinn had a heart for family. He remained grateful his only child was a happy young man. However, Quinn was uncharacteristically shaken when Simon's Peggy died.

Ginny and Quinn, now seventy-six and eighty, respectively, still found the energy to spend with their cherished grandkids. Darius and Fiona were the only two they had so they listened attentively to their conflicts, opinions, and yearnings.

With Charity and Kent on leashes, and mini Pru peeking out from Fiona's knapsack, the twins and their grandparents headed for a neighbourhood stroll. The clean-up crew arrived just before they left, and Quinn gave them a few instructional reminders about security codes.

A walk in this neighbourhood always provided visual delight. The wind on the water changed moods. A breeze offered lake ripples and the floating geese bounced contented. As the wind picked up, it slapped waves onto the rocks and the geese would honk, in chorus, hovering under a purple sky of moving pink clouds.

Directly in front of the Nesbitt house, the shoreline looped in and out. An arrangement of wide grey boulders placed one beside the other, about three feet high, created a border and kept the area safe from potential floods.

Already late summer, the fresh air was perfect for the strollers as the sun-kissed water spilled tiny waves onto the sand.

"Grandpa," Darius yelled over a sudden capricious wind, "don't you think these rocks look like the teeth of a grinning giant?" His hair shone an orange glow in the sunlight. Darius saw things differently. He saw fantasy.

"How right you are, Darius, my lad," Quinn answered. "You've got a remarkable imagination, grandson." He looked at this boy with love and wonder.

Darius did have an imagination...and some might say he was young for his age, compared to his almost seventeen-year-old twin, Fiona.

"Just look how tightly-joined these teeth are, but they have spaces in-between like you could floss there, eh, Gramps? Hey, maybe I should become a dentist someday, although I don't really think I'd like to be in people's mouths," laughed Darius, giving some extra lead to a tugging Charity.

Now, she was eager to sniff the tall oak tree's base and the surrounding ground. It was one of her favourite locations to dab her nose –that feature of hers, her most favourite asset. She left a urine message - the latest news, *p-mail* - as it were - for the next canine explorer to decipher and enjoy.

Regarding Darius, the family had an unspoken concern. What *would* he be when he grew up? How would the Asperger's affect him as an adult? But now was not the time. For now, Quinn and his grandson were on a roll, one which Quinn well-understood how to navigate. He focused on that rascal, Kent, who left his own news on a chosen spot.

They sauntered together on a path parallel to this lake in the direction of the wharf. Kent demonstrated skills as a vigorous explorer, and Charity found some climbing range, up and down, over the boulders, wagging that golden tail. Fiona set tiny Prudence down and slipped on her orange bling harness to offer her a chance to sniff around too. Dogs' paradise for all three.

Chapter 7

"Go prepare her"

"**S**chroeder!"

His jaw tight, Simon answered the call with uneasy expectation.

"Nesbitt, you clown. How did you *manage* this?" Schroeder drawled.

Doctor Jim Schroeder, experienced in his field where he could perform his dissection duties as though having breakfast cereal, tended towards irreverence and dark humour to survive his work of exploring the orifices and cavities of the dead. Thus, he often swashed the atmosphere with dramatic flair. He imagined funeral directors were like-minded in their artistic preparations of the freshly deceased. You do what you can despite life's cruel joke that we all end up the same. Cynical view? Or just a sane one.

Schroeder played *Neil Young* during his meticulous work – a favourite this day being the lyrics about an old man and comparing his own youth.

"Not the time for jokes, Jimbo," said Simon, "but I sure am glad you were on-call today. What did you find on my poor man?"

"Right, Igster, I hear ya."

'Igster'. Another nickname Simon's old school chums bestowed on him — once they learned his middle name, *Ignatius*, came from his uncle, a monk. Based on these tantalizing facts, the adolescent friends anointed Simon with a multitude of nickname variations. And they stuck.

"We were in luck today," Schroeder explained. "When I saw who they wheeled in, I snagged toxicology who agreed to test blood, hair, and gastric contents ahead of the line-up."

"Well?" Simon's oral juices dried up. He took a swig from his water bottle.

"Are you sitting down, Nesbitt?"

"Yeah. In the car."

"Fentanyl," announced the pathologist.

"What?"

Irritated, confused, Simon raised his voice. "What the hell *is* that?"

"Christ, Iggy, don't you follow the news, anymore?" Schroeder chided. His teasing sneer snapped like a rubber band.

The good doctor, as it were, lived in a world far removed from Simon's – one where it paid to be cynical – also having two expensive divorces, Schroeder didn't care for useless sentimentality or ostrich reality. At best, he had the bedside manner of a surgeon on speed.

"It's a deadly opiate, my man. New drug of the year, out of Vancouver. Your Carlos was a user. Face it. His recent ingestion gave him a head bleed – an aneurism – which finished him off when he hit the floor. Blessing in disguise, Nesbitt. He won't be in a bloody coma making the family feel fuckin' guilty for pulling the *pluuuggg*." This last word Schroeder dragged out like some weird chant.

Simon heaved at this information. He could not accept the sweet man working for him the last ten years as a drug user. It just did not make sense.

However, the true *non-blessing* in disguise, to which Schroeder tactlessly alluded, unbeknownst to either man in this conversation was the cross-country fentanyl epidemic which peaked in British Columbia and had not yet spread to national headlines as it would the following year of 2016. For ordinary people, fentanyl was an unknown entity, its dangers still hidden.

Schroeder can be such an A-hole, Simon thought, *such dickhead comments and disrespect, if not total indifference, of the dead. What a cold bastard!*

But then he realized few people would be capable of handling such grim work. Besides, Simon argued to himself, loyalty to family and even *flawed* friends were important to him. He recalled Schroeder's patience during the days at *KLA* as he gave his time to help Simon understand that miserable course in calculus.

"What do you think I should do now? Simon asked, his head splitting.

He was grateful for the softer tone from Schroeder: "Look, Iggy, go tell his wife. I'm required to submit this information to the police because of the controlled substance. Due diligence and all that. We can send the body over to *Corelli-Bauer* for you, and you or his wife can contact them later for further arrangements," Jim told him in a more matter-of-fact way. "The police will probably want to interview the missus. Go prepare her. No doubt it will be a shock to the family. Cops will want to speak to you, as well, since Carlos died on your property. Anything else I can do for you, Ig?"

"No, man, thanks." *Schroeder isn't such a jerk* – flashed through Simon's spinning mind. "Thanks again for your help. Let me know when you can drop by the house for a beer. Later."

Chapter 8

"Don't we always keep secrets from those closest to us?"

Marjorie didn't expect this call from Simon. *This could get messy*, she thought. *Filipe arrested and Carlos dead? Jesus, Mary, and Joseph. I must keep it together for Simon and his family.* She focused on her strengths - loyalty and passion – loyalty to her dear ones, and her passion for life. And she felt Simon appreciated her qualities. She would be there for him by tonight, as promised.

While re-playing a mind video of the last few months, Marjorie brushed her toenails from the *Purple Haze* bottle she bought earlier at *Shoppers' Drug Mart*. She and Hazel both laughed at the name, its significance of *Jimi Hendrix* and Hazel together. Purple was her favourite colour. Although, it was sad to think this twenty-seven-year-old Black musician died of a barbiturate overdose in the seventies, his hit, *Purple Haze,* still popular today.

Hazel left to have tea with a neighbour who suffered the loss of an elderly mother at a nursing home. Relieved to have some alone time, Marjorie felt shaken after this disturbing call from Simon.

Hazel's always full of sympathy, she thought, *but I wonder what she'd think of me if she knew. Don't we always keep secrets from those closest to us?* Her thoughts went 'on pause' as Beyoncé's *'Single Ladies Put a Ring on It'* played in the earbuds of her iPod.

Marjorie sang along focussing on her pedicure. *I could do this professionally*, she mused. But she believed her real skills lay in the practical ways of homemaking, childcare, and the culinary arts which she had studied at Naples' branch of Saunders College. She did well in school and landed a job with the best employer in town at the most gorgeous location by the lake's edge. Hired by Simon Nesbitt and his wife Peggy - to live in - when the twins were ten years old because Peggy was sick then and needed a housekeeper. Company cleaners came on a regular basis to handle the big stuff.

Fresh out of school, Marjorie was thrilled with this position overseeing the household. She was twenty-eight then.

What an excellent job she landed. Her own two-bedroom apartment attached to the house through a breezeway, afforded space and privacy. Her upstairs bedrooms could be reached with a charming, circular open staircase. She had her own little patio which faced the afternoon sun. Always great windows everywhere on the estate.

Since Peggy died, Marjorie felt like queen of the house, but remained humble, not to screw things up. Simon relied on her for many of the domestic decisions. She wondered why, in the last six years, he had never *fallen* for her. She found Simon decent and *handsome*, but she *did* sense how depressed he was after his wife died. Although in her heart she was tempted, she never dallied with the idea of flirting with her employer. Besides, she thought for some reason, not sure why, Simon might not be attracted to Black girls, even beautiful ones like herself. Well, Marjorie reasoned she was no Beyoncé, but she did have strong bones and a great ass. Her late mother, Heather, a white woman, was as pretty as her name.

Marjorie, herself, felt she looked a bit like Vanessa Williams. Albeit no 'Miss America' either, she knew she looked good. Once she thought it through, Marjorie figured *race* had little to do with it. A boss like Simon would simply never mess with an employee. He was *Mister Integrity* all right. Just so protective of his kids, too, and bottom line... he was *still in love* with his dead wife. End of story.

Toes done, Marjorie poured herself a coke and went outdoors to sit on the balcony. She sat upright in a canvas chair beside a planter of pink geraniums Hazel potted. She set down her plastic cup and looked at the city. Being in downtown Toronto turned her into a nervous wreck. All too much. So, despite this latest shocking news, she wanted to return to Naples and face whatever needed to be managed.

Chapter 9

"He absorbed her feral, pungent scent."

Simon pulled onto the blacktop driveway of the Delgado's red-brick, back-split. He parked beside Eduardo's yellow *Volkswagen*. Felt some relief the son at home and available to comfort his mother.

The porch, partly hidden by climbing vines over three arches, made it difficult to check if the garden chairs were occupied. He strained. Satisfied no one there, he placed his *Ray-Bans* in the holding slot and made for the door. Up a few concrete steps to the cement verandah. He drew a deep breath before he pressed the ringer. Moisture spread under his shirt - the dread of anticipation. How would he deliver this tragic news?

The thick door swung open. Behind the screen stood Albina. With heavy eyelids, she stared at Simon, her black, wavy hair unkempt.

Unprepared for her hostile glare, Simon received Albina's wild expression like a smack in the face.

"You son-of-beech, *Meester* Nesbitt," she growled through tight teeth. "Why you no tell me about Filipe?"

After that stinging greeting, Simon pulled open the screen door. He retained his manners and composure.

"May I come in, Albina?" he asked as he inched towards her.

She stepped aside.

Caught in the narrow entryway, his damp shirt stuck to his back, Simon brushed past Albina's ample bosom, aware of the awkward, involuntary contact.

"We need to talk," he muttered, suddenly feeling self-conscious. He needed to ensure restraint would be the imperative, singular reaction here.

"Hi, Mr. Nesbitt." Eduardo, the lanky, early-twenties son strolled from the kitchen, his wide-eyed blonde girlfriend behind him, absently holding a dish towel.

The two men shook hands. Simon nodded to Beryl.

"Let's have a seat." Familiar with this home, Simon led the way into the worn, but cozy living room. As he waved his arm indicating a place, the three of them slipped into a spot on the charcoal couch over which hung a blue, crocheted throw. Simon picked a hard-back chair from the adjacent dining room and turned it around to face them.

"So, the police called you about Filipe's arrest?" he asked the full-lipped Albina who crossed her arms over her chest and worked her mouth into a tight rope. Her raging display unnerved Simon.

"Yes, we were shocked," interjected Eduardo, eager to be helpful to his dad's boss.

"Just let me ask," Simon frowned at Albina, "why you're so upset with me?"

Albina uncrossed her arms and dipped her torso towards Simon inadvertently revealing more cleavage than he expected to see. She slapped her lap and shouted.

"Police inspector call me about Filipe, and you lawyer call me, too. Why you no let Carlos go home? I wait. He no call. No come home. We are in shame and trouble with police." Albina's face softened slightly, as she leaned back having made her point, but her dark eyes still radiated anger.

She continued, with a shaking of her head: "Why Carlos no here, now, eh?" In frustration, she raised a suntanned arm high, exposing a tuft of black, armpit hair. Simon pretended not to notice. But an unexpected blast of heat surged throughout his body and radiated to his own wet armpits.

He got up from his chair, looked at Eduardo, inclined his head to the right. Eduardo shoved over, as did Berri, who moved to the flat arm of the couch. Simon took the spot next to Albina. He reached for her hand, scrutinized her weary, intense face, albeit still youthful, and said in earnest: "I *did* send him home Albina. I did."

"Why he not here?" Albina tried to jerk her hand from Simon, but he held it, unyielding. He covered her hand with his own as he often did to a person he comforted. He knew his nature – as a sincere, touchy-feely sort of guy.

"Listen to me," said Simon. He looked directly into Albina's dark, fiery eyes. He absorbed her feral, pungent scent. Their joined palms, now sweaty.

Given this sincere, intense eye-contact, Simon's maleness sabotaged his poise – his cool. Unsure if just nerves or from his lack of female proximity, Simon felt the blood drain from his face to his privates. A firm urge of male stirrings flooded him. The unexpected and inappropriate nature of this sensation shocked him. *Sweet Jesus.* He had to keep his mind clear. What *was* this?

"Carlos had an accident when I was out with the kids. I had told him to get some bottles of wine from the cellar and go home.

When we got back, I found him on the floor in the basement. He fell off the ladder."

With arched eyebrows, Albina eyed Simon.

He felt his stomach contract, and his testicles shrink.

"Where he now?" She insisted, agitated, her tension rising.

Again, Simon inhaled musk pheromones. He felt drugged. Lost concentration. His head floated. Rare demeanour for him to lose control. Simon fought it.

"I sent him to hospital by ambulance," he explained. "You know Doctor Schroeder, my friend?" he asked. "He examined Carlos."

Then, Simon just spoke the words he had come to say:

"Albina... Ed...Carlos had a stroke." Simon turned to Eduardo, then back to Albina. He lowered his voice and squeezed Albina's hand tighter. "He didn't survive."

"What you are saying?" shrieked Albina. She yanked her hand from his and pulled her hair.

"Mama, Mr. Nesbitt is saying Papa is dead!" Eduardo dropped from the couch to kneel in front of his mother.

"*Oh, Meus Deus*" Albina wailed in Portuguese, visibly distraught. Suddenly, she burst into loud sobs. Inconsolable, this weeping widow.

Shaken from such display of dramatic emotion, Simon gathered the strength to mask his own distress. He hurried to offer how he would take care of all funeral expenses at *Corelli-Bauer Funeral Home*. They need not worry about finances. He would send the best flowers, too. He got up from the couch and paced while Eduardo and Berri hugged Albina, one on each side of her, with consoling soft words.

Simon felt the time was right to leave. With Albina supported, appearing more composed, Simon took this opportunity to *escape*. He mentioned he needed to get to his kids, explain what happened to Carlos. He told Eduardo to pick up his father's truck at his convenience.

Then, as an afterthought, Simon dropped the information that Dr. Schroeder found serious drugs in Carlos' body. He wondered if they *knew* anything. Albina and Eduardo both shrugged yet looked at one another with knowing eyes and remained silent. It seemed each one had something to say – but not in front of the other. Neither showed any surprise, which Simon found odd. Berri slipped back to the kitchen. Just the three of them stared at each other. Eduardo broke the spell of secrets.

"Let me walk you out," he said to Simon.

Outside, Ed's face took on a serious cast, and changed from boy to man. "Mr. Nesbitt, I want to talk to you privately," he said.

"It's Simon. You're old enough to use my first name, Ed."

"Well, that may take some getting used to, but thanks." Eduardo ushered them towards a large crab apple tree away from the house down by the pavement. Its generous shade - a welcome relief.

In a moment of circumstantial bonding, both men spoke at once. Eduardo deferred, but Simon insisted Ed go first. Evidently, he had something to share.

"You mentioned drugs were found in my dad's body." Eduardo ran his hands through his wavy black hair. He wiped sweat off his brow with the back of his hand. His long fingers trembled. He grimaced. The pain of the fresh loss, and the pain this information would soil his father's good name. It might be written in the newspaper because Nesbitt's were important people in town, and the *Naples Gazette* would leap at a story on the mysterious, drug-related death of the groundskeeper on their property.

Simon gave Eduardo a kind, reassuring look. "We all loved your father, Ed. None of this makes any sense to me. Is there something you know? Can share? We can keep it just between us," he said.

Chapter 10

"Naples existed as a global microcosm."

T he Nesbitt family reached the harbour, visited the wharf, heard the wind chimes of high masts attached to the slew of white sail boats. The grandparents, kids, and their pets continued to downtown's Mariner Street. Ahead lay the lush carpet of the private, lawn-bowling club, *The Naples Green*. The ubiquitous white picket fence corralled the space. Occasionally a *black-eyed Susan* pushed through the slats, to escape the clusters within. Oddly, her struggle simply enhanced the view.

"I'm tired, Grandma," moaned Fiona, twisting her braid, and keeping one eye on Pru's grass-eating activities. "Can we go back, now?" She squinted at Ginny, her tone whining. Unusual for this active teen.

"Of course, Darlin'." Ginny gathered her granddaughter and drew her in close. "You've been cycling, today, and then this unsettling business with Carlos..." she trailed off, sighed, looked to the sky for answers. Thanks to dark sunglasses, the *worry* in her eyes remained undetected by Fiona.

"No, Gran," said Fiona. "This feels different. Usually, I handle stuff. I just feel worn from the inside-out. Hate to admit it, but out of breath. You know how athletic I usually am."

Ginny rushed to rescue. Not to let the kids get depressed. "Well, let's get the dogs back and go for something to eat. I'll call

Lucio at *Buca di Bacco's* and have him hold us an umbrella table on the patio. You can have some wonderful spiced Italian sausage with ravioli to give you that needed burst of energy, honey." She reached in her bag for her cellphone.

"Sure, Grandma. Sounds nice."

While Ginny made reservations, Fiona retraced a few steps, called to her brother and granddad, "Hey guys, we're taking the pups home. Then going to lunch at *Buca's.*"

She watched them admire the grand sculptures on the forest grounds of *Aberdeen Museum.* A majestic Canadian moose, antlers extended, stood in the direct path of three approaching wolves, whose tails froze in an alert position. These wolves humbled the three Nesbitt dogs who stared with shyness at their *cousins.*

Most Naples' schoolkids took field trips to the *Aberdeen Museum.* Along with antique furnishings, century-old fashions displayed on mannequins, the second floor held a permanent exhibit of some serious history: The *Underground Railroad* story. Among sepia photos, old film, students learned of Naples' role as the town which offered refuge for Black people escaping American slavery before the 1865 abolition. Although, not a specific road, nor an underground trail, per se, the *Underground Railroad* acted as a metaphor for safe, meeting places. At significant risk to themselves, some runaway slaves were smuggled in large cargo crates out of their country. They arrived at a port of freedom in Naples, Ontario, Canada. Modern youth, fascinated by such trials of escape, left the museum in awe.

The Black population increased in the west end of Naples. The village of Bronte grew as a settlement for many African Americans. Many citizens earned respect in their support of other refugees. Furthermore, their enterprises contributed to the growth of Naples. Occupations such as blacksmiths, the need for shoeing horses, and hardware stores for outfitting schooners were necessary, significant businesses.

Later, faith-based gathering spots led to the opening of the *African American Episcopal Methodist* Church right on Lakeshore Road in downtown Naples.

In modern day, that former A-framed chapel was repurposed; now the *Olde Antiques Shop,* on Lakeshore, around the corner from Ginny and Quinn's Forest Street condo.

In this south Naples neighbourhood, of 2015, shady lanes led to the lake. The area spoke to dream-fulfillment for the privileged. The side streets held charming homes, each slightly different in character. Many sloping rooftops simulated antiquity. Delightful pergolas marked pathways to the homes, and held an abundance of trailing ivy, and colour-bursting red and purple wisterias.

Yet, like any modern reality, just blocks away, there also existed pockets of community where folks lived in bland, faded-brick apartment buildings. These medium to high-rise structures held old-style air conditioners jutting from bedroom windows, sticking out like somebody's ass full of stifling air. The constant buzzing no doubt left some tenants sleepless regardless of any cooling effect.

Naples even had homeless people. The *Kerry on House Ministrie*s, or *KOH* and the *Salvation Army* helped where they could. In such ways, Naples existed as a global microcosm, though hardly as congested and frenetic as its big city neighbour, Toronto.

These lower scale demographic patches were nowhere close to the Nesbitt's neighbourhood. However, Ginny, and her tender-hearted Simon, aware of life's injustices contributed in several ways to comfort those in need. Simon had his kids involved in community service. Food drives were particularly effective for the young people to organize at school.

It took effort not to raise spoiled brats, as a group of the students at their school, *Wendall Calbraith Secondary School* (WCSS) were reputed to be. Some kids from east Naples had gained reputations. Simon's twins attended WCSS, not private boarding schools. Keeping matters in perspective. The downside of money.

Virginia also contributed her time and efforts to *KOH* on a regular basis. Often, she brought food, or shared her time helping kids with homework, or just chatting to overstressed moms.

Chapter 11

"You got this, Girl!"

In Toronto, Simon's faithful housekeeper, Marjorie, lingered on the balcony of her sister's condo. She had loads on her mind. The breeze blew whisps of her naturally crimped hair while she tossed ideas around in her head. Should she *move* to Toronto? She treasured her position at the Nesbitt household. But things were changing, always changing...

In this year of late summer, Toronto, known as a city of sleek skyscrapers, appeared mangled with giant construction robots and grey nebulous dust. Old and new condominiums rising and falling like bars on a graph. Congestion whichever way one turned. Subways on main routes, closed for repairs, especially weekends, underground crumbling walls, flooded floors, electrical outages. Taxicab drivers irritable and snarky, even some new immigrants unfamiliar with the street maps. Driven by their own confusion, they ran up the metres - themselves a cause of snarled traffic. Pedestrians, forever in a hurry, hoisting a hot paper cup of *Starbucks* in one hand often able with a free one to flip the bird to those who ticked them off, since the raising of the third finger was not *yet* grounds for arrest. Many realized stepping off a sidewalk curb potentially became a life-risking activity. Statistically, at least once a week, somewhere in the city, a pedestrian was mowed down.

And it wouldn't be an exaggeration to say each morning upon turning on the television, or opening a morning newspaper, one could expect to hear or read about a new shooting or stabbing in the city overnight. And people would sigh and shake their heads and say we are like the Americans now, and it would be like a new board game to see in which *safe* area of this formerly benign metropolis these occurrences – a mark of modern times – had taken place.

Of course, this perception of the big city belonged to Marjorie, who secretly felt vulnerable and confused, and had critical issues to work out and decisions to make.

Hazel's impression of Toronto focused on its world-class status, with its spectacular hospitals, universities, ethnically diverse vibrant neighbourhoods, the CN Tower, a renowned film festival, *TIFF*, and an amazing basketball team called the *Raptors*. Oh, and not to forget, a cozy Gay Village right downtown where she lived to enjoy life.

Furthermore, holding it all together, a *new* affable, engaging mayor, John Tory. Beloved by Torontonians. Tory did his best to seek growth and security for his proud city and its citizens.

Still, Marjorie mentally explored various aspects of her changing future.

Naples with its air of nonchalance, remained a pleasant place to live. Marjorie appreciated this great position in Simon Nesbitt's house – among the plentiful ferns garnishing the front doors. Hazel could keep her big city and her career at a major hospital. Toronto life was not for her. Everything fit so well, but now this situation with Carlos. Unreal. And who knew *Filipe* would end up such a troublemaker?

Marjorie found Filipe rock-star handsome. With his dark hair and intense glare, he reminded her of *Heathcliff* from *Wuthering Heights*, the Emily Bronte novel she studied in high school English class. Yes, that Heathcliff, who was considered a brooding outsider, even an interloper, but sexy.

She spotted him one morning as she drew the drapes from her upper-floor window at *HR* – the west view which overlooked the back garden. He strolled beside Carlos to inspect the grounds. From her vanity drawer, she pulled a pair of opera glasses Simon gifted her one Christmas. She knew to expect this nephew, a recent arrival from the Azores. She adjusted the vision, brought him into larger view. Broad-shouldered, he appeared strong, tanned, and brooding. Marjorie felt that universal pull of animal magnetism throughout all her female parts.

But she was the housekeeper here and in charge. Not about to react to any vision of desire, muscles or not, she scoffed at herself.

Sitting on Hazel's balcony, Marjorie recalled how she checked her smile in the vanity mirror after dabbing on her violet lip stain before heading out to meet Carlos' new *assistant*. A glance at hottie Drake posted on her wall, and she was in control. But one more peek at this handsome man in the garden; she could almost see the veins bulging on this dude's exposed forearms — her weakness in male physicality. Then she replaced the binoculars. In the parlance of the day, she told herself, "You got this, Girl!"

Chapter 12

"Sisters from separate mothers"

Hazel slid open the glass door and stepped onto the balcony.

"There you are Margie. Pretty hot and noisy today in the big city, eh?"

Blaring traffic horns competed for attention over construction drills. Hazel lowered herself into the sling patio chair.

"Yeah, Haze – just thinking that, and..." Marjorie sipped her coke, unable to continue.

Hazel leaned forward. "You're worried about Simon's call, aren't you, Sissy?"

Margie nodded and exhaled. "It's awfully messy."

Marjorie knew her funny half-sister, a younger version of comedian Wanda Sykes, would *get* her dilemma. *Sisters from separate mothers* – often a joke- for people with a simpatico connection. For Marjorie and Hazel, it was a fact.

Hazel's mother, Maxine Reed, a Black woman, worked as a laboratory technician at *Brant Hospital* in Burlington. Her job in the early Seventies brought her into contact with Jeremiah Wallace, known as Jerry. His role as an orderly at the hospital gave them plenty of time to learn about each other through lunches in the cafeteria. As people of colour, they were a minority.

They sat together and joked around. They fell in love, married, and Maxine gave birth to Hazel in 1977.

When the bubbly Hazel turned five, tragedy struck her life. Her dear mother contracted AIDS from improper handling of blood samples. In 1982, no one knew enough about this devastating epidemic to take the necessary precautions.

Grief-stricken Jeremiah, a direct and proud descendant from the American fugitive slaves a century earlier, took up boxing, known as 'Big Basher Jerry.' No basher at heart, Jerry left that work with a battered nose, and entered the field of Real Estate. He signed on as a salesperson with *Powers Realty*. A personable fellow, Jerry charmed the staff, particularly one freckled secretary named Heather Margaret Dunlop.

Soon Jerry made a good living. He and Heather married. Her relatives visited from Edinburgh for the wedding. The happy couple purchased a corner house edged with large cedars which enclosed a hidden pool. A lovely location on Regal Road in Bronte. They raised Hazel as an only child until sweet Marjorie came along in 1986. Then they had their perfect family.

As any true cynic understands, in a changing world, anything goes. Marjorie and Hazel lost their parents in the Tsunami of 2004. Heather and Jerry took an anniversary trip with another couple, friends from their golf club. All four vacationers vanished in Thailand's natural disaster on Boxing Day. The presumption: they all perished.

The girls, eighteen, and twenty-seven at that time, clung to each other like the life-rafts their parents had never known, nor expected to need. Their American uncle and aunt, Benjamin and Celeste came from North Carolina to settle matters for the girls. They sold the house, invested the funds. They guided the girls to relocate to Naples where Marjorie would study at Saunders College. The girls found their bearings, shared an apartment for a while, until Hazel moved to Toronto to nurse at *Sick Kids*. Marjorie graduated college and landed her dream job at the Nesbitt's.

"My dear girl, go lie down and have a nap before we head back to Naples," ordered Hazel, the older, presumably, wiser sister. "You don't seem yourself, Margie… and I don't just mean this whole business about Carlos. Besides, Simon will need your support, and so will the kids."

"Hazel?" Marjorie whispered. "I'm pregnant."

"Go on, get moving! Do as I say." Hazel tugged her sister's arm. She heard nothing from that quiet voice over the high-pitched neighbourhood construction drilling.

Marjorie resigned herself to heed Hazel's advice. She realized Hazel didn't hear the information she tried to reveal. She took her confused and heavy heart into the bedroom, laid down on the bed and covered herself with the cozy comforter. She would *have* to deal with this secret, and soon.

She drifted to sleep with thoughts of her lost parents. Lost, never found.

And Marjorie began to dream.

And dreams create new worlds. One could swear to the reality. You were there!

Marjorie in the arms of Simon - the world's most tender and loving man. They sit on a blanket in the sand dunes by the sea. Their beautiful baby girl, Hannah, cuddles in-between them.

The sun shines. They are happy. Simon has no other family, but this one.

Suddenly, a wind blows. Its velocity whirls up a storm – tops of thick palm trees sway, no longer restful but angry. Marjorie and her beloved Simon hold baby Hannah close; they feel safe together.

Quickly, the landscape spins. Flying beach chairs hurl through the air. Clothing, towels, toy pails and shovels whip around in circles. Hannah's pink sunhat blows towards the growing whitecaps. Simon runs to retrieve it. He runs and runs in heavy sand.

Now she, baby in arms, runs after him. He is swallowed by the sky-high rolling waters which break over him. She, too, chokes, and coughs. Stumbles. Hannah slides from her grip... is gone.

Her dream-scene suddenly switches to Naples. A loud crack, louder than thunder, snaps a massive branch off the ancient chestnut tree which overlooks Simon's verandah, and crashes on them three. Silence. It's over.

Marjorie woke with a shudder and a slight scream. She reached for a tissue from the nightstand to muffle her sobs. *Having Simon's baby? How crazy, but how real it felt.* Wishful thinking. *But we were all destroyed! What hell.*

Then, Marjorie experienced her first real wave of nausea. She stumbled to the toilet and vomited. Finished, she lowered the lid and sat on it. She didn't want to come out of the washroom.

Earlier, at *Shoppers' Drug Mart* when Hazel flipped at the magazine rack through knitting patterns, Marjorie covertly purchased a home pregnancy test.

Hazel would make an excellent mother, and will someday, Margie mused as she admired her sister's enthusiasm for tiny-tot cable sweaters. But not in *this* way. Hazel was thick with Ellen *Fuyun* Lim, the anesthetist at *Sick Kids. No chance of either of them getting pregnant, like me. They would need a donor.*

Marjorie moved from the toilet lid, shoved the tropical shower curtain aside, to sit on the edge of the bathtub. She held her head in her hands and tugged at her soft black hair. *Simon will fire me when he finds out. I'll have to leave his house, his employ,* she thought, like Hagar from the Bible, dismissed to the wilderness with her *inappropriate* child. She crouched up, turned on the tap. Slapped water on her face. Peered into the mirror. Her usual confidence, deflated, her pretty eyes haunted. *No, he wouldn't, would he? How do I tell him? What about Fiona and Darius? What will they think?*

She sat back down on the lip of the tub and let her mind go wild. *With all my schooling, I'm going to end up being a babysitter at the YMCA!* Panic set in, catastrophic thinking. But not like her to panic. Yet she had never been in this state before. Now she had hormones to contend with, too.

What if I have to take a job as a receptionist or a cleaner? Worse, I could end up as a Walmart cashier. Not that it's an unacceptable job, but she was trained in running a home. Like a *concierge. How did I screw up so badly?*

Not necessarily a *pro-lifer,* Marjorie instinctively *knew* she would keep this baby. She wouldn't consider abortion. How many chances does a girl in her thirties get?

Okay, get a grip. I have to share this news with Hazel. Just hope she doesn't think of me as her sleaze sister. Life can be so unpredictable. I'm going for it. Meant to be.

A wry grin came over Marjorie's face. Now she thought of Hazel's happiness. Daddy would have been delighted Hazel 'landed a doctor' by working at *Sick Kids*. Not a Jewish doctor — the standard wish people always joked about — but a Chinese one. Yet would he have *cared* about the *gender* of said doctor? She wondered. Then, she threw up once more, and heard Hazel rapping on the door, calling her, genuine concern in her voice.

Chapter 13

"And Hamish…his gaze lingered on the distracted Simon."

"C an you meet me at *Orsino's*?" Simon spoke through his car phone.

Delighted, Hamish replied, "Hey, man, let me check with Esther – hold on Iggy,"

When he left Albina's after his talk with Ed, Simon couldn't wait for a drink with his best friend. They had a lot to debrief.

Why that wench, Albina! And why the hell was he getting a *boner* in her house?

"Sure thing, buddy," said Hamish back on phone. 'Twenty minutes, okay? How did it go at Albina's?"

"I'll save it till I see you, thanks, Ham. Tell Esther I owe her one – being a Saturday and all. Later."

What a day for the books, thought Simon. Concentration escaped him. All these unexpected events, and it was barely mid-afternoon. He called his mom and learned the kids and grandparents had a nice walk and lunch.

All four of them were sweet, thought Simon. Relieved they were unaware of the gravity of today's events, he relaxed some-what. This evening with Marjorie returning to smooth things over in her efficient way will lift the mood even more. How grateful he felt to have such a solid, loyal housekeeper.

Simon had some time now before meeting Hamish. He drove slowly. He clicked on Rod Stewart's the *Great American Songbook Collection Classics* album. His favourite piece was '*I'll be seeing you...*' the rich husky voice of Stewart created the perfect mellow atmosphere to match the lyrics.

Simon shivered, as though a hologram beam of Peggy sat in the soft, bucket seat next to him. He listened to the lyrics with his heart. They spoke of all the places they'd been together, liked Paris cafes, and playgrounds, and wishing wells. Would they ever meet again? Heart aching!

PAUSE... Simon clicked off the music. Far too painful. He stopped at the lookout point alongside *Caruso Park* and stared at the lake. He realized he was milking his sad feelings.

His overreaction to Albina's presence made him feel like he dishonoured Peggy's memory. *Nonsense.* Or was it? He was male, had physical needs, and no qualms taking matters into his own hands when the *urge* hit him – like other guys. But mostly he pictured sex in a romantic mood, Peggy as his fantasy woman. He had actually been hot for the mother of his children, not like those dudes who put a wife on a pedestal and find sexual fulfillment elsewhere. Peggy meant all things to him. But dead six years now. When she was dying, he promised her he would mourn her forever. And, he added, he would not look at another woman romantically for at least ten years.

Yet, he reacted to his dead groundskeeper's widow? Christ! Confusion.

Maybe I need to consider dating again, Simon thought. *Whoa, slow down, buddy.*

He started the car and headed towards *Orsino's Den*– his favourite pub.

Simon parked in his preferred spot, not busy midday. He looked around for the burnt orange of Hamish's Mazda. Didn't see it. He entered the pub, cave-like as its name, found instant darkness. Up a few steps, he pulled open the thick embossed glass doors into the cool afternoon ambience of a tavern. He paused — let his eyes adjust from the outdoor sunlight. He spotted the owner, who came to greet him.

"I'll just take my usual spot at the back, Enrico. I'm expecting Hamish. He's not here yet, is he? Didn't see his car in the lot," Simon offered a friendly smile, and walked along past the gleaming wood bar with overhead screens showing some tennis match.

"Sure thing, Simon. I'll send him down when he arrives," assured the owner and happily continued to organize menus passing them to a server in a black mini, with dark hair twisted into a trendy bun. Enrico already knew Simon's standard first round.

Walls of white stucco circled the pub's room. Pots of faux greenery gave corners a lift. Natural beams along the ceiling and a large stone fireplace created a relaxed atmosphere. Dark wood tables and chairs plus leatherette benches hugged the walls, pretty much standard fare, but there were areas in this pub which allowed intimacy apart from the general open space. However, this quiet afternoon he saw less than a handful of the usual, chatty Naples crowd.

Simon took the corner— slightly out of view. He sat on the hard-backed end chair of the small table and left the soft bench for Hamish. He checked his phone for alerts, then, gratefully, put it down, along with his keys and shades.

He looked up, saw Hamish approach. Simon stood, and the men gave each other shoulder hugs with back pats – greetings these days between close friends. Simon glad for this bit of modern culture. Hamish too.

Dressed in *perfect-fit* dark jeans, a collared, pale-blue short-sleeved jersey, and a tidy, thin leather belt, Hamish Deakin appeared as his usual immaculate self. His large brow showcased his fine auburn hair neatly gelled with a one-side wave. When dressed down, even as an adult, Hamish projected a clean-shaven, fresh, *prep-school boy* look.

He sat on the banquette. To impress Simon, he tried a *man-spread* of his legs as he leaned into the soft, back padding. After some awkward shifting, he adjusted his position. Not right for the elegant Hamish.

He leaned forward and crossed one knee over the other instead, trying a casual look; he swung a pointed toe of his chocolate-suede Desert boots.

Enrico sent a pitcher of draught by way of the Pixie who set the jug and glasses down carefully and couldn't decide which man was more breath-taking. A new employee, this young lady had not yet laid eyes on these two gentlemen.

Some small talk ensued as they asked her name and ethnicity. Russian, she told them. Her name, Natalya. She waitressed to pay for school.

She was beautiful. Yet, her teeth... less than perfect, although Simon did not focus there. His eyes dropped to her pale neckline.

Natalya asked the gentlemen to let her know if there was something else. Then she performed a tiny curtsy, and took her slight, but inspiring cleavage away with her to another customer. Simon watched her retreat, mesmerized by the flutter swing of her skirt off her petite backside.

And Hamish ...his gaze lingered on the distracted Simon.

"What a shit day," said Simon pouring Hamish a glass of suds. "In the first place, Albina was fuckin' hostile."

Hamish raised an eyebrow and his glass, as both men tapped cheers with a sigh and a first gulp.

"When I told her Carlos was dead – she bloody carried on... okay, we're all sad – but her reaction was over the top." Simon toyed with the napkin – folding a poor version of *origami*.

"Remember when we studied Hamlet? The widow Player Queen freaked out when her husband dies? And the real Queen – Gertrude, says while watching this play, 'The lady doth protest too much?'"

Hamish nodded, "Of course, Iggy. We use this a lot in law, too. Suggests someone is hiding something. Has secrets."

"Exactly! Well, you understand, Ham. That's how I felt about Albina. Like she was acting out this sorrow – trying to make a point of grief – which backfired as far as I'm concerned," said Simon, and downed another swig of coolness. "I hope I'm wrong, Ham, but my gut tells me her sobbing was insincere." He stifled a polite burp.

"What do you think it was?" asked Hamish, his lawyer's voice smooth and firm, his emerald eyes penetrating Simon's.

"Well, the thing is," explained Simon, "Eduardo and I talked outside afterwards and he gave me an earful. Said his parents fought a lot. Loud vocal fights. Embarrassed, he said he overheard his mother call his dad 'less than a man'. Apparently, they didn't realize he was in the basement. Then Ed told me his girlfriend Berri, and his mom had quite a little chat one night when he was out tutoring math to a high school kid."

"What kind of name is Berri?" asked Hamish. He knew Carlos, of course, and knew of his son Eduardo, because of their work at the Nesbitt's, but Hamish was too busy with his own family and career to think of Carlos' life beyond Simon's place.

"It's Beryl Webster. Her dad's an accountant at City Hall – Ron Webster. These two kids met at Saunders College. Well, God knows where Carlos was this one night, but with Ed out, the two women got drinking all comfy on the chairs of the front porch, and Albina spilled how miserable she was. Hinted that there's more fish in the sea than the one you get stuck with, or something along those lines, so warned Berri to be careful, not to rush and get tied down with the wrong man. She even told Berri that her husband - wait for this Ham – that Carlos was on Viagra. Now why in hell do you suppose she would tell a young girl that?"

Simon felt his moral indignity rise in the telling. He politely waved off more beer as the waitress, Natalya, tried to approach, all smiles, – they were both driving – one pitcher's enough.

"Guilt," said Hamish in his critical deduction.

"Well, that's the conclusion I came to, as well," agreed Simon. "I don't believe she was as broken up as she let on. Of course, I realize people handle shock and grief in different ways, but I'm going on a gut reaction, Ham. What do *you* think she was guilty about?" Simon asked as he raised his final glass to his lips. He knocked back his beer anxious to return home.

"Well, if she wasn't really broken up about her husband, then maybe she had someone else?" suggested Hamish raising an eyebrow, once again. Elbows on the table with his hands together, Hamish tapped his mouth in speculation. At the same time, he twirled his wedding band, mindlessly, as he waited for Simon's opinion.

"Albina? I never thought of her *that* way," said Simon. "Just thought of her as this nice little wife of Carlos." But then, he stared at the table through his empty glass. He felt a twinge of discomfort. His deceit. A stab in his gut; he realized that's not what he thought of Albina at all. Stuck in mire here, Simon raised his head and met Hamish's gaze with a sigh, said nothing more.

Simon wanted to tell Hamish about his unexpected physical reaction to Albina but held back. His best friend since grade nine at KLA, roommates in the dorm. Friends tell each other everything. He had no problem sharing about Peggy back in the day, but this felt different. Simon knew Hamish's secret. Talking about his sexual fantasies or, sexual urges would not help Hamish. Simon knew Hamish, a happily married husband of Esther and father of two, was bisexual, and also deeply in love with a man. Simon didn't want to stir the pot, sexually speaking. Both men grasped the unspoken: the man Hamish was in love with sat right beside him, looked straight at him.

When Simon, or Iggy, to his schoolmates, roomed with Hamish at the Kawartha Lakes Academy, they were both shy, sweet, and well suited. Hamish was sent to the boarding school all the way from Australia since his family, the Deakin's, planned to emigrate to the Niagara-on -the -Lake in a year or so after they bought vineyards in the region.

The two fifteen-year-old sensitive boys simply melded and were considerate of each other's feelings, helped one another with homework. They became inseparable. But in such close quarters as a shared dorm, secrets were hard to keep. One night, from homesickness, Hamish, overwhelmed by emotional need, cried. Simon sensed his friend's palpable suffering. He invited him to his cot to sleep and put an arm about him. That's when the incident took place. At the peak and mercy of hormonal impact, the boys expressed themselves in strong physical ways together, finding release stronger than guilt. Iggy was tender towards Hamish but made it clear he was *straight,* and this behaviour would not, *could not*, happen again.

But it did. Two more times that night. For Simon, he felt a lifetime connection to Hamish. For Hamish, it was a love never to fulfill, but a lifetime of devotion to his best friend.

The two buddies continued their conversation and came to the reasonable conclusion that Carlos probably got the Fentanyl from his nephew, and Filipe may have been providing him also with the Viagra, in addition to the mind-blowing pain killers which brought his demise. Hamish said he would visit Filipe at the *Metropolitan Toronto West Detention Centre* and question him. Hamish would not apply for bail.

Hamish also noted that Schroeder was wrong in calling Carlos a 'user'. Maybe it was just an accident, and they could put this behind them. All evidence pointed to Filipe as the user and dealer. The hope shared between Simon and Hamish: this was the end of it. They would give Carlos a nice funeral, and let Filipe pay for his damages.

Chapter 14

"He had charisma, but not the phony type."

Hamish and Esther Deakin met at the University of Toronto, Faculty of Law. Both pragmatic lawyers and somewhat introverted, they appreciated the life they created for themselves. They adored their boys, Bryan ten, and Gordie eight. They enjoyed an upscale lifestyle in a contemporary home off Lakeshore Road in Southeast Naples. They relished their successful careers and were proud of their *family-life choices.*

As a couple alert to each other's idiosyncrasies, over the years Esther recognized her husband's private yearnings for Simon. She trusted Hamish when he admitted to a few dalliances with males, but never with Simon, his *best* friend.

Esther tolerated Hamish's *extra-curricular* activities. Given his fastidious nature, he would take the necessary precautions to keep them safe. She preferred his brief flings with males over females. She figured she was better off with a bisexual hubby than a roving one, less threatening to her femininity and their marriage. This happy lifestyle was not for everyone, of course, but it worked for them. Hamish, always clean, kind, and considerate, understood her well-enough. More than most women got from marriage. Besides, he was a terrific dad.

Esther felt Hamish even *loved* Simon in a profound way. She also knew there was no chance in hell it would go anywhere beyond their friendship. Regardless of his ultra-sensitive nature, Simon was hetero as could be. Yet, due to his sensitivity, Simon seemed to appear on everyone's wish list. Who *wasn't* in love with him? Esther, herself, suppressed a little crush and she noticed how his housekeeper -that Marjorie - would *bonk* him in a flash, should she be so lucky.

It's true Simon did not engage in frivolous affairs. A monogamous man, he still missed Peggy and everyone in their circle knew it. Perhaps it was time for him to move on. Esther wondered who might be right for him. Yet, she realized he'd find somebody at his own speed and choosing. Not a shallow man, Simon oozed charisma, but not the phony type. He was solid.

Chapter 15

"This dude seemed like a mangy, abandoned dog."

On the drive home from Orsino's, Simon stopped at the traffic light where Mariner Street crossed Lakeshore Road. To his right, the impressive domed Central Library, and on his left, the popular *Paradis Patio*. He waited. The red, programmed extra-long at this corner, allowed high volume to flow across the Lakeshore Road bridge. Its narrow lanes often jammed bumper-to-bumper by weekend tourists.

Downtown Naples with its sophisticated boutiques juxtaposed by a scenic background of sky-high trees bearing the thickest trunks around, lured many out-of-towners on a regular basis.

Resigned to wait, Simon glanced at the diners on *Paradis Patio* seated beneath striped umbrellas. Chilling with their late-afternoon *Chablis*, they sat at outdoor tables graced with brown and white checkered linens. Epitome of subtle elegance.

As he looked right, he noticed a guy on the corner, faced away from him. Simon thought he seemed out of place in *downtown* Naples. His faded trousers, like someone's old dress-pants, perhaps a thrift-store purchase. The pant legs pooled to the pavement.

Simon stared from curiosity and sympathy. After leaving the impeccable, sartorial Hamish, he noted the contrast. The long-sleeved once *white* shirt, thread-bare grey. But worse, his greasy black and white limp hair hung to his neckline. The dude seemed like a mangy, abandoned dog. *Poor guy* thought Simon, *bloody injustice of poverty.*

Finally, the *walk* signal appeared. Abruptly, the pedestrian twisted to face Simon's car in case of a right-hand turn. Darting eyes caught his own, a haunted gaze of inquiry.

Simon gasped. Shocked, he realized this *vagrant guy* was a *female.*

Stunned, he shuddered, and felt ashamed for staring. He drove on as the cars lined behind him expected him to move it.

The image of this impoverished woman stuck in his mind and tightened his throat until he reached home.

Then Simon felt a lucky man. His parents and kids back from their outing. The dogs rushed to greet him, all wagging tails and licks, even little Prudence made her way over, hoping for a lift into his arms. She got her wish and a snuggle.

"Whoa, dark in here, guys," Simon pressed a button and activated a drapes retractor. The outdoor sunlight flooded the family room. "Sorry, guys, what were you watching?"

Darius paused the *Star Wars*: *Attack of the Clones* film they were introducing to their grandparents. Everyone shifted in their seats with 'hey dad, daddy, hi son, hello honey' practically all at once. He felt blessed by this chorus of love and by the universe regardless of this morning's events.

He slipped out of his loafers, padded over to deposit Pru in Fiona's lap, planting a soft kiss on his daughter's forehead, and then one on his mom's cheek, as she sat cozied next to her granddaughter.

"*Star Wars* dad. Grandma and Gramps haven't seen this episode, yet." Darius offered.

Simon leaned into the bowl of popcorn placed on the low rustic coffee-table, grabbed a handful, and then took a seat on *his* mustard armchair - which Darius bounced from without being asked, joining grandma and Fi on the oversized cinnamon sofa.

On the green velour recliner, Grandpa Quinn clicked into an upright position.

"Quite the day, son," he said to Simon, with a direct look full of implied meaning.

"Yeah, Dad, and it's not over. Thanks to you guys for being here for these two trouble-makers."

"Daddy!" interjected Fiona. "Nice one!"

"No honey," joked Simon, "I meant Charity and Kent, of course, my Beauty."

Home sweet home. Could he ask for anything more?

Charity and Kent collapsed into their former positions on the warm, sunlit floor.

Kent, reluctantly re-settled, remained assuaged by his proximity to Simon's ankles. Charity returned to Darius and turned herself into a golden bean bag. Prudence enjoyed having her silky ears stroked by Fiona.

Mom and dad - Ginny and Quinn - together kept wise looks of curiosity laced with patience. Life had schooled them on how to gauge a situation, when to speak. They, too, were grateful for this moment of togetherness – the now – all that anyone had.

Before the shit would hit the fan.

Chapter 16

"What *kind* of trouble?"

"**F**eels like we taking a fresh donor-heart to some recipient!" Hazel nestled the market fish onto the crushed ice and snapped the cooler's handle tight. She spoke in her relaxed *jive* or as some may say, *African American Vernacular English* when comfy at home with her sister or girlfriend. She chuckled at her medical metaphor.

"Oh, enough of your hospital humor, Sis," Marjorie shot back distracted; then embarrassed, she looked at her fingernails, and muttered, "Sorry, Haze."

"Why you in such a dark mood, honey? Having some PMS? Usually, you love my one-liners. Ahh, that boss of yours don't need no new heart, anyway. He's got a great one of his own, ain't that right?"

Moving about her condo's cozy kitchen, Hazel gathered shopping bags for the vegetables they would bring too. Not that he needs *our* food, she thought, but she knew, given the circumstances, he would appreciate the gesture. She remembered his kind and generous attitude towards them offering Margie extra times off when she had her own family needs.

Marjorie looked glum. She needed to tell Hazel *everything* before they left.

85

"Chill, baby girl," cooed Hazel. "Here's a bit of chocolate."
She opened Marjorie's palm and dropped a couple of silver-
wrapped *Hershey's Kisses* into it. "We almost ready. You already
packed; I'm packed. Cab is on its way,"

Marjorie unwrapped both pieces and popped them into her
mouth. Chocolate *was* a soother, her sister, a magician. Maybe
she *could* help. She turned and grabbed Hazel's wrist; halted her
movements. Hazel's metallic earrings jingled with the quick shift
of her head.

"Sit down, Sis," Marjorie pleaded, and drew Hazel towards
a yellow, leatherette chair at the small white table. "I have something I gotta tell ya before we return to Simon's."

Hazel paused. "Can't we talk about it in the taxi, baby girl?"
Forehead wrinkles replaced her bright smile.

"No. Cancel the ride. Please." Marjorie shoved the cellphone
across the table to Hazel.

"I'm in *trouble*," she wailed. Her jade eyes narrowed, but
engaged with Hazel's pronounced, deep-brown ones.

A moment of silence between the sisters.

"What *kind* of trouble? What the hell you talking about,
Margie?" Hazel raised her tone and arched an eyebrow as she
texted a postponement to her favorite taxi.

"There's no easy way to say this, Haze. I'm pregnant."
Marjorie waited for a reaction.

Relieved, Hazel exploded with laughter. "Pregnant? *In trouble*? Girl - *this ain't* the '50s! Nobody says *that* anymore."

"Well, I do. I have a '50s name, don't I? Marjorie pouted,
uncharacteristically. She suspected hormones.

"Don't gimme that! You know you're proud to have the
name of your Scottish grandmother." Hazel tried to calm her

dear Margie. "But, honey, the way you said you're in trouble, I thought something terrible happened!"

"Well, it *is* terrible. I could lose my job at Simon's."

"I must say, I am surprised, though. You didn't say you were *seeing* anybody."

"I'm not, really."

"Oh, lord, don't tell me it's Simon's?" Hazel's eyes widened and stared. She wiped the corners of her lips with thumb and index finger making an oval opening of her mouth.

"God, no!"

"Then, whose is it?"

"It's mine!" Marjorie sniffed, despite sounding ridiculous, even to herself.

"Well, we know *that* hon, but you're not the Blessed Virgin Mary. Who's the father?"

"That's part of the problem."

"What does *that* mean? Are you into one-night stands?" Hazel's anxiety swelling.

"No, Hazel. I'm not some *ho!*" Marjorie blurted a defensive reaction.

"So, who's your daddy?"

"You don't have to sound so frivolous, Hazel. I *am* upset about this."

"You don't want to reveal his identity? Is that it?" Hazel tried a calmer approach.

"I don't *know* who the father is."

"Damn! You're not making any sense, girl," argued Hazel. "And besides, as a nurse working with kids, I normally wouldn't recommend this, but you do *realize* you could get an abortion, Margie?" She tried restraining the sarcasm in her voice.

Hazel then turned and glanced at her girlfriend's cheeky photo pinned to the fridge door with a *Sick Kids Hospital Foundation* magnet.

"I must say, Fuyun and I are lucky we'll never have this type of problem," sighed Hazel, as she tried to comfort her sister. She took Margie's hands, and they locked their beautiful long fingers.

"You guys are lucky you're in love with each other," said Marjorie. "I'm not in love with the father of this baby. But I sure as hell do not want an abortion! I want to have this baby. What if I never get another chance? I'm no *spring chicken*, anymore."

"Look, I don't mean to be insensitive, Margie, but why won't you just come clean and tell me who the father is?" Hazel tossed up her hands in frustration.

"Okay, okay. Here it is then." Marjorie still felt safest when with her sister. She decided to lay it all out on the table.

"The father is either dead, or he's in jail."

"What's *that* supposed to mean? Hazel slapped the table. She grew even more frustrated. She puckered her lips.

"The father could be Carlos. Or, he could be his nephew, Filipe. Satisfied?"

"What the?" Hazel pitched high. "You were screwing those two guys at the same time? And Carlos was married?"

"It's a long story, Hazel. Please don't be ashamed of me," a weepy Marjorie answered and reached for tissues.

"Well, I'm listening, girl. You got some *'splainin'* to do!" Hazel shook her tight short dreads, crossed her arms over her robust chest, and was all ears for this one.

Chapter 17

"Why fight what comes naturally?"

Stirring a pot of spaghetti sauce for the boys, her thick, raven hair swept back and loosely twisted into a chignon, Esther offered her cheek for a peck as Hamish approached her at the Aga.

At the same time, he patted her round bum, housed in rose, slim pants. Then, he tasted the tanginess of the meaty sauce from the spatula Esther blew on and held for his lips to savor.

"Mmm, nice fresh basil, as usual, my love. And there is something so hot about *you* in that black apron, open in the back-side. Mmm, my imagination runs wild."

"Sexist." Esther shot back. She ushered a tendril over her ear. Her gleaming white teeth lit up her bronze complexion. "I'll give you imagination. *You're* wearing it tonight! Only accessory you'll need. And I'll have this," she declared, as she held the stirring spoon high with a warning glint in her eye.

They both burst into laughter.

"A little aggressive even for you, Darling," Hamish chided with a thrilling shiver. Then he moved to the sink to wash his hands at the touch-free tap and soap. Esther turned her head to follow his direction, still smiling.

Married to a bisexual had its playful advantages, thought Esther. It's like gays invented hotness. Always an underlining of erotica and fun. Always a pun or two of innuendo to feel your senses stimulated.

She often thought those who married - whether at the altar, in a park gazebo, or the offices of the Justice of the Peace – those who spoke vows of *socially enforced sincerity* – to NEVER ever, for the rest of their lives, have sex with another human being... well, nobody would ever marry! *Forsaking all others* –nicely couched in the speech– not realistic at all. In *her* opinion -boring! Small wonder so many divorces. It would be like promising to hold one's breath from this moment until the day I die – which, in this household, would take less than two minutes.

Esther joined Hamish by the black steel window frame over the deep kitchen sink. They looked to the boys kicking the soccer ball on the expansive grounds. Except for a few, well-spaced majestic white oaks, and graceful birches, the green stretch practically matched the size of a regulation field. Their view of knee and head bounces just in front brought them a feeling of pride and warmth. Their little guys.

"Shall I call them in?

"Not yet." Esther deliberated. "What happened with Simon? Fill me in first before they dash in hollering. Is he okay? I'm sure you were a comfort, dearest." She returned to the stove, dialed the burner to simmer, and angled a lid onto the pot.

They each rested a hip on a bar stool, and a foot on the chrome, lower ring as they leaned into the top of their ivory-speckled island. Esther's chestnut eyes, framed by extension lashes, focused with intelligence on Hamish's sleek, cat-eye gems. She studied his translucent freckled face, searching for information. She loved how beautiful her husband was, his straight nose worthy of ancient Greek artistry. Mostly, she cherished how brilliant a mind Hamish possessed. She felt lucky to have him. Hamish was her best friend even though he was also Simon's. She didn't mind sharing him in that sense, at all. However, she'd never admit to a fantasy of having them both to herself in bed.

As they entwined their elongated fingers, hers brown, his pale, the Deakin's discussed Simon's discomfort with Albina – how her anger startled him. Perhaps Albina had a lover. Perhaps she felt a bit of guilt over Carlos' death. Hamish was prepared to get further information from Filipe. And he wanted to question Schroeder, as well.

As lawyers, the Deakin's shared a wise philosophy: they believed the world is a less difficult place to navigate within a spirit of compromise. Why fight what comes naturally? People snap when bent too far – far beyond their natural inclinations.

They talked about how Simon always wanted to do the right thing. Perhaps - they tossed up between themselves - the right thing for him, what might have served him better, was less rigidity. They agreed, as much as they loved their friend, in the end they both felt Simon was a bit of a control freak. They thought maybe Quinn was responsible for the suppressed inner rebel in Simon. Although Quinn exemplified a loving father to this day, when Simon was young Quinn directed all his moves, leaving Simon unsure about some of his *own* decisions.

Even though they worried about their dear friend, with their practical outlook, neither Hamish nor Esther would snap easily. A focus on acceptance of their lives and a *make it work* attitude held them together.

Esther, a smart attorney, thought of by others as a tough, East-Indian beauty, herself came from an interesting mix of parents. Esther's father, Saul Greene, was a Jewish fine-furniture importer/exporter from Toronto, who met her mother - his 'Bombay princess' at the five–star *Four Seasons* in London, England, while on a shopping expedition. Bindu, a part-time concierge at the hotel, was an engineering student. She had a beautiful English accent which Esther emulated. The classy aura of education accompanied every word out of her mouth. The British.

Hamish's people were originally from Australia where the Deakin family, essentially the grandparents, did exceptionally well with their winery estate. The emigration of the next generation to Canada was successful in buying some vineyards and properties in the Niagara region. They managed to send their children to private academies and enjoyed a charming existence in a Victorian mansion in Niagara-on-the Lake where their daughter made a name for herself in the theatre community.

Amanda Deakin, the character actor, much beloved, drowned in a boating accident on Lake Ontario. Her host's thirty-foot *Islander* exploded one sunny afternoon. Three people died. Hamish tried to fill the aching gap for his parents; yet he never felt second best. He honored his older sister's memory by reciting her odd-ball risqué jokes at parties. She too had been gay, and they had shared many a laugh together of how lucky their parents were to have them.

Chapter 18

"We've got news!"

The cab ride from Toronto, jammed over the Gardiner expressway, finally picked up speed. The passengers remained silent. The driver, a gentleman in a mauve turban, complemented by strong, salt and pepper facial hair avoided conversation, kept his concentration on the road. He allowed himself to wonder why his female passengers did not chatter as women tend to do. At least the women he knew *relished* any opportunity to gossip with one another.

Leaning their heads into the shiny vinyl of the back seat, the sisters each looked out the north and south windows, respectively, seeing little, but their own thoughts.

So that's how it went down, Hazel reflected on what her sister told her in the apartment.

Just like Margie to be so kind, Hazel snorted to herself. *Carlos began taking little dick boosters which backfired on him. When kicked out of his wife's bed, he had nowhere to put his Mr. Stiffy. And when the boss and the kids were not around, my dear sis helped him out on occasion.*

God, thought Hazel, *Margie said he begged her. Ah, that's men for ya! And that nephew of his – shit-disturber. She did say he was so hot she couldn't turn him down. A total pig to hit on his employer's employee. Whatever happened to workplace harassment? Now, she's knocked up, and hasta face the boss, spill the truth... to the one she really wants. Bummer. Get ready, Simon, we've got news!*

She snapped her blue Nitrile gloves off one at a time and tossed them aside on the counter. Marjorie then donned the super-sized orange, silicone ones and slipped the lemon and chives dressed salmon into the oven.

'It won't be long now, everyone," she turned and smiled at *her* family. Yes, that's how it felt, especially today: Simon, Fiona, Darius, Hazel, Simon's parents, and Eduardo here, too.

Ed arrived to pick up his dad's truck, and sweet Fiona, brimming with heartfelt sympathy over Carlos, hugged him and insisted he stay for dinner. Her tenderness swayed Ed to agree. He needed a break from his mother – especially during this crisis.

Meanwhile, after Berri dropped Ed off outside, she returned to Albina to give her support with selecting an outfit for the funeral, but mostly to comfort her. They would have the stew Albina had prepared earlier, and they really *clicked*, enjoyed each other's company, almost a mother/daughter duo.

Faking their asses off, Marjorie and Hazel displayed inordinate goodwill, and spirit. They soon realized this was *not* the hour for their revelations. They kept their issues quiet.

The dogs delighted in *the more the merrier* experience although the occasion was less than mirthful. A distinct air of artificiality floated in the room to recreate an uplifting aura.

Just prior to Marjorie and Hazel's arrival at Hackberry Road, Simon broke *his* version of information to this little brood.

He let on Carlos suffered a stroke and died in hospital, not in this house. No telling how Darius would handle the truth. And, to further protect his family, Simon kept the business of drugs, and Filipe's arrest out of the general conversation.

Food usually made everyone relax, and Marjorie's arrival felt like a Godsend to Simon. He returned her smile with one of his own radiant grins, concealing his relief. What he revealed was his gap-tooth boyish appearance, which showed his happiness as Margie whipped around her kitchen, back in charge, and set them all at ease.

At the side bar, Simon prepared cocktails on the rocks, complete with limes which Hazel could not say no to, and with Ginny and Quinn, they toasted Carlos. Eduardo held an ale, and the teens their apple juices. The moment appeared special, yet there was a lump in everyone's throat.

Marjorie demurred from alcohol- insisting to keep her wits not to burn dinner. Ice water with a slice of lemon for her, *and her baby.* She chewed, discreetly, on antacid tablets she kept in her apron's pocket.

With everyone seated at the harvest table, a relaxed chatter broke out between forkfuls of salmon and rice, and the mixed arugula salad with feta crumble.

"I just can't wait for the new *Star Wars* movie," said Darius. "Yeah, *The Force Awakens.*" He shouted his enthusiasm. Suddenly, shy, he thought of the forever-sleeping Carlos. He lowered his eyelashes to his plate. Silent.

Marjorie, seated beside Darius, reached out and touched his arm with the warmth and gentleness of a mother. This gesture - not lost on Simon.

"Just look at that sky." Like a switch of the channel on a remote, Marjorie re-set the mood. Heads looked up to the sight of a purple heaven over their rippling lake.

Simon noted, "Ed, you know how we loved your father. We'll always remember him, his love of nature, and how he added to the beauty of this environment. He enjoyed working here, took pride in his accomplishments. If it suits you, Ed, feel free to carry on some of his work, if you like."

"I'd like that, Mr. Nes..." The raised eyebrow caught Eduardo.

"I mean *Simon*. Thank you, Simon, for everything you've done for my family." His voice choked, his cheeks flushed, and his dark brown eyes blurred with deep sorrow.

Eduardo dropped his chin, exhaled an audible, defeated breath.

For at this moment, in midst of a close family, Ed absorbed the full impact of losing a beloved dad. *His* family's father. Gone from his life. Just like that. Forever.

Chapter 19

"And we create our own families."

Sour-faced, Albina nodded.

On cue, Beryl picked up the pulsating phone. "Delgado residence," she announced, tone haughty. Following the Filipe disgrace, Beryl needed to restore dignity. *Imagine, a criminal had been living in their midst. And now, poor Carlos.* She curled the cord around her index finger and waited. She locked eyes with Albina.

"Hamish Deakin here. May I speak with Mrs. Delgado? Albina, please?"

"Oh, hello Mr. Deakin. This is Berri Webster. Eduardo's girlfriend? (A rise in tone). "Just a second, and I'll see if she can take the call."

Berri muted the phone. "Want to speak to him, Albina? You don't have to, you know." As she shook her head, her blonde pony-tail danced in sync.

"Give me, Berri. *S'okay*," Albina uttered, her voice cracked. She reached for the phone. The circles under her eyes, darker now, like the underarm stains of her blouse. Neither woman cared about the fetid perspiration in the air.

Quick press of a button, "Here she is, Mr. Deakin." Berri kissed the top of Albina's forehead, handed over the home phone, then disappeared around the corner into the kitchen.

Berri ran water into the kettle for their tea. Neither one of them felt hungry after she returned from the Nesbitt's. Besides, they had carrot muffins left over to nibble on.

Not a stupid girl, rather a bright psychology major, Beryl realized this attachment to Albina was a maternal *thing*. She admired Albina's emotional displays; they seemed raw, real. Her own dispassionate, self-serving, bitch of a mother ran off to British Columbia with a younger boyfriend when Beryl was twelve.

Left in her father's care, Beryl managed to love him in a perfunctory way. After all, he *was* her dad and he *wanted* her after the divorce, and *Mommy* did not.

Considered a bit of a snore by others, Ron Webster, a decent guy, appeared to exemplify the unfortunate cliché of an accountant's personality.

Beryl planned to do clinical counselling. Through her clients, she would resolve her own issues. *And we create our own families*, she thought. Albina might be the mother she always needed, and she wanted to be Albina's fortress. To get to Albina, people would have to pass through her first. Even Eduardo.

"So, what did he say?" asked Berri when Albina joined her in the kitchen.

Taking a chipped mug of mint tea from Berri's hands, Albina sighed, "he say sorry about Carlos. He say he go see Filipe in jail. He say too — his wife, Esther, will look at Carlos' *Will* – his wife take care of business side."

"Oh, right. She's a lawyer, too," said Berri. "Well, that's good to know. Now, shall we go upstairs and pick out something for the funeral, Albina?"

"What pick out? Most my clothes is already black." Albina made a weird face and took a resigned sip from her cup. The eyes of the two women locked over the rims of their mugs. Then, they set them down on the floral, vinyl table- cloth, and laughed. They laughed more because they laughed. Then, they began howling laughter, out-of- control laughter.

Suddenly, Beryl slapped her hand over her mouth, withdrew it and said, "I'm *so, so* sorry, Albina! It's wrong to be laughing at a time like this!"

"No, is not wrong, Berri. Is nerves. Is relief. Anyway, you know I sorry Carlos is dead, but we no *in love* no more. Justa Eduardo – I sad for him."

"You're right Albina. I know all about nervous laughter, but, duh, not when it happens to me. You know how much I care about your feelings. I'm sad for Ed too. I'll be there for both of you."

"You good girl, Berri. I glad you girlfriend of Eduardo. You friend for me, too."

"You bet I am, Albina. Let's take our tea to the porch. Looks like the sun is ready to set on this day."

In a rare, mosquito-free evening, a perfect light breeze greeted the women as they sank into the cushions of the lawn chairs. The sky offered layers of lavender streaks and the street remained still, no passing cars. They sipped and savored the quiet.

Footsteps broke the silence. They approached from the direction of the church a few doors down. A shadowy figure appeared from behind their crabapple tree which hid a section of the sidewalk. A skinny man with loose hair, a goatee, and blond sideburns strolled across the grass towards them. His long legs, in powder blue slacks, took long strides.

Albina leapt from her seat and clung to the man as he reached the porch. She wailed.

"Geoffrey!"

Geoffrey? Beryl couldn't make sense of this stranger. She wasted no time. She was on her feet. She stared at this interloper embracing Albina, who nestled into his neck.

"I'm Beryl," she said, clearing her throat, dramatically.

The couple turned apart from each other and looked at her.

Berri extended her hand, and Geoffrey crushed it in a macho handshake.

"And who, may I ask, are *you*?" she demanded, at least relieved he was no random killer off the street.

"I'm a friend of Albina's – from St. Basil's," Geoffrey offered, as he swung a sleeveless, rope-like arm in the direction from which he arrived. "We, ah, sing in the choir together," he drawled. "I dropped by the hall tonight to donate an item for the Bazaar next week, and Father James told me about Carlos. "

"Oh, right. Ed took over some of Albina's crocheting this afternoon for the Bazaar. He also wanted to tell Father about Carlos, and mention the funeral's at St. Jude's, because his employer offered to pay for it."

"The Nesbitt's?" asked Geoffrey. "Well, yeah, right, Albina *did* mention her husband worked for them. I've come to offer my condolences." Then Geoffrey took Albina's hand, held it, and gently lifted a strand of her hair which had drooped over her face, brushing it to the side.

This touch of intimacy shocked Berri. Her nostrils flared, and her face reddened but she hid her contempt like a suppressed hiccup.

"Maybe we go in house, now," coaxed Albina, flustered. "We make nice Geoffrey a good drink, Berri. We have Canadian Club whiskey with ice," and she added sheepishly, "We need cool off."

Berri reached for the screen door, held it open, and said, "After you two."

Chapter 20

"Esther embraced all things East Indian."

Hamish and Esther and their boys enjoyed a filet mignon, shish kebab barbeque with her parents, Bindu and Saul Greene. The grandparents arrived from Toronto's upscale Rosedale neighborhood for a sleepover to watch the grandkids. Bryan and Gordie *high-fived* their grandparents' challenge to play *Mine-Craft*. All four intended to build *Steampunk City*, controlling the blocks and squares, and seeing the results on the large wall-mounted screen. They stretched out on the camel leather sofa bolstered with sheen black and gold striped toss cushions and a pair of matching armchairs. Set to play.

Esther valued her parents' dedication to interactive playtime with the boys. She also delighted their home included a beautiful white, ensuite guest bedroom for her parents' comfort.

As she and Hamish prepared themselves at their double-sink bathroom, each with wonderful round mirrors paired with black sconces, Esther expected excitement tonight.

Recently, she re-watched her favorite film by the lauded 1960s director David Lean, based on the E.M. Forster novel she studied in university: *A Passage to India*. Set in the 1920s during the British Raj. And given her mother's heritage, Esther embraced all things East Indian.

A white woman from England, exploring the countryside, dismounts her bicycle, and finds herself in an overgrown field. Feeling the heat of India's sun, she moves towards shade where she stumbles upon large, erotic sculptures: a woman's rump lifted by her partner's hand while tongues intertwine...several lovers, in various forms of ecstasy. These statues, seemingly centuries old, were partially hidden by the long grasses of wilderness. The woman is taken aback as suddenly a pack of wild monkeys appear and leap about in a frenzy, frightening her to vanish.

Esther thought some Brit expats portrayed in the film either feared or repressed their sexual longings. True to herself, she found this wilderness scene particularly arousing. She craved to express her desires. She felt sex, a universal gift, needed to be celebrated at any opportunity. Hamish often told her that his darling was special because she had the instincts of a man. *Hah! Do men honestly believe they alone hold the bold genes of sexuality?*

Esther extended her eyeliner like the *male* 'Doctor Aziz' enacted in the film. She painted beautiful, black upswept strokes on her eyelids in anticipation of a hot evening with their male friends.

Hamish thought about his former school friend they were about to visit and his life-partner, Samuel. Great guys. Handsome, smart. Gavin had his own home-design show on television, and Samuel, a lyrical singer, paid tribute to Peggy Nesbitt at her funeral. He performed no less a beautiful rendition than would Andrea Bocelli, when he sang, '*Time to Say Good-Bye.*'

The audience found his singing particularly moving since Samuel sang from his wheelchair. Six months earlier, he suffered injuries from a motorcycle accident which placed him there, indefinitely. Hamish thrilled thinking of beautiful Samuel with charcoal eyes, and black curly hair, and a dark, sculptured stubble to die for. He could almost be Esther's twin – but he was full-on Jewish – no Indian in him that he knew.

Yet, as he shaved his own tender face, Hamish's big 'could almost happen' fantasy would be a Rufus Wainwright concert with Simon – not likely – but tickets for such an event would make a scintillating birthday/Christmas gift. Esther would go, of course, especially if held at *Royal Albert Hall*, London. *Let's be honest,* he thought to himself, it wouldn't create the same effect as a dream date with Iggy, *alone.*

They told her parents they would no doubt have a late night, would likely stay over just for a delicious sampling of Gavin's special breakfast cook-up. It had been hinted at when plans were discussed. They'd be available by text. Kisses to the kids, and they were out the door. Bindu and Saul were perfectly in tune with the arrangements, and gave their usual, not to worry, comments.

The Uber driver, deferential and quiet, loved these drives where people popped out of magazine mansions of elegance. *One day...*he dreamed. But his mind now on the pre-arranged short drive to Clarkson village, along the Lakeshore, just east of Naples, to the woodland shores of Mississauga.

The road, a winding piece of forest leading towards the water, with many trees blocked the home address. But it appeared painted on an antique mailbox. Given the latest government directives to use community stations for mail, the box was no longer functional; however, it added great charm to the locale, with its two iridescent surnames along with the digits: Shanks & Goldstein #325 – in gold lettering, no less.

Samuel greeted them at the door. His automated wheel-chair provided optimal mobility in the gracious ranch-style home. Wooden ramps outdoors, and one-floor spacious indoors, life was comfortable. Dimples and carved cheekbones gave Samuel the look of a naughty, grown-up cherub. Always bearing a wicked twinkle, Samuel received Hamish's gift of red Amarone wine into his lap. He and Esther exchanged double-cheek air kisses.

"You smell divine" he purred.

"Opium. Yves Saint Laurent."

"Woman after my own heart."

"Glad I don't have competition," Esther, slapped him play-fully. And in they went.

Tall, elegant Gavin appeared within seconds at the Spanish-tiled foyer. Subtly protective of his man, he lifted the wine bottle from Samuel's jeaned lap and welcomed his friends towards the screened-in sun porch.

The home smelled of a verdant freshness, amidst wooden beams. Subtle jazz sounds of Miles Davis streamed into the veran-dah. Straight ahead, the green lake with mossy sand and uneven rocks piled almost onto the back doorstep. A second wooden walkway created some separation as it led to what they consid-ered *their* beach. They were fortunate to find this house with its ravine privacy and stunning view, and suitable for Samuel's wheelchair. The latter, a permanent addition after Samuel's road accident.

Everywhere, the décor was simple, smart, and relaxing. Vases with branches and blooms provided hints of beauty. The heavy grey, wicker seating was top notch as one might expect from a designer. Gavin himself, in a body-fitting charcoal V-neck top, and expensive crinkled cotton pants walked with an air of casual confidence which he cultivated since their school days.

Samuel, however, was not one of the students from the boarding school, KLA. Rather, the partners met several years later, in the lobby of the Toronto Opera House at a performance of 'Les Misérables.' Samuel, a musicology professor, attended with some students. Gavin had taken his folks for an anniversary treat and benefitted with the treat of his own life.

During intermission, waiting for an order at the frenetic bar, the gentlemen locked eyes. Bang. Just like that. For Gavin, it really *was* love at first sight, clichés aside. A big dose of lust thrown in, icing on the cake.

Samuel, his loveable lunatic, music, and motorcycle fanatic, responded in kind.

Esther suggested they partner up for a game of Canasta. She had taught them before– a game she had played with her parents. Gavin arranged the glass table on the porch, so they could keep the view of the sunset and brought some crisps as snacks with their wine.

Crisps. His diction. So British. Esther enjoyed it.

Hamish and Gavin sat opposite each other in the wicker armchairs; Esther, comfortable on the couch, as she and Samuel faced one another. They nibbled, played, and laughed while Chet Baker now crooned in the background, blowing his trumpet. Suddenly, joyful with his second glass, and the game about to finish, Samuel urged Gavin:

"Babe, we need some Barbra."

"What about the Broadway Album, love?" Gavin held his remote.

'*Pretty women are a wonder...*' Barbra belted, from Stephen Sondheim's musical *Sweeney Todd: The Demon Barber of Fleet Street*. Music and lyrics so beautiful in such a horror story. The four card-players reveled in Barbra Streisand's magnificent rendition. Samuel loved sending it up with his amazing tenor voice, up to the rafters.

All three of the non-singers swooned, their hearts listening to the duet by Samuel and Barbra. '*Here's to the girls who just watch...*' Still in tune, the pretty Samuel moved back his wheelchair, and reached inside the drawer of the teak serving trolley. He removed a stash of weed, and papers. He sang and rolled a joint for sharing which they passed among the four of them, relaxed.

As the sky turned from pink to purple, they let the music play on, card game over. After a mass of giggles, they slipped into their dreamy stupors, Hamish slid off his grey suede wingtips and thought of Iggy's abs when they toweled off after swimming. Esther let her head loll back onto the couch and recalled Simon's firm ass when she saw him last in his cycling shorts.

Gavin imagined his lover's beautiful lips, his sensuous mouth which soon awaited him.

Samuel closed his long-lashed eyes and dreamed of Gavin's soft, brown beard when their faces touched and his lean, strong biceps when Gavin lifted him from the chair into his arms. How he loved and knew his man; he even felt Gavin's jealously of Esther's sexual presence.

They all had secrets and desires but knew how to make life work.

Chapter 21

"Struck by the familiar and welcome smell of his father…"

"I should be getting back." Eduardo turned to Simon. "Thanks, for everything." On the balcony, the men enjoyed the warm air and the beauty of the evening. The women *insisted* the men clear out during kitchen clean-up, and the gents, only too happy to oblige.

"Everybody is heading into a busy time," Quinn commented. "Are your classes at Saunders back next week, too, Ed? It's *IT*, isn't it?"

"That's right, sir. I'll go back after we bury my dad." Charity approached, as if on cue. Ed stroked her ear.

"You sure you can't stay a bit longer?" asked Darius, glad to have a young guy present, despite the circumstances.

"Berri's with my mom, and she'll need to get home, and I don't want my mom to be alone. But thanks, Darius. Good luck with school yourself next week- grade twelve, eh, Bud?"

"Yeah!"

"We'll all see each other on Wednesday at St. Jude's," confirmed Simon and pulled Eduardo in for a shoulder-hug, and a reassuring pat on the back.

Crossing through a gleaming kitchen, Ed paused, and said his goodbyes to the women. He received generous hugs from each of them, and the last from Fiona. She stalled, rested her head of red curls on his chest, then walked him to the side door. Prudence wobbled behind them. Ed scooped her up and allowed her to bestow her *Doxie* affection - tiny licks to his cheek. Then he handed her to Fiona and left.

He headed around the back. On this side of the property, with a moon high in the sky, he felt a brush of west wind on his forearms. He climbed into the white truck. Struck by the familiar and welcome smell of his father, Eduardo sat completely still. He inhaled his dad's warm, masculine body, plus a lingering whiff of Corona cigars.

Ed rested his forehead on the steering wheel. He closed his eyes and wept. His shoulders shook as he remained in that position for a good five minutes, releasing hot tears of grief for the man he loved with all his heart.

Then he was ready to turn on the engine. His father's favorite band, the *Gypsy Kings,* bellowed from the speakers; guitar strings, with those husky, rhythmic voices rising, and calling out, again and again, the pain of love and loss. His father's beloved piece, *Un Amor,* played on with lyrics Ed understood as 'Crying for you – with love.' No translation needed.

How would he live without his father? They were as close as any father and son could be. Still not ready to drive, Ed reached into the glove compartment in search of tissues. He touched one of his father's folded, white handkerchiefs, and brought it out to wipe his face. A small, plastic baggie spilled onto the passenger's seat. Ed picked it up, and a rock formed in his gut. He examined the contents. Blue and green tablets. The taste of bile rose into his mouth. His sorrow rapidly transformed to anger as Eduardo thought of his cousin, Filipe. *That bastard probably caused this with his drugs. If I ever see that son of a bitch again, I'll kill him!*

Gritting his teeth, Eduardo shoved the clutch into reverse, and backed out of the driveway. After a deep breath, he lunged forward, ready now to go home and comfort his mother, to share their memories of his dear father, Carlos Delgado, as fine a man as ever there was.

'Ting' - the sound of Beryl's iPhone notification. She looked down. "It's Ed texting," she said. "He's on his way back. At a stoplight now. He'll be here in about six minutes." Her face registered concern towards Albina who uncrossed her arms at once to this news and sprang into an upright position.

In a flash, Albina swallowed her whisky. "You go now, Geoffrey, go now!"

"Sure," Geoffrey muttered, surprised, as his narrowed eyes darted back and forth. He stood and stretched. "Ladies, my motorcycle awaits in the church lot. I'll be going then. Nice meeting you Berri. I'll see you soon, Albina. Stay strong, old girl." He gave Albina a meaningful look.

Beryl feverishly read between the lines. *This forty-year-old hippie is living in the last century, and he's definitely hitting on Albina. What's his deal?*

Through the screen door, all three heard a truck's motor pull into the driveway. No six minutes had passed. More like two. They froze in their spots.

The screen door clicked. Eduardo entered the narrow hallway which opened to a view of the front room. Preoccupied, he tossed his keys into a brass bowl on the tiny entrance table. He looked up, taken aback to see three people standing and staring at him.

"What's going on here?" He looked at Geoffrey. "Ma? Who's *this*?" he demanded, trying to be civil but a sense of intrusion stood his body hairs on end. "Is this a neighbor, Ma?' 'Who *are* you?" he directed to Geoffrey.

"My friend, Eduardo. He my friend." Albina stepped forward awkwardly to placate a possible, incendiary situation. She felt her son's hostility.

Beryl put her arm around Eduardo's waist, but he disregarded both her, and his mother. His instincts questioned the presence of this stranger, not to mention the dude's appearance.

"Name's Madison," Geoffrey extended his arm for a handshake. Eduardo ignored it.

"What are you *doing* here, Madison, with my mother and girlfriend? Do we even *know* you?"

"Actually man, my name is Geoffrey – Geoffrey Madison..."

"*Geoffrey Madison*?" Eduardo echoed the name, then turned to Beryl, "Why does that name ring familiar?"

"Oh, yeah. I remember now," Eduardo nodded to himself, dismissing the idea, ashamed to repeat his thought aloud in front of his mother. *Sounds like that website for adulterers.*

"So how do you know each other?"

"Me and your mother sing in the church choir together, Ed."

"It's Eduardo."

"Sorry, man. I came to offer my condolences for your loss – your father..."

Eduardo softened a bit yet remained suspicious. "Well, thanks for coming over. We'd like to be alone tonight. I didn't see any car in the driveway other than my *VW* bug. How did you get here?"

"I'm parked at the church." Geoffrey ran his hands through his greasy hair, and his yellowed fingers pulled downwards on his moustache in a few jerky motions.

"Nice meeting you Eduardo."

He bowed at the waist -in a fake-formal way - to the women. "Goodnight, Ladies." Then he vanished rapidly, past them, through the door, and into the dark night.

"'Night, Geoffrey," Albina and Beryl called out, in unison.

The two women hugged Eduardo, one at each side. There came a moment of released tension for them all.

"I'll take you home now, Berri," Ed said.

Albina began gathering up the glasses and took them to the kitchen.

"I want to stay over tonight," Berri whispered.

"No, not in my mother's house, not tonight," Eduardo's pulse quickened.

"I'll sleep on the couch, then." Beryl offered. "I just want to be sure you guys are okay.

"Of course, we'll be fine. Stay if you want."

"Ma, you go to bed and get some rest. Berri's staying over. I'll get the sleeping bag and extra pillow from my room for her. She wants the couch. We're just going to chat a bit in my room, first." Ed kissed his mom. Berri kissed her too.

"Okay, kids. Don't forget you call your father, Berri, so he know you stay here."

"Sure thing, Albina."

Eduardo's bed lacked a headboard, so the two of them leaned against the wall. They murmured feelings of fatigue. Ed rubbed his black, closely cropped head. Then, he picked up Berri's hand, and set it down between them.

"You take this comforter when you go downstairs." He indicated the blue, double-sized spread they sat on. "It'll be nicer for you, Berr."

"How was it at the Nesbitt's?" Berri asked, eager to know more about them.

"Oh, fine. You know Simon and his kids are such cool people. His parents, too. And Marjorie came back early, made dinner, and her sister Hazel is staying with her for a while. The funeral will be Wednesday at St. Jude's. *(Pause)* Oh, FUCK, Berri."

"What???"

"I found *drugs* in my dad's truck just now before I drove it back. That fucker, Filipe. It's all his doing. Getting dad on drugs."

"Jesus," said Berri. She chewed on a fingernail. "What are you going to do? Give them to the police?"

"I don't know, yet. Hey, who's this asshole who was here tonight?"

"I never met him before, either. He just showed up when your mom and I were on the porch having tea."

"Just showed up. Just like that?"

"Yeah, he looked like he had 'an in' with Albina."

"Don't stay that, Berri! What do you mean? *An in?* "

"Like he knows her well. Too well... if you get my drift..."

"What the fuck? Are you suggesting this creep is banging my mother? I can't hear this. It makes me sick! And disrespectful to my dad's memory!" He struggled to lower his voice.

"Well, why was your dad on Viagra? She told me."

"Christ Almighty! My poor dad couldn't get it up?"

"That could explain your mom's attraction to Geoffrey." Beryl tried to reason.

"Fuck Geoffrey!" I said, "Fuck Geoffrey!"

Eduardo muffled his sobs in Beryl's embrace as she stroked his head. They nuzzled together in their day clothes until the power of sleep blotted out the pain of feelings.

A few hours later, Eduardo awoke, removed his jeans, and covered Beryl with the comforter. In silence, he pulled his sleeping bag from the closet and headed to the living room couch where he remained till morning with a throb of grief stuck in his throat.

Chapter 22

"Filipe knew she worshipped
that lucky bastard..."

Not a half hour away, Filipe shivered in the damp holding cell. Despite summer outside, the concrete interior blocked natural heat. The only warmth within floated from his stream of piss into the steel basin.

He thought those bastards in the eating area mocked his accent. He ground his back teeth, then grunted. He needed a hit, something to pop. Hell, he'd likely be deported, even if Nesbitt's lawyer, Deakin, promised to help.

Filipe grabbed the cot blanket and yanked it tight around his shoulders.

He heard retching down the hall as he sat and eyeballed a cockroach crawl the white blocks. Then he stared at the darkened screen in the corner, the place *visitors* appear. Filipe didn't understand how it worked. Should he turn it on? Deakin might want to reach him, tell him he's free...

Only a year old, the prison was not just new, but large. Filipe didn't expect this. A guard told him welcome to the *Toronto South Detention Centre*. He felt lucky he didn't have a roommate. The guard said *don't get too comfortable* and warned another guy coming soon. Filipe hoped he wouldn't stay long. Didn't want to deal with some jerk - worse than himself.

Weird, when brought here, he had to sit in a chair called *BOSS*. How North American, he thought. BOSS! But another guard explained *BOSS* as a search device able to detect hidden metals in your arsehole. Like he'd put a gun in his ass! Or worse, a knife! Yet that guard wasn't a dick. Filipe saw he talked to him like a regular guy. Told him BOSS meant *Body Orifice Scanning System.*

Filipe didn't understand the English word 'orifice'. But he figured nobody would finger-poke him. Or he, too, would vomit all night. Still, restless as hell with eyes darting, leg muscles twitching, Filipe couldn't fall asleep.

He felt bad for Uncle Carlos, depressed his wife no longer wanted sex; worried she might get it somewhere else. Filipe hoped the *Viagra* he supplied his uncle would give him the stiff rod Albina, the bitch, could choke on. He smiled cause he didn't need that shit himself. Thoughts of the hot, bronze body of Miss Housekeeper kept him hard night and day. Who knew she'd be so easy to seduce? She was eager, willing. But he could tell she was worried her employer, Nesbitt, might discover them, which took a bit of fun out of it for her. Yet charged him up.

Truth was...Filipe knew she worshipped that lucky bastard, Simon.

For Filipe, forbidden fruit, almost caught – those highs in life, so worth it, like smack. He closed his eyes. Drifted off maybe a half hour. Then banging, rattling sounds. The cell door clicked open.

And in he came. One tattooed big *son-of-a puta*. White guy with a shaved head the shape of a huge egg, weighing about a hundred and thirty-six kilos. Used to the metric system, Filipe often had trouble with North Americans who still asked him his own weight in pounds. He learned he was a hundred and eighty-five pounds which meant this guy would be close to three hundred pounds. All in his arms and throat...and that massive head.

The door soon locked again. Big Guy grunted for Filipe to move his ass from the left side bunk. Each cot was pushed flush to the right and left sides of the cell. Only about two and a half feet of floor space between them.

"No, man, I here first."

Huge mistake. Claiming property rights.

Big Guy grabbed Filipe by his foot like a dog's rag toy and tossed him— whipped him across to the other side of the cell. His head just missed the concrete.

"Okay, okay, I *don* understand English *mush*." Filipe groaned in his Portuguese accent. He lay on the floor cradling his head, his gut queasy and legs still twitching.

Big Guy sat on the bunk trying it out, peered at Filipe as one might at vermin.

"Do what I say, shithead, if you wanna stay alive." Then he stretched his massive body into his full length. "What you in for, anyway, pussy?"

"Drunk drive, drugs, no Canada papers."

"Crazy bastard."

Big Guy punctuated his comment with a massive groaning fart. It left a trail of putrid stale cabbage in the cell. He snorted, pleased with himself.

"Sucker. You got the shakes now. You won't last long."

Filipe crawled off the floor onto the right bunk, curled himself to face the wall. He trembled all night. Meanwhile, Big

Guy hacked, coughed, and spit. He released more stale air from his body parts which polluted the shrunken cell. No fresh air, no window to open, just frosted glass to suggest the outdoors, and which allowed daylight to arrive far too early in the morning.

Chapter 23

"Virginia floated towards her husband."

Quinn stood barefoot. His posture still erect for a man his age. He tied the sash of his blue and gold satin robe around his narrow waist.

"Well, my darling, you still can't beat our view – those glowing lights from Toronto, and the CN Tower. What a wise choice we made moving here. It never gets stale, does it? Come see this full moon my Sweet."

Retracted, billowy sheers exposed the night's beauty, the condo's vantage point —a far perspective. Their gas fireplace flickered. Over the ivory mantle hung a painting of purple wisteria – Virginia's family heirloom from the Kentucky plantation. On a glazed chinoiserie corner table stood an onyx vase, arranged with blooms of pink and purple gladioli among shoots of greenery. Mango and violet cushions accented the lush sofa and armchairs upholstered in white and grey brocade. A swirl carpet cozied the oak floors and offered warmth to the glass coffee-table, arranged with a couple of classic books, and a small stack of *The New Yorker Magazine*. On the right, the condo's long front hallway held stunning black and white diamond-shaped ceramic tiles, a touch of Victorian glamour. The soundscape - a light Mozart concerto for flute and harp.

In a peach chiffon peignoir, and bling flip-flops, Virginia floated towards her husband. She circled his waist, proud of his fitness, his lack of paunch, as some men his age gained. She rested her head on his back and pressed her bountiful bosom to meld into his body; always an erotic sensation to rub up against him. She purred, contented.

Portia, their Siberian kitty, a ball of champagne fur, broke a reverie from her place and with a tiny leap descended to wind about Ginny's ankles expecting appreciation. Ginny lifted her, gave her a snuggle, then set her down. Ginny's interest now lay with intimacy towards her man. Portia scattered down the hall-way towards the bedrooms.

The couple returned the short distance from Simon's to their penthouse by cab. Just in time to change and watch the windows in the gracious building ahead transform into a magnif-icent, metallic pink. This small miracle - a reflective cast of the setting sun. Beautiful. Until they grew black. The building, itself, housed corporate offices on the lower levels, and residential suites above. Later, tiny glows from lamps in private units exchanged the magic for a cozy, nighttime charm.

"I feel sad for our baby," sighed Ginny; she pulled in tighter to Quinn.

"I know Simon has a lot to deal with, Precious," Quinn turned to face her, "but we raised him well. And please *must* you call him baby? We've got to stop babying him – he's forty-eight years old – and he's got companies to run, as well as his family. He's becoming a bit soft these days..."

Rarely shaken, but often stirred, Ginny let this comment slide. For now.

"The moon is beautiful tonight; I'm with my love alright," she sang. They both laughed at her attempt at poetic levity. Sliding up beside him now, Ginny shared Quinn's view of the sky, yet each of them sensed something unique in the moon's image, the shapes and forms the eye of imagination creates for each individual soul.

"You know, when we were out for our walk this afternoon, Fiona ran out of steam," said Ginny. "I didn't want to say anything at lunch. But I *worry* about our lovely granddaughter. It's not like her to complain of lethargy, is it?"

Quinn turned his head to meet the kind, velvet brown eyes of his wife, and seeing her usual sparkle absent, offered his look of compassion. Lifting her chin, he aimed to console, but keep it light.

"You know, Precious, I do believe at this stage of life, our main job *is* to WORRY."

Not believing his declaration for a second, Ginny played along. "It's an occupational hazard, which we love," she retorted. It was their way to balance each other - attempts at understanding core disagreements. They knew how to play the game of marriage, to stay together.

Stretched out on the luxurious sofa, and feet propped onto the coffee-table, the two mature lovers dimmed their pot-lights, turned on the side orbs and settled in for their evening entertainment: reading to each other. Some time ago, they decided to *do* the classics. On their agenda this month, Daniel Defoe's *Moll Flanders* – with her fortunes and misfortunes. Moll Flanders' entanglements with sex for money, and several marriages kept the Nesbitt's engaged in discussion – what it meant in the eighteenth century to be a woman born into poverty and use her beauty to gain social status for herself. *How did that fit today?*

The couple raised their stemware of chilled white wine, ready to enjoy their reading romp, taking turns with chapters, when Quinn's grandfather mind flashed to the kids. "Simon needs to do more for Darius." He followed his comment with an eager swill from his glass. Then set it on the mirrored tray.

Virginia looked at him, took a sip from her goblet, and voiced her opinion.

"But, Sugar, all research points to allow the child to grow out of the *Asperger's* a bit, doesn't it?" Portia hastily returned to position herself on the book in Ginny's lap.

"Well, as I said, before, Precious, it *is* our job to worry. But it's no longer our place to solve anything. Somewhat disconcerting, hmmm. Well, then, shall we begin, my love?"

"Maybe we should just talk tonight, rather than read," said Ginny. "This rascal is not going anywhere. She looks so comfortable; I hate to move her."

"That's fine love. It's been an exhausting day." Quinn's voice dropped low, deep. "Besides, we can't sweep events under the rug. Carlos died. That's a big deal. And the collapse took place in their house. Imagine that. The kids are unnerved, to say the least. Poor Eduardo, too. How did you find the grown-up gals? Marjorie sure knows how to take charge, eh? A wonderful housekeeper. I hope Simon keeps her on."

"Why wouldn't he? Carlos' death has nothing to do with her. What were you thinking of Sugar?

"Nothing special. Just that she appeared...hmmm...how should I put it? Robust somehow?"

"Robust? What's *that* supposed to mean?"

"Robust. Full. Maybe she has a boyfriend and wants to leave."

"Where do you come up with these ideas, Sugar?" Ginny sipped her wine, her eyes twinkling once again, looking at her man.

"That Hazel seems funny and smart." said Quinn. "Actually, maybe Simon can check with her for a *Sick Kids* work-up if Fiona's feeling ill." Quinn took his wife's glass and set it down not to disturb Portia's catnap.

"I could mention it to Simon. I don't have to tell him it's your idea in case he bristles - you know how he gets if *you* think of something which he's already planned..." Ginny said as she hooked her glasses over her neckline.

"And, Sugar, this reading of Moll Flanders stirs me to do more charity work at *Kerry On House*. I've seen people push their grocery carts down the street – it breaks my heart how needy some folks are who live just blocks from us. This disparity always troubled me. But it's hard to help and not seem patronizing." She stroked Portia's thick fur.

Quinn leaned in and kissed his wife, tenderly, on her full lips. His grown-up *Shirley Temple* is how he often called her; kind, so good-natured about everything. And he loved everything about her: that generous smile, her humor, her loyalty, her patience and understanding ...qualities which, occasionally, overwhelmed him, as he compared his own character to hers - he knew he fell short. But he could show his appreciation:

"You're a great broad, Ginny! Give me that pussy."

"Quinn!" shrieked Ginny. "WHAT? Are you Frank Sinatra, now?" Her smile enormous, her chest heaving.

"I'm moving this *kitty*! Portia's returning to the armchair. I need to hold my woman."

And Quinn did just that. First, he inserted the CD *American Classics* Simon had bought him one Christmas, not sung by Sinatra, but in the gravelly voice of Rod Stewart. Something in common, father and son shared a love for *old- fashioned* music.

"You *are* a great broad, my lady. Up." Quinn helped Ginny stand and enter his arms to dance and sway to *"It Had to Be You."* They moved together, bodies touching, and Quinn so grateful for his good fortune in life, in love. Together for many years, a few indiscretions behind him which never surfaced; so unfair to Ginny, but he loved her despite any long-distance fling with any stewardess on flights to France – business trips, and jaunts to see his mother in her Paris apartment. Stewardesses, now known as flight-attendants, catered to his *needs* while away from home, but he never *loved* anyone else.

Quinn reflected how bittersweet his only child had found love, and lost it, through no fault of his own. However, since the flip side of Quinn's good fortune in life was tarnished with specks of guilt, his attitude towards Simon often took on a harsh, and perceptibly demanding tone. *Do better, be a better man.*

As they hugged and rhythmically moved in short steps to the romantic lyrics, the pair continued their silent thoughts. Ginny felt like she danced in the arms of a movie star. Young people she worked with occasionally asked what her husband was like. Instead of a photo display, she liked to say he's the Captain in the movie, *The Sound of Music.* Everybody knows that character, still familiar after forty years. She'd add, he'd be a bit older now, of course, but still handsome, and just as ornery. Sometimes she had to explain *ornery* to the youth. It did not begin with the letter *aitch.* After the first big laugh, people relaxed, got the idea, young people relieved it did not mean sex-fiend.

For his part, Quinn told himself he did not deserve this fabulous and vibrant woman, still with such gorgeous tits, at her age. His memory of the young Ginny included the scent of hay, honey, and fresh air. *I feel like a scoundrel — a- son-of -bitch - but a contrite one, a grateful one, and I'm never letting her go, God willing...*

"Let's go to bed, my darling." Quinn, the tough guy, whispered, choked with sentiment.

Ginny let her hand slide. *Good lord!* She felt his stirred passion in every sense.

They left the music playing, the fire burning. Holding hands, they reached the bedroom, and collapsed onto the exquisite, white-cotton sheets spread across their queen-sized bed. Quinn's silver hair on the pillow, silver stubble nuzzling Ginny's ear lobe, and suntanned neck. They clung to each other with great comfort and surrender. The robe and peignoir quickly tossed off to the creamy carpet below, freeing their naked bodies. And the sex? Elevated to a sacrament. With faces open to each other, they took communion. *No prior confessions mandatory.* And images of Shirley Temple had long disappeared at the bedroom door. Quinn hardened and dissolved in Ginny's mouth. They were charismatically *speaking in tongues*. The only religion that mattered. Love.

Chapter 24

"It became a refuge, each evening, for the three of them."

Given his respect for ritual, Simon worried their bedtime chats could suddenly stop. Lucky so far. Six years as a *single* parent solidified his closeness to the twins. Yet, he expected changes; teens eventually pull away from parents and live their *secret* lives.

Darius, stretched on one side of Simon's king-sized bed, explored his phone. His legs extended over the charcoal quilted duvet, his head down.

Simon's master bedroom faced south. He kept the room simple and clean. Across the wall of windows, retractable blinds either remained open to a splendid vista of the lake or closed for evening rest. The eastern sunrise demanded blackouts. However, before bedtime Simon left the blinds open to watch the moon, catch the streaks of cloud, or see the dazzling shapes the starry sky provided. The other walls, designed with textured paint, hues of clay and light brown created a roughed-in cave effect, a coziness. The sandy hardwood floor gleamed as a sunlit beach. A couple of bamboo floor mats tossed at each side of the bed added to an island mood.

Oasis, cave, whatever this bedroom reflected, it became a refuge each evening for the three of them. Charity and Kent, also welcome, spread out in front of the screen door of the upper balcony and sniffed the lake's night air.

"Dad?" Darius, thumbed through *Instagram*, stared at his cell. Propped against the high, padded headboard, he appeared comfy, clad in plaid boxer shorts, and an orange tee-shirt.

"Yes, Son." Simon searched through a drawer of his wicker bedroom desk, his back turned away.

"Where's Carlos? I mean – now? Is he in the morgue?"

Simon returned to the bed, sat down with a brochure in his hand, looked Darius in the eye and said, "No, Son. Carlos is in the funeral home now."

"Same one mom was in?"

"That's right. Same one."

"Do we *have* to go there?"

"We do."

"Can't I stay home? Fiona can go with you."

"What about the church, Dare? Will you be okay with that?" Simon needed to bargain for Darius' comfort zones.

"St. Jude's? You said that earlier to Ed. I guess, for Ed's sake. But you know I hate it."

"I know you do, Son. You're a brave young man facing your fears."

"It's not a fear, Dad. It's more like a nightmare!" Darius looked up from his phone and sought understanding in his dad's soft eyes.

"You and Fiona will sit with me. You'll be fine. You can be in the middle."

"What's that, Dad?" Somewhat comforted, Darius looked to the yellow sheet in Simon's hand.

"It's a brochure Hamish dropped off when I saw him earlier. It's about the *Ripley's Aquarium Centre* in Toronto. He's taking his boys before school starts and thought you and I would like to join them."

"They're little kids, Dad! I don't hang with kids that age. At least not in the big city."

"It's for everyone, Darius. Adults, kids. I hear it's wonderful."

"What's the fuss about, guys?" With Prudence tucked under one arm, Fiona entered in her two- piece turquoise lounge wear, bare toes painted to match. She wore a twisted thick topknot, with loose tendrils spilling from her red hair.

She let Prudence down gently on the bed, and nudged Darius with her knee to shove over.

"We're talking about the Toronto Aquarium," Darius piped up. "Dad wants me to go with Hamish's kids. Wanna come, Fi?"

"That's the spirit, Dare," Relieved, Simon pat Darius on the shoulder. "Let's wait until we pay our respects to Carlos and his family, after the funeral..."

"Dad, I need to get school supplies from *Staples*" said Darius, eager to change the subject.

"Sure, we can do that after Wednesday. I'll check on some business appointments I had lined up, but I'll clear time. You guys will get what you need before heading back."

"I need to get some stuff too, Dad," said Fiona, turning on her side to face Simon. "Maybe I could go with Marjorie and Hazel because I'd like to drop into the Mall and pick up some new tops and jeans. Hazel's got great taste. Could use her advice. That okay, Dad?"

"Of course, Sweetie."

"I also want to apply at the library. Mrs. Chambers at the Central Library branch - she said to call her Suzanne - told me I could probably complete my volunteer community hours there."

"That's sounds like a plan, honey. Simon looked pleased. Needed to hear positive things from his beloved kids.

"But, Dad, I feel really tired lately. I told grandma earlier about it today." Fiona petted Prudence and was careful to keep any whining out of her voice.

Simon's gut took a wallop. Looking at his daughter, Simon tried to conceal his feelings and his high cheekbones kept his expression cheery. "Okay. Not to worry, Sweetie. I can arrange through Hazel to set up something at *Sick Kids* for you – a thorough check-up before you head back to school."

"I'm not really looking forward to going back to school," said Darius. "Are you, Fi?"

"Actually, yeah, Dare. I want to audition for the musical. Why don't you help with Props? You could find some cool stuff. And I hear the new Vice Principle is directing. She used to be a drama teacher."

"How do you know all that?" asked Darius.

"Duh. I've got friends!" Fiona teased with her upward pitch. "Sophie told me. She's got the inside info. I told you before." Fiona elbowed his side with a giggle. She loved her twin. One-minute younger, he needed his big sis to set things straight.

"Alright guys let's sit on the balcony for a few moments before we call it a night." Simon offered. "We have a lot of goings-on coming up. Let's take these three beasts and get some night air. And look at that amazing moon. Let's go wish on it."

"I wish Mama is happy," said Darius.

"Me too," Simon and Fiona said together, and joined pinkie fingers.

And out they went. Simon would lock up later.

Chapter 25

"Can they even *get* samples from a deceased person?"

Two ghosts in white frocks, Marjorie and Hazel also took the night air but from the northwest angle of the estate. Hidden from view of Simon and the teens, with voices low, the sisters felt free to chat unheard. Nevertheless, all shared the same light beam, the full moon in its western sky, and its varied effects on the human mind.

"I feel like a fraud," Marjorie sighed. "Did you see how *happy* he was tonight, despite all the day's shit? He *believes* in me. He thinks I run his household like a ship, and everything is chill. Wait'll he gets my news! I'm nauseated, Haze, and not just from this pregnancy! I can't *bear* deceiving Simon."

Sitting together on the stoop, Hazel put an arm around her sister's shoulder and pulled her close. "It can wait a few days. Tell him after the funeral. There's just one thing..." she pulled up a blade of grass.

"What's that?"

Hazel took a big breath, then exhaled.

"Don't you think, Sis, maybe you should get a DNA sample from ..." she was about to say *the body*, but caught herself, "from Carlos' remains? I mean before he's buried?"

131

"Why? What does it matter now? It feels creepy to think about it."

"Well, if the child is *his*, it would have a right to an inheritance as Carlos' offspring. There could be a dispute with the son, Eduardo, not to mention the widow."

"Geez, that sounds complicated, Haze. I never thought that through. What if it's *Filipe's*? What a damn mess! If ever I wanted a smoke and a drink, it's now." Marjorie's stress reminded her when she smoked a pack a day after their parents died.

"Can they even *get* samples from a deceased person?" Margie asked her sister.

"I could call Fuyun and see what she thinks can be done. With her mom being a pediatrician... Patricia...Dr. Lim could get some info for us. And *fast*." Hazel's words poured quickly from her protective heart – trying anything for her Margie.

"But screw anyone who tries to make you feel bad about your own baby. Still, it would be good if you find out who the father is. At least *having* the DNA sample, you could use it closer to time of birth to sort things out."

"Okay, Haze. But shouldn't I also have a backup plan like after I *tell* Simon, and depending on his reaction, what I'm going to *do*?"

"I doubt he'll give you the heave-ho. He's one, kind-ass dude."

"Doesn't mean I should take advantage of him - his good nature!" Marjorie felt defensive of Simon. She would remain loyal, regardless of the outcome.

"I would just like to know how you pulled it off. I mean working out here with the two men, and with Simon, and the kids around?" Hazel's curiosity bursting in full form. "The logistics of it, hon."

"Well, my *Sista,* I ain't no *ho!*" Charged up, Marjorie shook her head.

"Stop it. You know I'm not implying anything. Just don't go there. You know me. I *love* you. I need to understand how this kind of thing happens to a good girl like you." Hazel rubbed Margie's back in a nurturing way, softly up and down.

"I guess I'm touchy now," Marjorie, about to supply more details, needed to frame this right to her loving sister.

She began, "It was back in May when Filipe arrived in the country. He took English classes, and Carlos didn't bring him around right away. Carlos himself was in a bad state. I felt so sorry for him, Hazel. The kids were still in school then, before summer break, so they weren't around during the day. And Simon had appointments booked in Toronto with accountants, and *Nesbitt Holdings*' board meetings.

"Often in June, we were the only two on the property."

"What? You did it *here*? In the house?" Hazel whispered, slightly shocked.

"God, no! I would never risk it, nor desecrate Simon's house with an *affair* under his nose! Not that it even *was* an affair, per se." Marjorie insisted.

"We chatted in the garden, and he told me how his wife rejected him, and he needed sex. We'd been friendly for years, remember. Carlos was no stranger to me. So, I agreed to help him out. He booked a room one afternoon at the *Holiday Inn,* the one up by the highway, and we had sex there. It only happened once. Afterwards, I don't know what he did. Maybe he stopped taking the pills, maybe he jerked off, maybe he found someone else, but we both felt ashamed because of our respect for Simon."

"So, that doesn't sound too bad," Hazel purred, reassuring. "What happened with the nephew, then?"

"Hazel, this guy was so hot. Just my type, physically, I thought at the time. And I had no boyfriend."

"Well, I know how you had a crush on Simon, right? That must have been tough and confusing. I can't say I blame you for finding another dude attractive. Did Filipe come on to you?" Hazel was finally getting the full story.

"Actually, a few times he showed up in Carlos' truck because he was supposed to pick up plants from the horticulture center when Carlos had a doctor's appointment. Filipe would swing by and ask if I wanted to go with him. My schedule, pretty much my own, and sure, sometimes I got bored, so I jumped at the chance to get out. Summertime, beautiful weather, he found a spot outdoors, where it was private for us to talk. Then he suggested to spread a blanket, and one thing led to another. After we started kissing, it was hard to stop nature taking over. Plus, we had the vehicle, for privacy."

"I guess you spread more than a blanket," Hazel couldn't help herself, and laughed.

"You don't need to be *vulgar* about it, Hazel!"

"Okay, you're right, Margie. I'm just trying to make this feel less heavy for *you*. Bring some levity. You know, people of my *persuasion* are more comfortable with sexuality."

"You mean gays and lesbians, right?"

"Of course! We enjoy stimulation humor. But let's not stereotype my people, Sis."

The sisters hugged lovingly. Exhausted from the excitement and drama of secrets - so much to hide. For now.

"I hear, ya. Let's go in, watch your taped *Kardashians*. We can still talk if you want, put TV on mute, cuz they *look* better than what they got *ta say*. I'm telling 'ya Margie, those gals have worse problems. Even with all their money. *Think they all happy?* You're a good person, Margie, babes. That's what counts."

Chapter 26

"Time to start looking at the internet."

E sther reached behind her firm chest, unhooked her red satin bra, and let it float to the floor. Like a concubine, she languished in the velour armchair. She stretched her tanned legs, bent her knees, slightly, and extended her maroon-painted toes to rest on the edge of the grand bed facing her.

With her libido stimulated, Esther watched. Moist with lust, she absorbed the view in front of her. The men appeared like naked wrestlers: muscles glistening, tight buttocks, strong thighs, heads bent, and arms entangled, as they emitted a tang of fresh male sweat. Reminiscent of D.H. Lawrence's 1920s, novel, *Women in Love*. Literary erotica.

No artificial sound or lamplight lit this room; rather, guttural moans while a filter of moonlight streamed through shutter slats. A few nightstand candles quivered. Outside, a stiff breeze slapped waves against the rocks; each retreat a sound of slurping, replicating nature's rhythm inside. Esther, the *voyeureuse*, with erect, dark nipples, enjoyed the flesh and the men 'making the beast with two backs' as Shakespeare referenced in *Othello* - the sexual act, powerfully animalistic. Here, the two men who held the third gently on his back, firmly positioned their sensual Samuel for deeper pleasure. Esther's penchant for voyeurism, sex as sport, contributed to their gratifying orgy.

And furthermore, she loved how these refined males were respected as upstanding gentlemen in any polite society.

Despite high security at *HR,* Simon continued the nightly ritual of cursory door and window checks to assuage Darius' imagined fears. A promise to his beloved son.

Charity and Prudence, each in their own teens' rooms rested quietly. And no longer on high-alert, Kent dozed at the foot of Simon's bed.

On the main floor, by the breezeway's yard side, Simon noticed a white figure. He found Marjorie in a light shift sitting on the stoop.

"You still up?" he whispered.

She startled at the unexpected sound of his voice.

"Didn't mean to scare you – thought you and Hazel were in your apartment. I'm just doing locks."

Marjorie understood, of course, knowing the habits of all family members.

"Simon." She stood, and he indicated she sit. He joined her.

"I need to talk to you..."

"No need, Marjorie. It's been a rough day. I'm grateful you came back. Hazel, too. She's so good for you, and so much fun."

"She's snoring away, now, dear thing," Marjorie said, "overdue for a vacation and here's all this excitement. We took some air out here, had a little chat, but after we went up, Haze fell asleep with the TV on, so I slipped back out. Such a lovely evening."

"Sorry to bring you back from Toronto..." Simon looked directly into Marjorie's moon-lit cognac brown eyes as she angled her head towards him. She leaned her forehead into her hand. Then, she swiped her loose hair back a couple of times in a soft, self-conscious way. An awkward moment of silence, like breath withheld, between these two friends, employer/employee.

"I", Marjorie began, but faltered. *Should she wait until after the funeral to tell him?*

"Com 'on, young lady, best go to bed. We can talk another day. Get some rest. We rely on you, so much." He reached for her free hand, the one closest to him, and slightly pulled it towards himself. She lost balance and caved over to his side. Loose strands of her dark, blonde-streaked hair fell over her face, as she looked to her lap. She wondered if he felt as uneasy as she did. This weird *intimacy*....

He stood and helped her up. Then, he placed a spontaneous peck on her cheek. At once he mumbled finishing the task of doors. He'd see her tomorrow. She slipped away. He watched her climb the circular staircase to her apartment, watched her short garment flounce around the top of her long, smooth legs. It reminded him of the waitress with the fine derriere this afternoon at the tavern. *Ah, beautiful women,* he sighed in a dream-like state.

Then *WTF?* She is his employee! What is he doing getting all cozy with Marjorie? She could even sue him for coming-on to her. Embarrassed, he planned to apologize tomorrow.

Time to start looking at the internet - those intimidating, boring dating sites. *Peggy, forgive me. I finally need to be in a relationship with a female. And the kids won't like that, either!*

Chapter 27

"So much for fantasies..."

Spent and satisfied, the hosts of the Mississauga waterfront cottage invited Hamish and Esther to take the guest room. Sleep or not, their own desires. Gavin and Samuel curled up together with hoarse whispers of goodnights to their friends.

Across the hall, naked and at peace, Hamish and Esther drifted off, arms and legs interlaced under the summer duvet.

A text notification beeped through Hamish's mobile on the side table.

Dr. Jim Schroeder.

Hamish read the text aloud to include Esther in the information.

'Unable to reach Iggy. If you do, tell him Dr. Patricia Lim's request for paternity DNA on Carlos Delgado DONE before body sent to funeral parlor.'

"What the fuck? *Paternity* test done on *Carlos*? Iggy will shit himself! What do you think's going on, darling?" Hamish turned to his wife as his dreamy state instantly dissipated.

"I don't know, baby, but I'll figure it out by morning. Let's try to sleep, now, love. Simon will need our help tomorrow, and all week," said Esther. She leaned into the pillow, and thought, *what the fuck, indeed! There's a story here...*

Except for that fleeting moment when Marjorie slipped off her blush panties, straddled him, and lowered herself onto his lap with his large hands supporting her round buttocks, offering them both a spell of ecstasy, Simon's night was restless, unsatisfying.

Even with his phone off, his sleep proved fitful, achingly wanting, and disappointing. He woke several times to sip his water bottle, each time a hope to resume that incredible welcome dream. But it didn't return. *Do they ever?*

He rubbed himself, felt too exhausted, and gave up. *So much for fantasies.* He flipped his pillow to cool off. *Lots happening this week.* He needed his self-control and good sense.

Now that it's started, any kind of shit could hit the fan.

Chapter 28

"Afraid to stir the sleeping giant beside him…"

SUNDAY MORNING – August 23, 2015

He knew he was in withdrawal, and it hurt. Hurt bad, more than being tossed from the bunk last night. He awoke before daybreak and as the drugs left his system, his thoughts found comfort in Marjorie.

Filipe fantasized she might even *love* him. No longer did he tell himself she was just a hot screw. He hoped he could get her pregnant; maybe she would even marry him. He could stay in the country, and they would get a little place of their own. She was *uma alma bonita* -such a beautiful soul. Good to him and Carlos, and Simon's kids. She was a queen. Margie.

Soon the automated door locks of the cell units popped open. These modern devices - such a surprise. He heard men with deep voices in the common area; early-bird risers. Some joked with the guard whose station was central to all the units. Others shouted about showers before breakfast.

Filipe didn't want to move, to disturb his cellmate who breathed loudly, like someone with a nose problem. He recalled sometimes Uncle Carlos had that trouble. His cousin Eduardo called it 'sleep-app', something like that.

Filipe's thoughts switched from the world of sleep-apnea as he tried to control the pressure to relieve his bladder. Afraid to stir the sleeping giant beside him, he couldn't hold it much longer. He let his thoughts wander how he got into this drug use. Marjorie wouldn't like this at all. He blamed that *malvado* he met at the *YMCA*.

Grateful when Uncle Carlos added him to the family membership, Filipe liked to build his muscles on the machines. So convenient, just a few blocks from home. And Albina used the pool a lot, too. Sometimes they went together.

Then this dude, Geoffrey, with stringy greyish hair, like a bird's nest, started talking to him in the guys' change room close to the corner lockers. Said he had stuff for cheap could make him get a nice high and give him confidence with any woman. Would keep his young dick hard, and listen, man, he said, that's all women really want, don't kid yourself.

Filipe didn't understand half of what Geoffrey said but it sounded like important advice - man to man – from this older guy, experienced. Geoffrey even offered his car to Filipe to make a few drug deliveries. Only for a while. Told him he'd make money and attract women. And Filipe had just met the housekeeper at Uncle Carlos' jobsite. She was single and lived on the property. Filipe knew he would love this job with his uncle, just to glimpse this beauty who brought cool lemonade to them as they tended the gardens on the grounds.

Several months earlier, Filipe's life in the Azores came to a halt when his parents died. His father and mother worked in the exported canned tuna fish industry and leased a villa on the island. Filipe thought of taking courses in marine science; despite his learning disability, he felt he could do alright now in his twenties. Everything had just taken him a bit longer.

But life took a strange turn for Filipe when late one wet night, over rural roads, his parents, in taking a corner, became the victims of a fatal car and truck smash up.

The authorities, fortunately, found personal records at the cottage. They contacted next- of- kin, Carlos Delgado, the brother of the deceased male, in a place called Naples along the shoreline of Lake Ontario, Canada. The kind uncle offered to bring his brother's son across the Atlantic over to live with him, and his family, for a few months of mourning and moral support. This would do until they figured out the next step after the tragedy.

Out in the foyer of the prison, the lobby officer Glen, new on this shift, heard screams coming from cell four; most inmates had left for the breakfast area, so it wasn't as noisy. He hurried to investigate. He pulled open the unlocked door.

An inflatable monster gorilla—the kind one sees in cheap, used car dealerships – engulfed the tiny cell. Officer Glen quickly realized it must be the gigantic, latest inmate dubbed, *Big Guy*.

With a foaming mouth, the stunned prisoner stood legs spread wide. His orange jumpsuit stained dark, from the crotch to his ankles.

On the ground lay the foreign, dark one — his face blood-splattered, his forehead squashed like a pumpkin. A quick assessment led the guard to determine the boy may be dying from a severe headbutt and the larger inmate pissed himself in this clearly unfair fight. Definitely an attack, he surmised.

Officer Glen tried to summon help, but his partner was already on it. After shouting, "hands behind!" she snapped cuffs on Big Guy. And Big Guy knew he was done for. A temper he couldn't control.

The first guard about to call for infirmary help checked and found no pulse on the young, prostrate inmate. Another write-up. Another black eye for this new, ultramodern institution. The big man, and the dead one, both, were removed from the cell.

Sunday morning blues at '*The South.*'

Chapter 29

"Boss needs to see me…"

Sunday morning brought a text from Simon to meet him in his office.

"Boss needs to see me," Marjorie shared with Hazel. "Wonder what's up?"

They agreed Hazel would go down and make coffee while she took a quick shower. She texted Simon back: "There in ten minutes. "

Marjorie stood at the threshold of his office, stomach in a knot, her round brown eyes, questioning. She knew his body language: tense shoulders, his stubble more pronounced. He hadn't yet shaved. Evidently this *talk* would differ from last night's soothing moonlit chat. But what changed? Last night was tender, sweetness personified.

Seated and grim-faced, Simon observed Marjorie with gentle eyes, then waved her forward, "Please, come through and close the door behind you," he said.

She recognized this soft, formal tone usually meant trouble. Something awkward adrift in the air. As she shut the door, he began:

"I asked you to join me in my office this morning Marjorie because I need to speak to you now not as a friend, but as your

employer. Please... sit in the armchair. And excuse me for address-
ing you from across my desk. Although, I may get up and pace."

Marjorie walked past the windows and sat in the soft
rawhide to his right. Antsy, she swiveled, glanced towards the
misty lake with its low hanging clouds, turned back to him, then
remained still. Her eyelashes down, she fixated on her mulberry
nails. With fingers linked in her lap, she awaited *something*. She
felt every bit the *employee,* now.

She didn't care for this condescending version of Simon,
when he wore his invisible business shield, and appeared talking
down to his employees. Patronizing. But he *was* the boss, after
all. And the bottom line – everyone knew it.

"We have Carlos's funeral this week," he began, as though
delivering a speech. "You didn't know this but when I told Albina
yesterday, she didn't take it well. In fact, she became hysterical.
Over the top." Simon shook his head.

"I'm so grateful to you and Hazel for giving us your free
time to be here for us. To deal with this emotional impact on
our household, particularly the kids. You know those kids must
always be put first... and protected," he added.

Marjorie darted a nod of agreement at Simon, then lowered
her eyes again. She struggled with direct eye contact, but hoped
he imagined she hung on his every word. In truth, she saw a
sermon couched in a benign attitude. She braced herself, held
her breath, panicked about a possible explosion for which she
was unprepared.

Simon continued his speech:

"I had noticed you always had a pleasant smile for Filipe,
and it makes us all feel bad that he's been arrested and in the
detention centre. A lot happening at once. That cliché 'when it

rains it pours' never seems to fail in real life, does it? First Filipe, then Carlos. What's next I shudder to think. So, let me get to the point.

"Last night, Marjorie, after we all said goodnight, I silenced my phone. This morning I found a text from Hamish. He and Esther stayed overnight with their friends in Mississauga. Apparently, our mutual friend Jim Schroeder tried to reach *me* - in his role as *pathologist*. Evidently, a significant issue, but he didn't leave me any text, rather turned to Hamish."

A thunderbolt of lightning cracked the morning sky. They both jolted.

Simon continued. A tone of resentment crept into his voice.

"Does *any* of this have to do with *you*, Marjorie?

Then, he tossed in a sincere plea: "Perhaps you can fill me in – help here."

Marjorie now turned wide-eyed to face him. Shocked. *Where was Simon taking this?* Despite her own secret, she glued her eyes to his without a blink. Waited to hear more.

"Schroeder told Hamish that his medical colleague, Dr. Patricia Lim, needed a future *paternity* test on the body of Carlos Delgado. So, she made this request, this last-minute thing, for a rushed DNA sample on a deceased person. On our Carlos!

"Is there something you need to tell me? Are you involved? By the way, Schroeder also said, earlier, toxicology found drugs in Carlos's system. Fentanyl and Viagra. Carlos was not a drug-user. We both know *that* don't we, Marjorie? What can you share with me here? Here's the tissue box; I can see how distressed you are hearing this."

Marjorie flushed at this uncommon interrogation from her usually kind employer. Perspiration built under her bra; the wetness accentuated her natural scent and intensified her lavender body spray. Her head throbbed.

Simon paused, cleared his throat, gave her a moment. Drawing his eyebrows together, he took on an expression of deep concern. His face appeared like a mask as he methodically, continued to grill her.

"Now isn't Dr. Lim — a professional with clout — a close friend of your sister? Isn't she Hazel's partner's *mother*? Why would *she* be requesting a paternity test on Carlos for God's sake, and whose blood or urine sample would she be wanting to match? And what business is this of *hers*?"

With clear puzzlement and plain irritation drawn on his forehead, Simon persisted.

"This is one helluva unexpected shake-up Marjorie but listen to me here -whatever the heck is going on, you have my full support. Do you hear me? You know you can lean on me, whatever shit is going down. Now fill me in before somebody else does, Margie."

In his attempt at strong eye contact with Marjorie and offering his reassurances of her safety with him, Simon noticed the wafting lavender fragrance in the room.

He concentrated on her face, but his mind took in the fullness of her light purple lips as though seeing them for the first time. His need for a reply caught him in a spell of desire to physically connect with her mouth.

"I'm pregnant," she announced.

Boldly, with deliberation, Marjorie held his gaze. She knew her defences were up, so she went for it. She wrapped a loose lock of hair around her ear and waited for Simon's reaction.

A shot of adrenaline exploded from Simon's temples straight with a blow to his gut. A sense of hot and cold. A second of blackness. His limbs weakened, and a flood of heat overwhelmed him. *This must be what it's like to faint, to suffer shock,* he thought. He tried to cover his struggle, this momentary wipeout, to hold it together in front of her as he gripped the edge of his mahogany desk, unaware he left fingerprints on the glass overlay.

"Okay, I 'm stunned," Simon admitted. Clearing his throat, he continued, "You're pregnant. So, you requested this paternity test on *Carlos*? Why the hell for? You don't *know* who made you pregnant? I'm still in disbelief, Marjorie. It's one thing to be pregnant, but another to confirm if *Carlos* is the father? What the hell is going on?"

Simon felt an enormous tightness in his chest, as well as a dry throat. Then he realized the edge of nasty creeping into his voice and aimed to reduce his volume.

"Are you saying you were having sex with Carlos, and someone else? Right here, under my nose? It's none of my business who you have sex with, except if it's someone from this household. Do you read me, Marjorie? Fill me in. I can't say I'm not shocked by this news." He felt his skin crawling. He needed to move.

He stood up and headed to the windows. A sudden violent rapping of raindrops on the windowpanes blurred his vision yet muffled the pounding in his chest. This Sunday morning summer shower lashed out swiftly, and as Simon turned to look at Marjorie, nausea arose in his throat, followed by a suffocating swell of melancholy. Even his innermost feelings challenged him: *Why couldn't her unborn baby be mine?*

Time stopped. He stared at her.

He saw her kindness. He saw her gently brush Peggy's hair before she was moved to the hospice; the way she made Peggy's sallow face pretty again with a blush of pink powder. He saw her place a roast into the oven, gather the young twins and their two pups, and head off to the playground while dinner cooked. She gave him his office time to get work done. He saw the wind blow her hair wild like his own family's as she helped Carlos with replanting when he struggled, exhausted. He saw her dance with Darius to calm his nerves and teach him some cool steps before the junior prom. He saw her sit with Fiona at the kitchen island and encourage her to solve math problems before she faced a major test. He saw when she bathed Kent after his skunk attack. He saw her deal with the stink to comfort the frightened dog, without complaint. So much to admire about Margie, he knew she was special. And now she had her own issue at hand, and he was stunned, hopeless.

For Margie to be pregnant with someone else's child rattled Simon. Not to even know who the father is? *How could he allow such loose behaviour in front of his kids?*

More ruminations arose in his mind. Anger directed to himself. *Marjorie fucking Carlos, oh man! Was he jealous of poor, dead Carlos?* He felt ashamed of those thoughts, and for the mess that lay ahead. *In his household!* His father will humiliate the ass off him when he learns this. *Simon unable to control his own home and employees.*

He paced up towards the bookcases and tried to think. *Why isn't she saying anything more? Why do I have to pry information from her?*

"Marjorie, please, let's cut to the chase. I didn't know you had a boyfriend. And please try and explain why Carlos and you were lovers. Work with me here."

A scratching at the door. Simon turned to allow Kent to slip in, gave him a reassuring head-rub. Sensitive to thunder, Kent sheepishly disappeared under the desk. Nonetheless, Simon now had a comrade in the room. He returned to sit at his desk where his ankles were licked. Better prepared, he listened to his housekeeper's story.

"Me and Carlos weren't *lovers,* as you call it, Simon." Marjorie wet her lips and dabbed at her nose with a tissue. "I can explain some of this. I was helping him out."

"*Helping* him?" Anxious for Marjorie's explanation, Simon tapped his fingers. He detested confusion, feeling out of control. He felt trapped, like on a midway ride, stuck high at the top, but turned upside down and left dangling!

"He told me he was having trouble with his wife. She didn't want him to touch her. So, he thought maybe she had someone else. He tried to be more amorous and started using Viagra – to get her excited, but she still rejected him. Then he turned to me. He said he felt desperate. I felt sorry for him. He *was* a nice guy... with a sexual problem. I was only trying to help."

"Viagra? Where did he manage to get that? Carlos wouldn't be the type who'd know about these pharmaceuticals."

"Filipe got them. And he might have gotten them mixed up with the fentanyl which Filipe had on him." Marjorie felt like letting it all out now. She was screwed anyway.

"Jesus Murphy!" Simon spit out. "That's probably what killed him, you're right, Margie. This fentanyl is some new deadly drug Schroeder told me about.

Suddenly he felt some relief; they were like buddies solving a problem together.

"So why the paternity test? No condoms? What about your boyfriend?" *God almighty there was so much more ugly stuff to get through,* thought Simon.

"Dad! You in there?" Fiona rapped on the office door. Simon raised a finger to Marjorie to hold on and went to open the door part-way.

"Marjorie and I are having an important chat, honey. Can you and Darius make a nice breakfast for Hazel if she's up? Don't wait for us. We're going to be a while here going over some details. Pru and Charity okay after that thunder? Kent's here with me."

"Yeah, dad, they're fine now. Okay we'll manage on our own. Catch ya later." She gave Simon a peck on the cheek, could feel his endearing, scratchy stubble. Could see he was flushed about something. *Leave him be.*

"Alright, where were we, Margie?" You were going to tell me about your boyfriend."

Simon's mouth dried up, but he persisted.

"Did you meet someone on your trips to Toronto? Somebody you met through Hazel, perhaps?" His prying embarrassed even himself, but he needed to know everything!

"No, Simon. I *said* I don't have a boyfriend," Marjorie emphasized.

She added, "I can give my notice if you'll keep me on for two weeks. Then I'll move in with Hazel until I get a new position."

"Whoa, slow down!" Simon took sharp, small jabs to his gut.

"This is all moving too fast for me."

"Well," said Marjorie, "I know you wouldn't want me to be pregnant in front of the kids, right? How to explain my *situation*."

"Well, you're a grown woman. We're in modern times. We could explain your *situation*, as you call it, that there's a special someone in your life, or whatever. Or maybe you won't need an explanation. Have you considered termination? Modern women do it all the time."

Fuck you, Simon.

Chapter 30

"The more she revealed, the more he felt vulnerable."

T hose words exploded in Marjorie's mind. However, she replied with respect to her employer.

"I repeat, no boyfriend. And...I intend to *keep* this child." She folded her arms across her chest to punctuate her resolve. *What a good sensation to feel strong again.* Once she decided she would leave anyway, she sensed a huge relief.

Simon washed over once more with a burst of sweat, a spell of some sort...he wasn't used to this... at all. The more she revealed, the more he felt vulnerable. And just to see her now, he noticed her bustiness. *Why were women's tops in the last few years all cut so low? A guy doesn't know where to look...*

He tried to lock eyes with her but lost at that game and flipped open his daybook. Feigning busyness, he examined his timeline, as he fought the vilest lump in his throat, twice the size of his Adam's apple. He knew it resulted from tear-suppression, the male kind. *He would bloody-well miss her.*

"You don't have to leave, Marjorie. Not so soon. But after the funeral it might be wise to stay at Hazel's for a bit, until I figure this out, explain things to the kids. Go now, relax, get something to eat, lie down. I'm sure the third degree from me wasn't pleasant. For the record, I'll honour your wish to keep your baby business private. We good?"

The *woman* in her arose. With female hormones in full glory, she stood with pride, and he stood too. They entered a friendly – albeit awkward - chest embrace across the desk. "Thanks, Simon. We're good." And she left.

Simon sat down. The rain had stopped. Waves splashed the boulders. His head in his hands, he released some throat pressure with a sniffle. Kent appeared and placed his black and white snout onto his master's lap.

Marjorie took the back hallway and ran into Hazel on the small staircase.

"Thought you were in the kitchen with the kids," she whispered.

"Just came back for my phone. Did something happen, Margie?"

"Fuyun's mom called Schroeder for DNA on Carlos. Simon found out and grilled me. So, I told him about my pregnancy."

Hazel grabbed her sister's hand and pulled it to her heart. "OMG!" she uttered.

"We'll talk later," Margie added. "I'll be down soon. Go. Act like nothing happened."

"Did you say anything about Filipe?"

"No, Haze, one mistake at a time. Go now."

The sisters hugged strong.

Chapter 31

"Being an open-minded person will take you far in life."

When Simon and Marjorie had conferenced in his home office on the lower level, the kitchen on the main level then buzzed with chatter. During breakfast, the kids relished gabbing with Hazel. When they shifted to the Family Room, they quizzed her about her work at *Sick Kids*. They raised questions about her partner Ellen, Chinese name *Fuyun*, and *her* special bond with little ones as an anesthetist.

Often lacking a thought filter, Darius jumped in and asked if they planned to marry. Hazel laughed, said she hoped so. She wanted to raise a few kids of her own.

"I'm going to join the *Gay-Straight Alliance* group at school, this semester," Darius shared with a shoulders-back determination.

"Why that's great, Darey," Hazel reached and tapped his hand. "Being an open-minded person will take you far in life." She wondered if her comment didn't seem too preachy and turned to Fiona with a tender glance.

"You're so right, Hazel. I joined last year," Fiona added, "and I learned a lot about understanding the points of view of others.

Dad approved the idea, didn't he Dare? So, are you and Fuyun planning to adopt your kids?"

"Not at that stage yet. We're hoping Fuyun finds a sperm donor. Oh, sorry, not sure if we should be talking about *this* stuff. Your dad might not find it appropriate." Hazel raised her shoulders and slipped into a small neck cringe.

"Nah," Darius erupted. "Our dad is a cool dude," he gushed. "He worries about us, but he is … what's the word, Fi?"

"Understanding?" Fiona offered, with a tiny smirk.

"Yeah, that's it. Understanding! He's totally a fair guy." Darius relaxed back into the sofa, crossed his arms behind his head, and linked his fingers with conviction. Then, he nodded to punctuate his satisfaction.

"Your dad *is* a fine gentleman, guys. Margie talks about him constantly when she's at my place. She has ultimate respect for him and loves her position here. It doesn't feel like employment, she says. She calls it her *cocoon*. And she just adores you guys, too."

Smelling a good mood in the air when the word *kids* was tossed about, Charity and Pru took a keener interest in the conversation like they really understood this human dialect. They had at least several words down, of course a favourite being 'walk' which they expected might come up anytime soon.

They sniffed the air and wagged their tails.

Chapter 32

"They're sending him for an autopsy."

L ying down in her sanctuary, Marjorie's thoughts whirled. *So, out in the open now to Simon. That's it. What's next?*

She knew the kids awaited her downstairs, puttering around. They needed to discuss the loss of dear Carlos, consider some ideas for the funeral. Fiona might choose to write a tribute song. Plans needed to be made. She bolted to her washroom and heaved. Stomach empty. Head heavy. *Pull it together, girl,* she ordered herself.

Marjorie removed her top and pants and after a quick wash, slipped on a fresh, bluish-green cotton shift Hazel had sewn for her. It felt cool and loose. She twisted her unruly hair into a bun and applied fresh mauve lip-gloss. She'd go to the kitchen and pick up the pace for the family.

A ting phone-text.

Simon. Asking her to return downstairs if she was feeling okay. He needed to gather everyone. Marjorie's heart skipped, *had he decided to tell the kids now about the baby, and her leaving them?* Simon wouldn't. She had to trust him. She replied, *in a jiffy.* Convincing herself to act normal, she felt a bit lighter.

What Marjorie did not know after she left Simon's office: he intended to pull *himself* together, and after some deep breaths to return to the family room, when Hamish texted: *'Bad news, Ig. Sorry. Call me ASAP.'*

He did just that. "What now, Ham?"

"There's no easy way to say this," Hamish sighed. *"The South Detention Centre* just contacted me as Filipe's attorney. Filipe was murdered early this morning by his cellmate."

"What the...?" Simon grabbed his head. "What the hell happened, Hamish?"

"Apparently some huge asshole assaulted him with a head-butt. Smashed his cranium. They asked me what I wanted to do with the body. They're sending him for an autopsy."

"Jesus Christ. Are we on a streak of bad luck or what? For Carlos' sake, we'll have to do a double funeral. I'll call *Corelli-Bauer*. Listen, Ham, do everything you can, to keep this low-key. I appreciate it, man. Oh, and that DNA paternity test on Carlos? Keep that under your hat too. We'll deal with that later. Thanks, buddy. Wish me luck. The shit really *has* hit the fan. A lot to handle with the kids. Why don't you all come over later, today, with the boys? Lighten the atmosphere. I feel like I'm suffocating. And thanks for being there, Ham. Always grateful to have you in my corner, pal."

Marjorie brought her best face downstairs. Simon came up from his office just about the same time. Each bearing a new *secret*, they looked at each other, discreetly. The kids still chattered with Hazel as she kept them laughing with her playful mimicking of some doctor from work. Marjorie passed to the kitchen island, turned to the fridge to get the carton of milk, picked her favourite plastic tumbler from the cupboard, and poured to the rim.

"Hey, guys, anyone want anything? Thanks for stacking the dishwasher, by the way."

"No, we're good, thanks, Margie." Fiona tossed a warm smile in her direction.

Simon, reading lenses still perched on his head, just came out with it. "Listen up, everybody, there's something I need to share. Can you gather round? Marjorie remained in her spot. But she looked in his direction.

"What's up Dad?" from Darius.

Simon sat on the edge of the armchair facing the kids, Hazel, and Marjorie also in his view. "I didn't tell you what else happened. Friday night, Police pulled Filipe over on the road, for DUI, and because he didn't have proper ID papers, he was arrested."

Oh, no's came from everyone at once.

"I didn't even know he had a car," said Darius.

"Or even a license to drive," added Fiona.

"That doesn't matter right now. But before we went on our bike ride yesterday, I told Carlos about the arrest. Naturally, he was shocked. And ashamed. I believe this information had a direct bearing on his accident in the wine cellar.

"I immediately put Hamish on it. I asked him to deal with the police, the detention centre, and the legalities to have Filipe released as soon as possible."

"Well, Dad, that's some relief," Fiona went to put an arm around her dad's shoulder. Kent appeared and made his way to sit by Simon.

"Wait, family, there's more. Hamish just contacted me now and gave me some dreadful news. And there's no easy way to say this, as Hamish just put it, himself."

Now, Simon had Marjorie's full attention. She placed her tumbler on the counter and held her breath. What the heck was he going to tell everyone? *Dreadful* news? She hoped nothing to do with these paternity tests on Carlos.

"It's about Filipe. He was killed early this morning. In the detention centre."

Marjorie gasped, knocked over the milk carton, and sank to the floor. Milk drained onto her belly.

It was only for a moment Marjorie lost consciousness. Hazel wiped the milk from her sister's dress as Marjorie raised her head. Simon wasted no time, scooped her from the floor into his arms. The twins stood in stunned disbelief —how quickly their world was spinning. Darius felt queasy, and Fiona managed a good front, but sniffled at news of another death, and a young man at that. The dogs barked, then backed off, strangely silent, allowing the humans to deal with this situation.

"I'm okay, Simon," Marjorie whispered, mortified in front of the others. "Please put me down, thank you." Always respected as the strong one in this household, she didn't know how to deal with her unexpected reaction to this news and the humiliation. In addition, a huge wave of sadness overwhelmed her.

Both potential fathers of her unborn baby dead. No future for her only child.

"Well, at least let me help you to your room," said Simon as he placed her on her feet and put her arm around his neck as he encircled her waist. A pool of hopelessness collected in his belly. His once solid Marjorie now emotionally fragile with this unforeseen pregnancy. His mood couldn't be lower. But he made his usual *I'm in-charge* effort.

"Give us a minute, kids, Hazel. I'll take her up. Margie's in shock over losing such good friends, as we all are. Fiona, Darius, try to chill, calm each other. Hazel, I'll take it from here. You might want to make some personal calls. I know this has been rough on all of us. I'll be down soon."

The kids stretched out on the sofas. They turned onto their sides, and just looked at each other, communicating only with their eyebrows and groans.

As they inhaled the somber atmosphere, the big dogs collapsed onto the floor space between the couches and behaved with proper dignity. Tiny Prudence lay curled on Fiona's midriff.

"I'm going outside to call Fuyun," said Hazel. "You kids be okay? Just rest. We all need us some quiet sanity to absorb all that's happened."

Fiona grunted, waved her on.

Hazel stepped outside and strolled in her flip flops to the lake's edge. She sat on a warm boulder and inhaled the fresh summer breeze. The air felt good blowing through her short wiry hair and her white V-neck tee-shirt. The bright morning sun and clear sky offered a feeling of peace. She took her mobile from her jeans' pocket and squinted a 'call me' text to her love at work. Seconds later, her phone chimed.

"I'm here babe. I'm on a break. Glad you caught me." Fuyun 's soft voice felt like a cup of comforting tea. "What's going on?"

"I love you. I miss you, Fu," Hazel half-sobbed. "All hell broke loose."

"What's happen now?"

Knowing Fuyun's hospital break to be short-lived, Hazel filled her in on the morning news from the Nesbitt household.

"So, Margie is resting upstairs. Simon took her up. After your mom contacted Schroeder to get Carlos' DNA, he couldn't reach Simon. So, he texted Hamish, who told Simon this morning. Simon called Margie into his office for a formal talk, and she spilled her pregnancy news. She pretty much had no choice."

"*Tian a*"! I should have told mama to keep it down-low," lamented Fuyun.

"Not your fault, Fu! We got you and your mom involved in this. But honey, the awful big news is that Filipe was *murdered* in his detention cell last night and Simon just told us now! Margie's a wreck cause she doesn't know which guy is her baby daddy. And now they're both dead. (She heard Fuyun gasp.)

"Listen, sweetheart, I think Margie will move in with me later in the week after the funeral. There's no way she can stay here and face this family in her mental condition."

Fuyun stunned, *not another death*. A fatherless baby on the way. And her family involved in this drama, her mother being a catalyst of sorts. Fuyun's thoughts flashed to Marjorie moving in, a compromise of her and Hazel's free time together. She needed yoga or meditation break, not this news today.

"Anything else, my girl?" asked Fuyun.

"Well, actually, yes, babe. Glad you asked. I'm hoping you could arrange a 'work-up' for Fiona at *Sick Kids*. She's been lethargic, and that's not like her. Simon wants her to have a complete assessment. Can't blame him after losing his wife."

"I can take care of this, sure," Fuyun glad to help her beloved.

"*Ni tai bang le! Wo ai ni,*" Hazel expressed awesomeness, and love to her partner in Mandarin. She thought she'd better keep up her Chinese classes. It felt wonderful to touch Fuyun's heart in her own language.

"Love you, too, Haze."

"Alright then, text ya later."

Chapter 33

"We've been through hell this weekend."

That Sunday morning took its toll on everyone's nerves. Hamish drove to Hackberry Road to offer Simon support. As his lawyer, he would also visit the Delgado home to deliver the tragic news of Filipe's demise in prison. He suggested he'd drop Simon's *girls* at *Naples Mall* on the way.

Fiona, Hazel, and Marjorie needed a break from the house. *Shopping therapy for women is such a healer* thought Hamish. Sheepishly, he admitted to himself the sexist attitude in *that* one. Ironically, he loved a bit of retail therapy for his own dapper self. He lowered the visor mirror to check his complexion before he got to *HR*. His usual pale cheeks, already pink. A tough task lay ahead for this day.

Content to stay home with Charity, Darius relaxed with headphones. Pru napped nearby. And, after Hamish and the girls left, Simon craved alone time with *his* dog,

He and Kent strolled the shoreline. They reached a grassy clearing at the water's edge bordered by a white, weathered fence. The view highlighted moss-coated craggy rocks where strong-rolling whitecaps slapped over them. Simon absorbed the healing power of waves, watched them smash then dissolve into foam. They melted into the sand and the pile of tiny pebbles at the shore. A small roar accompanied the wave action. Nature's mesmerizing repetition offered Simon some blessed moments of peaceful nothingness.

On an extended leash, Kent kept his nose to the ground, sniffing, but strained to move on. Simon obliged and called his mom while walking. He regretted to share more bad news, yet immediately felt her soothing, warm comfort.

"Oh Darlin'," Virginia sighed after Simon told her about Filipe. "That poor family. We'll do what we can to support them. Hamish will find out how Albina wants to handle this. Bless his heart. And our sweet Ed. Such a lovely boy."

"I don't think Ed cared much for Filipe, Mom," Simon said, "but he wouldn't have expected him to end up in a violent death, either."

"Of course, not," Ginny agreed. "But you know there could have been some young male rivalry for Carlos' interest. I noticed some tension between those boys. Still, it's all too sad. You take it easy today, Sugar. I'll tell dad. He's in the shower just now. He wanted me to join him. Glad I didn't, or I would have missed your call, Precious."

"Mom! TMI," Simon shouted into the wind.

"What's that, Darlin'?"

"Too much information, Mom. You should know kids don't want to hear that stuff about their parents!"

"Well, you're an adult, Darlin' and you know dad & I are always *close*." Ginny emphasized this euphemism with great pride in her voice.

"Okay, that nice, but I don't need the details. Tell the *Captain* it embarrasses his son! Keep it to yourselves. But Mom, of course I'm glad you guys are so happy together."

"You bet, Sweetness! By the way, tomorrow I'm meeting a new gal who needs some help at *Kerry on House*. But remember, you can reach me anytime, Sweetheart."

Doctor Schroeder visited late Sunday afternoon. A rare break for this medical man who seemed like a caricature when in a social setting. With his long arms and legs, brush cut, and bristle moustache, Jim appeared *unique*, perhaps one might simply find him unconventional. A description to which this pathologist would readily agree.

Simon offered him a beer. The women returned from shopping by cab and quickly dispersed. Schroeder nodded to Marjorie before she disappeared up to her suite with Hazel, and Fiona dashed off to her room.

"Man, your Marjorie's looking hot these days." His attempt at praising Simon's housekeeper fell flat. Simon thought *thank God they had moved into the office.*

"Not now, Jimbo! We've been through hell this weekend. Gotta find your own woman. Eyes off my housekeeper! So, what happens to the DNA? "

"We freeze it until there's a *baby* to test the match. Who's having a baby that you know? The request came from Patricia Lim, a colleague from medical conventions. How is she connected to *you*? She claimed *you* needed this evidence. I arranged for the DNA on the body, but when I couldn't reach you, I went to your right-hand man." They both took for granted Schroeder referenced Hamish.

Simon took a swig of his beer, then cradled his head. "Let me fill you in."

Chapter 34

"Would that make her some *mother-stalker*?

Albina no longer wanted a *church* service. She didn't want *coffins* from any funeral home, either. After Hamish told her about Filipe's murder at the detention centre, she flipped out. She wanted both men cremated, *the drug users*! She screamed at her son.

In turn, being a man, Eduardo hated the expectation to take charge as taught from childhood. He ached to mourn his beloved father properly, not disrespect his mother in the process, and still tolerate this unfortunate incident, *maybe a godsend*, his cousin's demise in prison.

And so, the church had to be cancelled.

Mother and son were at odds. He called Beryl. She would comfort him, buy him some thinking time.

"Yah, honey, what's up now?" Beryl whispered as she answered her cell. She knew her voice modulation would keep her boyfriend calm. She had been reading through elective course descriptions for last minute changes in her program at Saunders College.

"Do you think having a cremation instead of a funeral would be disrespectful to my dad?"

"Well, Sweets, what did he ask for in his Will?"

"Nothing in particular. I think he just expected a traditional approach, and never expressed it in writing. At least I can't find anything here as I go through his papers."

"I'm guessing, then," said Beryl, "if your dad did not specify anything, he would want you and your mom to do what you feel is best. After all, you're the ones left with your bereavement. And he would want you at peace. Whatever that would mean to you."

"I suppose true enough, Berri," Eduardo sighed audibly into his phone.

"How's Albina doing? Do you want me to talk to her?"

Glad to comfort Ed, Beryl held a bizarre passion for his mother. She admitted to herself since her own mother took off years ago, she transferred tender feelings to Albina. She wished Albina could be her mother. In fact, *she* also wanted *to be* Albina's *mother.* She felt this symbiotic relationship between herself and Albina, at least, she hoped Albina felt the same way. What if she didn't? Would that make her some '*mother-stalker*?' Beryl thought about herself and shook her head. *Psych classes*!

The young couple agreed to try and keep everything on an even keel. No coffins then, just photos. She would come over and help Albina find the best pictures of both Carlos, and the nephew he cared for, Filipe. However, a small blessing - with Carlos deceased, he would never learn the ugly truth how his only late brother's son ended up *murdered* in a Canadian prison.

Chapter 35

"She knew when she knew *something...*"

Betty Andrews, manager of *KOH*, didn't need to look far to spot the person she was to process. This individual—definitely older than the *kids* who hung around after school at *Kerry on House*.

"Miss Reichert? Is that *you*?" Betty cocked her head in a friendly way.

Seated on an orange plastic chair, Frieda Reichert closed the *Naples Community* magazine. She turned and saw the kind face of the woman who addressed her.

"*Ja*, I'm Frieda," she stood, blushed, and jerked up her oversized pants. The women shook hands.

"Good. Let's go to my office down the hall, shall we?"

Settled with a cup of Betty's coffee, Frieda burst into tears of relief. Betty wanted to hug this sad woman, but she relied on professional training to remain empathetic from her desk. She passed Frieda a tissue box.

"We're glad you're here, Frieda, and not to sound trite, we *are* here *for* you! I just want to make that clear. This is a *safe* place. We can help you organize financial aid and help you find a better place to stay. As you've noticed, the lobby shelves have healthy grocery donations. They arrive fresh daily. You are welcome to take what you need.

"Can you fill me in on your personal background? I know you're originally from Europe and were treated in Vancouver for your illness."

"It's alright, Ms. Andrews...you can say it, I am narcotics addict. Dr. Devon Ranger helped me, fix me out there. He so kind, not judge me. He saw my pain," Frieda explained in her best English.

Frieda set her cup on the side table. With caffeine in her system, she began to fidget and run her hands up and down her arms. "Doctor Ranger wrote big book, name is: *Understanding Addiction*. Do you know this book, Ms. Andrews? Maybe, I am not saying it good?"

"Call me Betty, please. And no, I have to say, I'm not familiar with it, but I'll certainly look into it. I have heard of Dr. Ranger's excellent work through a documentary."

"Thanks for suggestions. I feel okay now. I feel better for new life. It's been long fight. When I was teenager, I lived with my mother in Frankfurt. I was *rebel* as you say here. Got trouble with bad crowd, I run away from home lots. My *Mutti* was much gone to her work at airlines, and I did not know my *Vater*. I wasted many years in drugs. My mother died from injury after Lufthansa airline crash in 1990s. She survived crash, but some trouble, later, complications, and doctors say she suffered *aneurism*. By that time, I was twenty-one, and a real mess."

"How did you find yourself in Canada?"

"My *Mutti* had good friend, Greta...they worked together, and Greta's family tried help me. Greta say I have real father in Canada. Greta and her *Mann* helped me get passport and stuff.

Greta said my father was important man. I thought to start in Vancouver and search whole country. But I fell back to drugs for years, was lost."

"Well, Frieda, I have a wonderful volunteer who will work with you. She will be here soon. Her name is Virginia Nesbitt. You will find her a warm and lovely person."

As though the timing were planned, a gentle rap came at the door. Then it opened to reveal the most cheerful face Frieda had seen in a long time.

"Well, speak of the devil," chuckled Betty. "Here's Ginny now."

Virginia extended her hand to Frieda and felt an *affinity* when their palms touched. Sometimes a handshake is indifferent, merely a perfunctory action as one might open or close a door, without much thought. However, like a spiritualist, Ginny now *felt* a *person* at the other end of this social encounter. She *became* a palm-reader. Her husband would have called it her 'Voo-Doo' again. *Call it what you will, Quinn*, she would smart, but she knew when she knew *something*. Often it just took a bit of time to figure out what it was.

"Ladies, would you like to take it from here?" suggested Betty.

"If it's okay with you, Frieda, I thought maybe we could go to *Horton's* on the Lakeshore for a chat. Oh, you already have a coffee, I see?"

"No, that is okay, I drink much coffee."

"Wonderful. I have my car in the lot, out back. Do you have any belongings to bring with you?"

"Just my knapsack, here."

Ginny wheeled her Honda Odyssey minivan towards the coffee shop. On the way, Frieda mentioned how roomy it was. Ginny said she drove twin grandkids around, almost seventeen, a boy and a girl. Frieda delighted in being with this lady who obviously loved children. She wanted some of that *love* for herself.

Although she was no longer a child at forty-one, Frieda was skinny enough to look like a teenager, except for a few white streaks in her thin black hair.

With the lunch crowd gone, the two women sat at a window table, each with a mug, and a glazed donut, not feeling rushed. From her street view, Ginny had the funeral home at the corner, which triggered the thought she'd better not mention the business happening in her family, just yet.

"You seem to have a French accent, Frieda, mixed with German, am I right?"

"*Ja*, that's right. You have good ear, Virginia. I lived in France, the north of Paris, with my mother until I was ten. Then she lost her job with Air France, and we moved to Germany where she worked for Lufthansa."

"So, you're schooled in both. You Europeans are so clever with your languages. My mother-in-law was from Paris, as well."

"And you, Virginia? You have an accent, too, not so much Canadian?"

"Yes, Darlin', I'm from the American South East...Kentucky, originally." Ginny smiled at this intelligent young woman who could use some TLC. She noticed specks of blue emanating from those haunted grey eyes.

"Oh, *ja*, I hear that now" Frieda looked interested. "You African American?"

"Oh, no, Darlin'! Not that there's anything wrong with *that*...I mean, it's just the way we all speak in the South. I grew up on my Daddy's plantation. He raced horses."

"I just thought you remind me of some people I knew in Germany, with your warm colour, and soft skin, Virginia. And your accent. I am not offending you?"

"Of course, not. Don't be silly. But tell me, Frieda, Betty says that you also had to deal with abuse in Vancouver. That must have forced you to hide the pain, contributed to your drug use. Is that right?" Ginny tenderly examined those sunken, too-old-for-forty, eyes looking back at her.

"Hard to talk about, Virginia...but you feel so comfortable to me."

"Well, in that case, thank you Darlin' and please feel you can call me Ginny...almost everyone else does."

"I will tell you, then. I was raped by doctor. Radiologist."

"A radiologist?" Ginny widened her eyes, set down her cup, and wiped her lips with the napkin leaving slight traces of red lipstick. "I would think there's rarely direct contact between radiologists and patients."

"It was not office visit. We met in bar, strangers, downtown Vancouver. He was high with cocaine. Come sexy on to me. Seemed nice.... Said he had room upstairs in hotel, and he could share some goodies with me. Me, then addict, interested, so I go with him to his room."

Ginny reached across the table and put her hands gently over Frieda's. "You don't have to elaborate if it's too painful, Sugar."

"No, is okay. Now I talk about that nightmare. But I was stoned. Still, I will not share details, maybe another time. Just you know he was arrested and lost his doctor license. I told my counsellors. I want to forget his name but will remember forever: Raymond Douglas Hitchcock, M.D. I will never forget it, but I try, Ginny."

Frieda's eyes welled up. She hoped Ginny wouldn't think she was lying. She blew her nose into the napkin, then crumbled it. "I probably deserved it, me a druggie!"

"Stop that right now," Ginny ordered. "You've had an illness. You've been hurt and neglected during your lifetime. You need love, and that includes self-love. I'm going to see about getting you a better place to live, and maybe, just maybe, I could help you find your father. Do you have any inkling who he could be?"

"Yes, I do."

Ginny's eyebrows shot up. She leaned forward, "Well, who do you think he is? That could give us a place to start looking, Darlin," she said as she tapped Frieda's hand.

"I think he is Roman Catholic priest."

"What? A priest? She pulled her shoulders back. "Why in heaven's name would you ever think this?"

"Because why else *Mutti* not tell me? Why else my *Vati* be such a big secret, my whole life? Why, else? Why else would she be fired from Air France? I think all those things, Ginny. It makes me crazy, yes."

"Alright, Darlin', we'll leave this topic for the moment," Ginny tried to diffuse Frieda's distress. "We'll have time to explore this later, and we will. Let's talk about a nice place for you to live. Where are you now?"

"I have subsidized room in the *Queen Isabella* apartment building. Volunteer church lady, good person, offered me to stay for a while. I am there four weeks now. I met her brother, a nice man too. I need some friends."

"Glad to hear that, Frieda. I think I can find you something more permanent." Ginny started wiping little circles on the table, mindlessly, the small coffee-drops from her cup as she told Frieda about her widowed friend who owned a lovely home in Naples' Bronte neighbourhood. She had a small, but cozy basement apartment which she would rent for a reasonable rate, a bit of household help, and companionship. Ginny also suggested Frieda could probably find part-time work in housekeeping at the YMCA. She would investigate all this for her. For now, she would return Frieda to her apartment. At the drop off, Ginny gave her a big hug, and a promise to stay in touch. But now, things in her own family were charged up, and Simon needed her attention.

Chapter 36

"A *saint* could not have expected a better send-off."

Choral sounds of Albinoni's Adagio — *The Beatitudes* — soul-gripping sopranos, akin to the voice of the late Peggy Nesbitt, vibrated with heart-piercing clarity through the speakers. The piece, itself, induced tears in any listener; hence, the mourners dabbed their eyes. The classic organ contributed just the right celestial gravitas to the occasion. People fanned themselves. Most attendees contemplated thoughts of grief...or relief.

Angelic in a white muslin dress, Fiona, too, brought tissues to her eyes as this music stirred her tender emotions. She missed dear Carlos, and she let herself feel this loss. She focused on his photograph, displayed on an easel — a bushy mustache, a gentle smile. She imagined Carlos' warm eyes looked directly at her.

Then Fiona glanced at Filipe's picture and wondered. Why such negativity towards this nephew? Was he somehow to blame for Carlos' death? They were *both* dead. What did it matter *now*? She bent forward and looked across the aisle to Eduardo. Her heart broke for his massive loss.

The abundance of florals— on tall stands and in urns positioned on lower levels— appeared outstanding. Yet, for people not used to funerals, the thick air overwhelmed from the varied scents of sweetness.

In consultation with Marjorie, Albina, and Eduardo, Simon provided the funeral home with fresh-cut flowers from local florists. However, the kids suggested to choose from their garden, also, to honour Carlos' work. Thus, plants Carlos lovingly nurtured stood alongside the purchased ones.

Florists' recommended the family choose flowers for their beauty and symbolism. Four-foot pink gladioli conveyed strength of character, moral integrity. Violet and white chrysanthemums, arranged in bunches, signified grief and truth. White and purple hydrangeas displayed a gift of thanks. Furthermore, hung on easels, wreaths of crimson roses signified respect, love, and appreciation. Only a hard-core cynic would view this display of floral opulence a touch overdone. A *saint* could not have expected a better send-off.

Solemn faced, Eduardo, handsome in a dark green blazer and black dress pants, sat in the aisle seat. His mother, dressed in a black skirt and long-sleeved blouse with a purple ribbon at the throat, remained sheltered between him and Beryl. The girl, somehow too fresh, in a lavender sleeveless dress, clutched Albina's moist hand. They, three, were the only *relatives* in the front pew of the chapel's right-side.

Several people from Albina's church and a few classmates of Ed's and Beryl's occupied the other rows. Word of the family tragedy spread rapidly throughout — *Facebook* attracting both friends, and the curious.

Some rows back, the person Eduardo met as Geoffrey sat alone. Restless, pulling his nose, Geoffrey fidgeted with his facial hair, and fumbled with his red necktie. His grey sports coat looked borrowed and hung loose on his bony frame.

Simon, Fiona, and Darius, whose brooding expression felt right given the occasion, sat on the chapel's left side in the first row. In the second row, grandparents Quinn and Virginia, whose pink faces accentuated their white hair, suffered the humidity of late summer. They wondered what happened to the air - conditioning. Beside them, Marjorie and her sister Hazel assumed formal positions with hands in their laps. Hamish and Esther and their young sons took the pews behind the sisters. Gavin and Samuel, also present, stayed in back where Gavin parked Samuel's wheelchair. Dr. Schroeder was not in attendance. Some people from *Nesbitt Holdings* came to show their respects to Simon and sat scattered here and there on the left side as well.

"We could have done with less flowers. We overdid it," a desperate Marjorie stage-whispered to Hazel. This first trimester of pregnancy had her gasping for clean air. All odours, fragrances, particularly sweet ones, turned violently offensive to her. She felt she might have better tolerated the rancid smell of death, itself. She held a tissue to her nostrils to block the vapors. She figured no one would consider it odd at a memorial.

"I know, honey, but he *was* a gardener, after all. It's a great tribute. Hang in there," replied Hazel, and squeezed Marjorie's hand.

Simon, with a fresh, close haircut, wore a charcoal two-piece single button suit, a crisp white shirt, and a sheen purple tie. As the music faded, he moved the few steps towards the front of the chapel and faced the mourners. His earnest eyes warm, his forehead furrowed in the spirit of genuine compassion, Simon addressed the audience without papers.

Good morning, Family and Friends:

Thank you for joining us here today, and not at St. Jude's, on such short notice for this memorial.

Carlos was much loved at our home. Many of you noticed his shy, warm smile as he went about his work. For us, he was simply the best groundskeeper in Naples. He wasn't only a wonderful landscaper, he became family. (Simon's voice cracked as thoughts of Marjorie's unborn baby invaded his psyche. He noticed her, caught her eye, and she held his, not looking away.)

Carlos regarded us as his own as we did him. He also had the love and support in the garden of our wonderful Border Collie, Kent. They were good buddies even though occasionally Carlos worried the rascal Kent might rip through his radishes on a chase after a young fox. Just doing his job. Audience murmured a hoarse group chuckle.

And by extension our love and respect go out to his dear wife, Albina, and beloved son Eduardo. Ed has agreed to continue some of his dad's work part-time with us for this season, when he feels up to it.

For those who are not clear about what happened, let me tell you that Carlos had a fatal stroke last Saturday in our home when the twins and I were out, and our loyal friend and housekeeper Marjorie was visiting her sister in Toronto. (At this point a more perfunctory glance at Marjorie sitting beside Hazel sufficed.) *Sadly, and shockingly when we returned home from our outing, we found him collapsed. I called EMS and when they arrived, they declared our dear Carlos deceased.* (The twins looked at each other; *not* something dad told them at the time.)

We gathered from his records that Carlos did not wish a casket and a funeral in a cemetery but rather a cremation. His family will advise where to spread the ashes, and we will be ready to help with this honour.

As you see beside the picture of our dear Carlos is a young man who lost his life strangely on the same night! This young man was Filipe Delgado, the son of Carlos' late brother and sister-in-law of the Azores, Portugal.

Filipe had only been in Canada a few months staying with Carlos and his family after his parents passed from a tragic accident on the rural roads of the Azores.

Right here in our town, sad to say, Filipe ran into some unsavory people who took advantage of him. He landed in trouble with the authorities, was placed temporarily in detention and shockingly, he was murdered by a brutal inmate the same night.

Our hearts are heavy. One small blessing, if I may use that word, blessing, is that Carlos predeceased his nephew and did not learn of Filipe's cruel and shocking fate in detention.

*Both men have been cremated, and today we mourn them. I would like to say we celebrate them but I'm not ready yet, myself, to assume **that** position. I will mourn for more than a while. Perhaps a celebration of Carlos's life will be more proper at a garden party next summer on our grounds at home, and we plan to place a commemorative bench somewhere in our Naples' neighbourhood.*

For now, we want to comfort each other as we say goodbye. Fiona has written a song for our Carlos. And afterwards, Eduardo will speak of his father.

Before closing, Simon noticed the presence of a female reporter from the *Naples Gazette* sitting in the back. He had met her on several occasions when *Nesbitt Holdings* held special promo events. He wondered if *more* journalists and media were present.

Thank you again for being here.

Simon returned to the pew as Darius shifted over, allowed Fiona to come forward.

Her guitar, placed at the front and ready for her, Fiona picked it up, strummed gently, and sang close to the standing microphone.

> *Ooh, lah, lah,*
> *Ooh, lah, lah,*
> *The summer winds.*
> *Now blow our way,*
> *To take you to another place*
> *Our dearest friend*
> *Who knew us well,*
> *Carlos Delgado*
> *We let you go.*
>
> *With broken hearts,*
> *We weep for you,*
> *But know dear friend,*
> *You're in God's grace.*
> *You've always lifted up our hearts,*
> *With your beautiful works of art*
> *Which will continue, on...and on...*
> *Each year,*

Each summer the flowers will bloom,

And your beautiful memory we'll embrace.

Ooh, lah, lah,
Ooh, lah, lah,
We love you, Carlos,
As we say goodbye,
We love you,
We truly do.
We thank you, too.
Ooh, lah, lah,
Ooh, lah, lah,
And now, to you
Adieu.

After Fiona set down her guitar and took her place in the pew, Rachel, the funeral director, nodded for Eduardo to approach.

He stood in the space between the two easels: photographs of his father Carlos, and his cousin Filipe. The paper in his hands shook, but Eduardo spoke without reading, and without the microphone. He looked only to his father's picture, then to the audience, his eyes red-rimmed and face, dark-shadowed. When he raised his masculine voice, he lifted a gentle power of conviction, and a sound which resonated from the ceiling to the seated and might have been heard by the public on the street had the doors been open.

My dad was a good man, a kind man. He taught me the beauty of nature in the world. He loved his flowers; he loved his job at the Nesbitt's. He loved his music, particularly the Gypsy Kings, their flamenco guitars, and soulful vocals. You'll hear some today. Dad also enjoyed his pipe, his cigars, and of course, fishing, which he did off the pier in Bronte. He had simple tastes, but he was an authentic person, a dad that I wanted to be proud of me. I was always so proud of him.

And I knew he loved me, and my mother.

Also, he offered to help my cousin who he took into our home when Filipe lost his parents in Portugal. From the goodness of his heart, he gave Filipe a family again and included him in his landscaping work.

Now they are both gone so suddenly. I can't speak about my cousin, but I will always honour, love, and remember my dearest father. His loss is almost unbearable.

I love you, Papai. Rest in Peace.

Eduardo returned to his seat and blew his nose. His mother rubbed his back.

Uncomfortable, even in her loose brown shift with its white lace collar, Marjorie carried more than this baby; she felt encumbered by a mantle of guilt. Yet, she reasoned it wasn't her place to say anything. Not here. And the scent of the pink and red lilies overwhelmed her as she swallowed the bile of nausea. She fought her gag-reflex and discretely sipped on a bottle of water.

Hazel looked at her and could almost feel Margie's cheeks burning. Symbiotic sisters. She'd help her through everything once they were past this awkward day. She had not packed funeral clothes, and Margie's size was tall girl. So, when the sisters, along with Fiona, had popped over to the *Naples Mall* they picked out something right for themselves. And now, to her discomfort, even Margie's bustline clearly had swelled.

Moments of silence and reflection took place as music played once again. The instrumental version of 'Inspiration' by the *Gypsy Kings* streamed through the speakers. Guitar strings, quick and strong movement of encouragement to continue life for the living as Carlos would have wanted for his beloved son.

Finally, the number *'A Mi Manera' My Way*, as a final ending. Carlos lived his life his way. Ed's shoulders shook with sorrow. Beryl moved in closer to embrace him. Albina turned and glanced behind her to see who was in this congregation.

Those mourners who knew and loved Carlos wept during this last number. They wished him to *rest in peace*. The music stopped. Coughing, shuffling, the sound of tissues put to proper use. The memorial was over.

Geoffrey, first to flee out through the heavy wooden doors, unknowingly fled not only into the shock of bright sunshine, but also into a media mob with reporters and cameras pointed *at him*. Several uniformed police officers from the drug squad approached him. He was surrounded. They made official statements and placed Geoffrey in handcuffs.

Chapter 37

"Police cars with lights flashing..."

Frieda worked a couple of pins through the waistband of her pants—those she bought from the thrift shop. Still a bit loose. She needed to gain weight, but she also craved the healthy feel of running lakeside. She'd eat more carbs in the future. Now she needed motion and a breeze on her face.

From her apartment, Frieda ran south towards Forest Street. Sunshine beamed on her forehead and cheeks. She stopped by the lavish condo on the coroner. Jogged on the spot. Waited for a green light. She took in the height of this building, and thought, *wow*!

Who lived in such luxury, while others have so little? But useless to puzzle over the injustice of life. Some suffer hardships more than others, still we fight on. Never give up, as her *Mutti* would say.

Frieda realized her good fortune to meet this warm person Ginny - a wonderful, kind, and helpful lady. This new *friendship* boosted her spirits. Though she knew in her heart they could never be *real* friends, coming from such different walks of life.

The light changed. Frieda skipped across the road. Down the south side of the bridge, she ran, then slowed her pace to view a marina full of tall sail boats, docked in the passageway where the green river spread open to the bluest lake of Ontario.

When Frieda reached the waterpark, a paved path curved between lofty, oak trees. She darted through a children's play-area, then jogged as far as Hackberry Road, and bent over, hands on knees, to catch her breath.

She rested on a bench outside a grand, yellow house and wondered how long the family lived there. Seemed quiet. No people sat on the huge verandah. Just a regular work weekday. Maybe only a housekeeper inside. Rich folks at their busy desk jobs. She imagined how it would feel to be the caretaker of such a place rather than pushing a towel cart at the YMCA.

Frieda glanced at a gleaming plaque attached to the bench. Dedicated to someone called Seraphina. Frieda couldn't make out the details. Her eyes needed a checkup. Also, a slant of sunray flickered through the leafy tree branches and glazed the bronze plate.

She grew hungry, and weak. She had just enough change for a coffee and a muffin.

Frieda walked the return route past pretty shops on Lakeshore Avenue and found her way to the *Horton's* café. The coffee *hit the spot* as her Canadian friends would say.

When she looked up, out the window, suddenly the street filled with people spilling through the double doors of the funeral home. Police cars with lights flashing arrived including a CITY TV station van which pulled up to the curb.

Munching on her carrot muffin, Frieda swallowed quickly and washed it down with her coffee. Her eyes grew wide.

What was happening? One of the people dressed nice who came through the heavy doors onto the sidewalk among the crowd was her new friend Ginny. A man beside her, an older gentleman with silver hair, took her arm. Maybe her husband?

Wow. Was ist das?

Simon also came out the front doors facing Lakeshore Road. He was surprised to see a crowd had gathered in the bright noon sunshine.

He had told his parents to leave by the side doors and to take the kids home. He would join them, soon, and he'd bring Marjorie, Hazel, and some of the flowers. He'd have the funeral home donate the rest.

As CEO of *Nesbitt Holdings*, Simon expected *some* word would get out, but he was jolted by this gathering and the media throng outside. *Why this attention?*

With sunshine in his eyes, he slid on his shades. What were his *parents* doing milling about? He jerked his head to the left for them to take off. *Now.*

Indication understood, they reached for the kids' hands and disappeared around the back of the building.

The police had a strange-looking guy in handcuffs. *Who was being arrested at Carlos' memorial?*

"Good morning, Mr. Nesbitt."

A petite woman approached him. A busty lady with brown, blunt cut bangs and cat-eye framed glasses. She handed him her business card. He took it, read, it, and removed his aviators to squint at her.

"You're from *'The Star'*? Surprised to be noticed by Toronto's influential newspaper, Simon dropped his defenses, and laughed.

"Well, Agnes Sybil Sharpe," said Simon, "your *initials* even beat mine! "And he noticed her impressive derriere. Round. He felt an instant connection.

"What can I say? Named after two grandmothers." She laughed. "And how were my folks to know I would marry a Bradley *Sharpe?*"

"*The* Bradley Sharpe? Award- winning animator?" Simon was impressed. "But he..."

"Yes, he plays for the 'other team' – now," Agnes admitted with air quotations. "But *your* initials are public knowledge, and all over *Wikipedia.*"

"Well, you're right, Agnes. Sorry about your personal upheaval."

"Still besties, no kids. That's what divorce is for." Agnes brushed off the topic of her marriage breakdown. *She had other sexual ambitions. No worries.*

"Well, what can I do for you?" Simon asked, feeling impatient, but with an effort to be polite.

"You can do lunch," said Agnes. "I need a follow-up on your staff and the dude just arrested."

"For you," Simon retorted, "I'll do my best. But I have to get my family back now. I'll call you, Agnes."

"When?" she held him.

"This evening, Madame," he promised.

In spite of the serious occasion, Simon felt uplifted. They shook hands. Then he noticed Eduardo and Albina with Beryl holding on to her.

"Hey, guys," he did a shoulder hug with Ed, full hug with Albina, and nodded to Beryl.

"So, they finally got this pig." Ed grunted.

"What?" Simon asked, unclear of the reference.

"This Geoffrey was getting Filipe to move his *shit*. Even gave him his car to do his dirty work. Then Filipe got caught. Now my cousin is dead, too."

Eduardo's pain was beyond grief. It embodied rocks of anger.

"It's not just that he gave drugs to Filipe, the son-of-bitch *killed* my father."

Manly behaviour aside, Eduardo overwhelmed by the reason his father died, sobbed openly. Then he glared at his mother next to him.

"And you *knew* about this, Ma. You were friends with this Geoffrey asshole! I hope he gets locked away forever." Eduardo took Beryl's hand and moved through the crowd. Albina glanced at Simon, then shrugged. She turned and followed her son to their car.

Across the street, positioned at a window table in the coffee shop, Frieda Reichert continued to watch the commotion on the sidewalk in front of the funeral parlor. That's when she had recognized someone. *What did the nice lady, Ginny, have to do with all this police business and whose funeral was it anyway?*

Chapter 38

"I'm usually the last to know anything,"

"**W**hat a zoo!" snorted Darius from the front seat of his grandma's *SUV*. "We were lucky to get out of there, eh, Gramps?" He loosened his plaid tie, sighed, and began tapping his knee.

Quinn gripped the wheel of the family van and nodded, "All a bit shocking, indeed." He maneuvered through the back roads towards Forest Street. The river separated this section of downtown from their neighbourhood. He headed for the Lakeshore bridge, just blocks away from the funeral home.

"I feel sorry for Ed," said Fiona, sitting beside her Granny Ginny in the middle row. "I just hope he's not implicated with that creepy guy they arrested. "Did you know anything about him, Grandma?" She raised her voice also to reach the driver, "Grandpa? Did you?"

"No, nothing at all," replied Quinn. "I'm usually the last to know anything these days, it seems."

"Well, I never knew anything about him till today," said Virginia, vaguely lost in her own thoughts. "Apparently he caused trouble for Filipe. I overheard the reporter ask if the car Filipe Delgado drove when arrested belonged to *him*."

"Dad's bringing Marjorie and Hazel back," noted Fiona. "Marjorie didn't seem too comfortable, poor thing. I guess it's just as well that Albina nixed a catered lunch at our place. So much unresolved tension, I think everyone just needs quiet time to rest, be alone. Although, I do wish Ed would come by. But he's got his girlfriend for company," Fiona trailed off.

"Well, Everybody," said Ginny, "in this hullabaloo, we didn't even get a chance to tell Fiona what a lovely song she wrote and sang. You did a beautiful job with that Darlin'," Ginny tilted her head towards her dear granddaughter, and held her hand. Fiona returned the love, leaned in to place a kiss on her grandma's soft cheek.

Given the short distance, they soon arrived at Hackberry Road.

Ginny and the kids plopped onto the sofas, their pups rushed forward to greet them. Quinn excused himself out to the verandah for a cigar; he had craved one for the last hour. The memorial for a father and nephew and a mourning son unnerved him.

Simon returned soon with the Wallace sisters. All three carried flowers. They placed vases on the kitchen island, some on side tables, and the dining room. Everybody inside helped. Then genuine hugs all around from one to another. A warmth for the *living* extended among this family. Simon and Fiona fixed drinks.

Hazel called *Chopsticks House* for a delivery which would arrive in an hour. Just light and tasty enough. She ordered extra fortune cookies for fun.

As they all took a comfortable seat in the family room, with friendly pups bringing forth some licks, they began chattering to themselves about the ceremony, the music, the people they noticed and said hello to, and more than a tear was shed for the two dead men who were such a familiar sight in this home just days ago. It's as though they were suspended in a bubble of floating unreality.

"Where's dad?" Simon noticed his father's absence. "Gone for a lie-down upstairs?"

"He went to the balcony," said his mom.

"I'll go check on him," Simon offered. Kent followed Simon through the doors.

The women continued chatting.

"Oh, Dad, give me that!" Simon approached Quinn who stood watching boaters on the horizon, smoke clouding his dignified profile.

"Sorry, Son...I'm setting a poor example," Quinn muttered.

"No apology needed, Dad. I just want a puff. *I need* a puff from that corona."

"Well, now I can *see* I'm setting a bad example, here," said Quinn. He passed the stogie to his son. "You sure?"

Kent circled and sat tall between these two fine men.

"You are *never* a bad example, Dad," said Simon, taking a puff followed by a slight cough. It *did* feel good holding this piece of archaic masculinity.

"You're a great dad, and today is a perfect opportunity to appreciate you. As poor Eduardo loses his father, I feel so grateful to have my old man." Simon placed his hand on his dad's chest and said, "I mean it, Dad." He puffed again and returned the cigar.

"I've not been a perfect man, Simon," Quinn narrowed his eyes, "don't put me on any pedestal." He wiped his brow with his gentleman's handkerchief. Even with good bone structure, his handsome face drooped in sadness. He placed the cigar in an urn.

Soon the men removed their suit coats, tossed them onto the porch swing, and sat on the steps, their view - the placid lake. As a sentinel, Kent rested one step below.

"Listen, Dad," Simon continued, "you've been a loving family man. That's quite an achievement. You love mom, and me, and your grandkids. Even your sisters you visit annually wherever they find themselves and you're good to their kids with cash gifts. Dad, you're loyal. Loyal. That's what you are! And I admire that in a man. Hate to sound soppy, Dad, but... I love you. End of story."

Humbled by his son's words, Quinn kept silent. *Verklempt.* At this age, he felt appreciative. Not his nature to be sentimental, he fought an unsettling guilt of nostalgia. Lucky to still be alive, have a family who loves him. With all his heart, he hoped *sleeping dogs* would lie. As if on cue, Kent stirred, and stretched out on his paws.

Hazel appeared to announce food had arrived, then disappeared quickly indoors.

"Thank you, Simon," said Quinn. "I hope I continue to live up to your good graces." A shoulder embrace between father and son felt strong and safe. Then the men returned to join the family for their luncheon.

During lunch, the family spent about an hour at the dining room table. Hazel and Marjorie had spread out the bamboo placemats, and dinner plates. The kids had arranged the serviettes and chopsticks. The mood was lighter than they expected after a memorial. The Chinese dishes arrived steaming hot, the shrimp and fried rice, the chicken and broccoli, colourful mixed vegetable bowls, and many spring rolls with plenty of plum sauce. They ate and laughed about the Chinese fortune cookies which they would read aloud after the meal.

Food, a way to process the pain of losing people dear to them, acted as an unspoken understanding by everyone around the table.

"Well, should we break open our fortune cookies now, Dad?" asked Fiona. The younger kids and the older, grownup ones always enjoyed this ritual when they had Chinese food.

"Sure, honey. Why don't you start?" answered Simon.

"They always sound the same," interjected Darius.

"Ah, no they don't," argued Hazel. "Let's give it a try."

The bowl holding the fortune cookies made its way around the table from Quinn at one end, until everyone chose theirs. Crackling cellophane broke a fresh silence in the dining room. With genuine interest, the dogs perked up. Maybe a cookie for them. As they made their obsequious approaches to his chair, Simon gave each one a doggie treat. Respectfully, they retreated into a corner.

"Okay, I'm reading now," Fiona announced:

Your challenges will be many, but you will come through even when moonstruck.

"*Moonstruck?* What's that supposed to mean, Dad?"

The adults jumped in, voices climbing over one other. "Love, it means love!"

Fiona blushed. "Whatever..." she groaned.

Hazel went next:

You are a bear, and your home life will be safe with good fung shui at the door.

Hazel burst out a hoarse laugh, "Guess I'd better return to my Mandarin classes, keep Fuyun happy." Everyone smiled not really understanding what her fortune meant. Except maybe Marjorie.

Then it was Quinn's turn. He unrolled the little paper strip and raised his bushy white eyebrows, over his reading glasses. He cleared his throat and read with his faux Shakespearean voice going for a bit of levity:

The past will return and bring you renewed life. Count your blessings.

"Well, isn't that odd?" Quinn said. "Who wants the past to come rushing in? We look *forward* in life. Don't we, family? Sort of hogwash. Anyway. Marjorie, you're next," he practically ordered.

"Relax, Grandpa," uttered Darius. "It's just BS, isn't it?"

"Ah, com 'on," from others around the table. "Don't spoil the fun, Dare!"

Marjorie, next in the seating lineup, brought her most indifferent tone to the reading:

The future is in your own hands. Make decisions wisely. Your joy will swell.

Everyone made ooh, sounds... except Simon. He read something else into that last word of Marjorie's fortune.

"Okay, Grandma, your turn," said Fiona, increased excitement in her voice again.

Since Virginia had laser eye surgery a couple of years earlier, she often went without the reading glasses. "Let's see..."

Your heart breaks but also mends. You are needed by others. Go there.

"My heart breaks? I guess it means for some of the folks I meet at *KOH* – many who have so little. I guess it sounds a bit like me, doesn't it? It's getting spooky like in some *Agatha Christie* play. What do you think, family?"

"Grandma," said Darius, "don't get caught up in this superstitious stuff...like grandpa calls your voodoo. It could have landed in any of our hands, remember. It's so random."

"Stop wrecking Grandma's fun, Dare!" bossed Fiona with a wink.

"Well, it's down to me and dad now. Want to choose first, Dad?" Darius offered.

"No, son. That's alright. Let's keep it in the order it's been going."

Darius cracked his cookie. Made an exaggerated move to extract the tiny paper, waved it in the air, and said, "Ahem!" Then he brushed his fingers through his short red waves, adding some flair.

Make up your own mind. Be true to yourself. Honour plays a role in your life.

"Well, then. That sounds intriguing. Maybe I find a lost wallet, and turn it in?" Darius said looking around at everyone, as he came down a notch in his skepticism and played along.

"You're it, Dad." Darius moved the bowl with the final fortune cookie toward Simon.

"Suddenly I feel in the hotseat. Thanks, son. I'll read my fortune in a sec. But before I do, I just want to say how grateful I am for all of you here today. This means so much to me. We've all been through a rough time losing two people so suddenly who were in our lives just up until a few days ago. And thanks to Marjorie and Hazel for being here with us at such a troublesome time. Mom, Dad, kids, I love you guys. Okay, so here goes:"

Not even Buddha holds all the answers. Remain open to the world. Meditate daily.

Silence.

"Any takers?" Simon looked around the table. "Any commentary on *my fortune?*" he asked the group.

"I told you this was crap," Darius burst out. "We'd be better off holding hands in a séance."

"Well, it was fun. Let's not read too much into this or be disrespectful given the occasion. Maybe we can all chip in to clear the table?" Simon faked an upbeat mood. "I've got to call that reporter back. I promised."

"What happens to Ed now?" Fiona wanted to know.

"We give him time to process this tragedy, and then invite him over to join us, maybe pick up where his dad left off, if he wishes, like I said at the memorial."

"Simon," said Marjorie, "may I say what I need to *now?*"

He locked eyes with her, then replied, "Yes." Others looked bewildered.

And then, Marjorie, with a slight tremor of her bottom lip, made her announcement:

"Simon and Hazel are aware of this, but Mr. and Mrs. Nesbitt, kids, I have to tell you I am leaving here... indefinitely." Simon's gut tightened at her words. Expected, but still a visceral blow.

The shock was palpable. Four faces looked at her, stunned. Marjorie was the woman of this household for the last six years. *No notice before this?*

The kids and grandparents looked to Simon. He nodded with visible discomfort.

Fiona shoved back her chair and rushed to the other side of the table to embrace Marjorie. She hugged this woman who had been a mother-substitute since she was a child.

"Why, Margie? Please don't leave us. You're family, you *must* know that."

Marjorie stood from her place, stroked Fiona's face, and held her tight. "Thank you, sweetie. I will always love you guys." She choked up.

Simon hurried to the rescue with words of comfort. Loosening his tie at the throat, and spreading his arms, he began the repair work.

"Sit down girls. Everyone listen up. Let's just stay calm. I know this is a shock...one of many lately, but we will get through this *together*."

"It sucks!" Darius pounded a fist onto the table. The dogs grunted and came forward.

Grandma Virginia reached out and stroked his arm. "It's okay Darlin' — let dad finish."

Margie sat back down and held Fiona on her lap as though she were a ten-year-old again. All eyes riveted on Simon at the head of the table. His father stunned into silence as well. Getting too old for all these new events, these changes he mused. His son has the reins. And that's alright.

"Look family, yes I knew about this for a few days. With all that was going on, I needed to pace out the news and changes in this household. Marjorie is still a young woman, and she has the right and the need to *expand* her opportunities."

He practically choked on his choice of word. He started to feel a bit of a fraud in his pained gut and took a sip from the water glass in front of him.

"Living in Toronto with Hazel," Simon continued with a strong voice and a nod to Hazel who watched him with laser intensity, "Marjorie will be able to discover what other life's options are open to her. We can't be selfish here. She needs to make a life for herself, enjoy new experiences."

Simon started to feel a little weak in his argument but moved forward.

"You kids are older now, have different needs, and I work from home a lot. And we've got your wonderful grandparents too."

Virginia and Quinn looked at each other, and had an unspoken understanding between them that *more,* rather than less, may be expected of them in their senior years. Both a plus and a minus in *their* minds.

Darius grabbed his plate and stomped towards the sink. Fiona stood up and graciously said to Marjorie, "Is there anything I can help you with, Margie?"

"Thanks, honey," Hazel interjected. "I've got some of Margie's things packed. But you can scout up some photos of you guys – if you can spare those ones in the frames?"

"We all sure can," Simon felt compelled to speak for everyone. "Right Fi?"

"It's been a long day," said Virginia. "I think dad & I will head back."

Chapter 39

"*Danguole* Valaitis reinvented herself."

S ince his family experienced painful changes losing their groundskeeper to sudden death on their property, followed by the resignation of their beloved housekeeper, Simon braced himself for other unexpected developments.

Fiona's fatigue demanded a medical workup. Through Hazel who nursed at Toronto's *Sick Kids Hospital,* and her life partner anesthetist Dr. Fuyun Lim, Simon arranged appointments with Fuyun's mother, paediatrician Patricia Lim, and her team. These professionals would check Fiona's bloodwork and perform the BRCA2 genetic tests to rule out the breast cancer which took Fiona's mom's life six years earlier. Simon pressed to complete this *asap.* The twins expected a great, final year of high school.

A month prior, a Ms. Jorgensen arrived in Naples as the new administrator for *Wendall Calbraith Secondary School,* the one attended by the Nesbitt teens.

Danguole Valaitis reinvented herself. Irritated with the mangling of her Lithuanian name by the English-speaking community, she changed *Danguole* to Daphne. She felt the Chinese had the right idea. They took a name like *Min Li* and anglicized it to Mandy. She kept Jorgensen, her married name, even though Lars was now her *ex* for five years. They had a son together. Nils. Lars was reasonable; Nils created trouble.

Daphne trained as a secondary school drama teacher and took principal's courses over the summers to land this plum position at WCSS. Initially hired as *acting* vice-principal which indicated a time limit, the Halcyon District School Board hinted this post may be open for a number of years.

Located in southeast Naples, the school acquired a reputation among her former colleagues as a haven for 'spoiled rich kids'. But gossip didn't bother Daphne. She believed in a firm discipline, and besides, she would bring her talent and experience as a drama instructor and produce a school-musical to wow them all, involve not only the student body, but staff too. She would draw participation from every department, including secretaries. She had ambition.

Daphne leased a 'cottage' house in Naples' downtown, on Calbraith Street. She couldn't believe the coincidence – same name as the school. She knew the *Calbraith* family history - founders of the village of Naples, now a large town. Already set up, her front garden, small but delightful, flaunted hostas which spilled their thick leaves over the tiny plot.

Daphne braced herself for Nils, who would soon join her. He completed his grade eleven in Mississauga City and spent the summer there with his dad. In a couple of weeks, Nils would be at Daphne's school for his senior year.

Chapter 40

"Simon felt damaged and ached inside."

S imon's house fell silent in late afternoon. After the memorial, the lunch, now Marjorie's pronouncement further altered the dynamics of the Nesbitt family. Stunned by these new circumstances, the grandparents returned home. The teens, followed by their pets, vanished to their respective bedrooms to contemplate how quickly their lives changed.

Hazel and Marjorie packed only personal items. Of course, the furniture in the loft apartment stayed with the property. Hugs and kisses to the kids occurred upstairs. No cause for celebration, the separation on both sides left a low-keyed mood.

Simon offered to drive the women into Toronto. They preferred a taxi to avoid further conversation. Some awkwardness relieved only by Hazel's news to Simon: an appointment for Fiona with Dr. Patricia Lim and team was rushed through in two days: hence – Friday.

He sighed, relieved. In addition to arranging top care for his daughter, Simon now clung to keeping a connection to Marjorie open. Yet, despite holding himself together Simon felt damaged and ached inside. He struggled with the appearance of control but unaware even to himself, Simon's warm amber eyes betrayed his feelings, reflected his pain. Marjorie's departure was total shit.

Losing Marjorie felt almost worse than losing Carlos. He swallowed some guilt over *that* one. But it is what it is, he thought. After the cab pulled away, Simon went for a swim. He swam until his limbs felt heavy, exhausted. He climbed from the pool, pulled on soft track pants and tread into his office. Kent padded at his heels. No doubt, the kids were napping, something he could use himself.

He clicked on his music, sank into the leather chair. He closed his eyes and listened. Bon Jovi sang a heart-wrenching track from *The Glory of Gershwin* album: 'How Long Has This Been Going On?' As the lyrics poured out, he, too, felt 'salty tears.' He ached. He loved. She was gone. He now realized his *she* was Marjorie.

Peggy became a sweet memory, and like one of the ribs in his chest, would forever be a part of him. Only that clear thought allowed Simon to admit Marjorie's true significance in his life. She was real, alive, beautiful, sensuous, and pregnant with God knows whose baby. Still, he loved her even with her complications. But he had the kids to think of, and he needed space in his head to process all these changes rushing into his once calm life. Like a man lapping up self-punishment, Simon decided to *let her go*, at least, for the time being. He would call the reporter, Aggie, and maybe ask her for a date. He felt desperate for an emotional distraction.

The taxi driver requested permission from the ladies in the back if he might play soft music to offset this heavy traffic into Toronto. To his credit, he sensed they were dealing with issues and their conversation needed to be muffled for their own privacy.

Marjorie surprised herself again; she wept.

"Don't be mad at me for saying this, hon," offered Hazel, "but it really could be these pregnancy hormones."

"I agree with you, it's okay, Haze." Marjorie wasn't about to fight this new reality anymore. "Once the senior Nesbitt's get a wind of this, they will judge me harshly."

"I don't think so at all...Virginia is such a warm person. She strikes me as kind and understanding."

"Well, what about Quinn? He will definitely lose respect for me when he learns of my pregnancy. I don't think I could ever face him again," Marjorie blew her nose, then looked at Hazel with a heartbreaking expression, a sad puppy.

"Oh, why give a damn what *he* thinks!" blazed Hazel, her eyeballs on fire. "*He's* probably got skeletons in his own closet. In fact, these *perfect* people often do; they just hide it better than people like us." She squeezed her love into Margie's palm.

The sisters quieted down and watched the stunning landscape. The iconic CN Tower straight ahead, high-density traffic and sky-high shapely condos bordered the winding shore of Lake Ontario on the south, and the new construction business cloud-busters appeared on the left. Downtown Toronto officially claimed its fame as 'world-class.' Signs of the annual 'September International Film Festival,' *TIFF.* were posted on billboards with recognizable faces of both Hollywood and European stars.

Marjorie felt her life turned into a movie, albeit not the happy-ending kind. She wondered at the future. She thought of her deep devotion to Simon. She truly wished she could make this baby in her belly his. Why couldn't life be that simple? Simon's role changed for her, *now former,* boss. He never indicated he was interested in her beyond admiration for her household talents and her loyalty. She wiped more tears. No job now. No more sweet Darius or Fiona. Sad, sadness.

Then Marjorie revised her focus. *Lordy*, as Hazel would say. Her love and attention will be on *her baby* now. She brightened at this thought. A new happy place. She would love it. She would be a great mother. Both she and Hazel lost their mothers, and the dad they cherished. This baby deserved at least one good parent and the aunties. Marjorie felt her entire inner view shift. Just like that. New determination.

This would be the new goal, the new future. With or without a man involved. Well, maybe she might find a part-time lover. She could visit a boyfriend, and the aunties would babysit. It could work out nicely. She smiled to herself. Like the old movie she saw on television, *South Pacific*, she thought, of the nurse's song, "Gonna wash that man outta my hair..." She had *Googled* the actor: Mitzi Gaynor. Maybe I'll call myself Mitzi instead of Margie. Her heart flooded with a renewed sense of peace and hope, and heavens, even joy. Her moods were fluctuating, alright. Bring it on!

The cab headed down the quiet, leafy Gloucester Street in *Gay Village*, to Hazel's building which housed her seventh floor two-bedroom unit. Considering his discretion, Hazel paid the driver a generous tip, thanked him, and the sisters actually smiled as they wheeled Marjorie's luggage towards the glass doors in front.

"We're home, Baby Girl," Hazel said, head tilted to the sunshine and then she flashed her brilliant warmth to her younger sister. Marjorie felt the comfort, determined to enjoy the moment.

Chapter 41

"Seems he was hitting on her."

They ordered *Kentucky Fried Chicken*, takeout. But Albina wasn't hungry. She went to lie down. The scandal Geoffrey created outside the funeral parlour gave her a pounding headache. He concealed his illegal activities from her and romanced her on false pretenses. Now she felt livid, used, and sad. Carlos wasn't *that* bad. This younger guy just made her feel so special. The familiar trap. *Fool,* she admonished herself.

In the kitchen, Beryl put dishes into the sink, and looked through the window at the green yard when Eduardo's phone beeped.

"Oh, hi Fiona," he answered. "No, I'm fine, it's okay."

Beryl's ponytail whipped around as she looked at Ed and mouthed 'FIONA?'

"We've just finished some fries, a little self-indulgence given the day..."

At home, in her bedroom, Fiona stretched her legs on her pink shaggy bedspread, and stared at her blue polished toenails, absent-mindedly. Next to her, Prudence snoozed on a fluffy pillow.

"I wanted to check how you are, Ed," Fiona whispered with reverence. "Your speech about your dad was *so* sweet."

"And your song, Fiona, just beautiful, too. Thanks for writing and singing."

Beryl took a seat at the table and stared at Ed as he spoke to Fiona. He got up and began to pace, felt her attention claustrophobic. He muted the phone for an instant and told Berri he would take this call to the back deck. And out he went.

"So, I've got news to share, Ed," Fiona pitched her voice. "Marjorie is gone! I mean she actually moved out."

"Come again? Marjorie left her job, her life at your place?"

"That's right. And we're all just numb about it. So unexpected."

"Well, what reason did she give?"

"Nothing much. Dad went into a speech to cover for her like she needs new opportunities, that sort of thing. I just found it strange. And I'm sad because of that, Ed. One sadness after another."

"Well, maybe that's how *she* feels." Eduardo offered his best to comfort Fiona. "Maybe she needs a break from your place and these deaths. She was close with my dad, too."

"I guess...you know, we studied *Hamlet* last semester, and a line from that play stuck with me. '*When sorrows come, they come not single spies, but in battalions!*'"

"I remember that line too. Claudius, right?"

"That's right, Ed. But how would you remember who *said* that?"

"Guys. We dig war words. Battalions!" Ed laughed, facetiously.

"Anyway, Hazel managed to set up an appointment at *Sick Kids* for me on Friday. Dad wants me checked out. You know the thing with my mom and all..."

"Well, I wish you the best with that, Fiona," Ed switched to a gentle tone.

"Thanks, Ed. I'm sure it'll be fine. Parents worry. But, Ed, who's this dude at the memorial police arrested? D' you know him? What was that about? Can you talk?"

Ed strolled to the end of the yard and rested on a small bench where he had helped his dad prune their pear tree. He sat in the shade but saw Berri looking at him through the kitchen glass. He thought she might be jealous of Fiona. Fiona? Just a high school kid. No way.

"Yes, Fiona. He was an associate of my mom's through the church choir. Seems he was *hitting* on her. I hate the thought. Looks like he was dealing drugs and got Filipe involved. He lent Filipe his car."

"How do you know all this, Ed?"

"We got this information from your dad's lawyer friend, Mr. Deakin."

"Wow, that sounds pretty messy. Your poor cousin getting involved in this and then being murdered in jail. It all sounds so unreal, like some bad movie. Well, I guess I should let you go. You're probably wiped. Oh, just remembered, did you want me to put anything on Facebook about your dad? I thought I'd better check first."

"No, Fiona, it's okay. Just want to keep things quiet, but thanks for suggesting."

"No problem. Give your mom my condolences again, Ed. I hope we'll talk soon. Stay in touch. We'll want to see you *here*. Please come by - not just for the gardens but to visit us. Big hugs." She braved on that last word.

"Sure will. Hang in there, Fiona. Thanks for the updates, and good luck with your health appointment. Talk again soon, then. Bye, bye."

Eduardo clicked off his phone. His blood rose. He hated this fuckin' world. Fiona - so damn sweet! He knew he had feelings for her, but what the hell...it didn't make *any* sense. While grieving his beloved dad, seemed all emotions were on the table.

When Ed came inside, Albina was in the kitchen.

"She's gone," she said to him. "She took cab home."

He stared at his mother, stunned. Then he hugged her and held on.

"You okay, Mom? I have to go for a run. I have things in my head. Will you be okay?"

"I okay. You go. Go, my boy."

He changed into shorts, running shoes, and clipped on his waist belt for keys and phone. With buds in his ears, dark glasses on his face, and a ball cap pulled down low, he listened to his dad's favourite music and ran like his life depended on it. It did. He clenched his teeth hard.

His depression overwhelmed him.

Chapter 42

"Why did you leave without saying goodbye?"

Esther tapped her elegant nails on Simon's office door. Kent yelped.

"You in there, Si? It's me, Esther."

Groggy, unaware he dozed off, Simon got up and opened his door. Kent zipped to the kitchen to lap from his water bowl.

"Esther. What's up? What are you doing here?" Discreetly, he wiped his chin drool.

She brushed past him and plopped into his office chair at the desk.

"Go back to the swivel, Si, and we'll talk. You invited us, and here we are to check on you, my dear." An unconscious preener, Esther pulled on the loose black strands of her low messy bun. Her sleeveless arms, toned and tanned, were up for admiration.

Simon sank into the softness of leather, turned to face his intruding guest.

"Oh, that's right. Where's Hamish... and the boys?"

Lost in a flash of self-indulgence, Esther stared at Simon's rugged, stubbled jawline then moved her focus from his full lips to his intelligent, sultry eyes. She sighed.

"Outside playing with your kids and the dogs. Maybe in the pool now. They brought their swimming trunks. I just wanted to come and talk to you first. Sorry if I disturbed a nap."

"No, it's okay." Simon stretched his defined swimmer's triceps forward with a quiet grunt and intersected his fingers for greater extension.

"So, I heard your Marjorie left. Quit. What's up with that?"

"Why are you smiling, Esther? Are you gloating?

"No, Simon. What a thing to say! I am *not* gloating. Why *would* I be?"

"Because I know there was no love lost between you two. But I have to say in Marjorie's defence, she never had a problem with *you;* it just seemed to me that you disliked her. Isn't that true, Esther?"

"Let's not talk about it. I'm here to support you, not get into an argument. We brought steaks and Hamish can barbeque on your beautiful new machine. We also brought asparagus to roast, and I threw together a kale, chickpea salad. Want to invite your parents?"

"Thanks, Esther. Sweet of you. But, no, my folks are drained. Besides, earlier we all had *China Chopsticks* delivered for lunch. They're probably only glad to be home resting after all this drama."

"Alright, so are you going to tell me why she *really* left? You know, pillow talk and all that stuff, because I was *there* when Ham got the text from Schroeder about the DNA on Carlos, bless his soul."

Esther's edge of nosy grated on Simon. He felt her probing lawyer-attitude pushy.

"Oh, that reminds me, "said Simon.

"What reminds you?"

"I forgot to call back that reporter I spoke to outside of the funeral parlor. I promised I would."

"Simon, honey, as an adult you don't have to keep every promise you make, you realize *that* I hope." Esther didn't shy from her own boldness towards friend nor foe.

"And you don't have to patronize me, Mrs. Deakin. Mind your own beeswax. You know, Esther, you never look good trying to make someone else look bad. Besides, successful people never worry about what *others* are doing."

"But we're your friends, Simon! Okay, keep it to yourself, then. It all comes out in the wash. Some things you just can't hide. I'm going outside. Shall I tell my gorgeous husband to fire up the *barbie*?"

"Sure. I'll be out soon."

Esther clicked her tongue and gave Simon a wink. She'd keep the upper hand thank you very much.

He couldn't stop himself from looking at her ass when she sashayed from his office. Hot pink pants. *Women! Can't live with them; can't live without them! An old cliché, but it's the damn truth that makes it one.*

By the time he reached Lakeshore Road, Eduardo headed west and gained speed. He forgot sunscreen, but the fuzzy black hair on his limbs would supply some protection. This long street, a mass of giant leafy trees, oak, and chestnut, offered shade. Adrenaline fuelled by depression and his pulsing playlist pushed him for a couple of miles. He stopped to grab an energy drink from the shop across the road from Appleton College.

Eduardo entered the school grounds, accessible to pedestrians, gated for vehicles. He circled the security booth, then ran along the paved pathway past the antique chapel, the modern residences, and classroom buildings until he hit the grassy areas which led towards the lake. At the water's edge, a cliff brought him to a dead stop.

He dropped to the ground and stretched out on the manicured grass. He stared at the outstanding sculpture several feet high, smooth stones piled on top of each other. He saw its beauty and its simplicity in its symbolism for Inuit North peoples, as travelling directions for hunting and fishing areas. The *Inukshuk* known as a symbol of survival. He needed this calming presence, to cope with the events of the last several days.

Somewhat rested, Eduardo heard shouts in the distance, and dogs barking. He turned and saw tennis courts in the valley, people playing, having fun, tossing balls for their dogs to chase. Summer students perhaps. Life being enjoyed.

He pressed Berri's number on his phone. Her recorded voice asked to leave a message.

So, he left one: "Why did you leave without saying goodbye?"

Chapter 43

"The subject turned to sex."

S imon read her business card. Tapped it on his desk. He deliberated. *Another woman. What does this Agnes reporter really want?* He thought of Esther... even his best friend's wife always such a flirt, like now. Was she just being a *bossy* girl? Stories of his aunts bossing his dad surfaced. He recalled Quinn's joking tales of *girl grief*.

Was Fiona bossy? Perhaps, but his darling girl, just a teen, needed to explore her sense of self. Dear Peggy, not at all, and Marjorie...well, she *did* boss him indirectly, but used tact to let him feel in charge. Afterall, he *was* the boss there!

Ah, female manipulation. He shook his head. *Lose the cynical ideas, man!*

His mom was no manipulator, rather, a guiding light. He felt blessed with both parents. Sure, it would have been helpful to have had a sister to understand the nature of women better, but alas, that wasn't in the cards. The downside of being your parents' only child.

Thus, Simon refused to stereotype women. He saw *individuals*. Each one unique, and he'd approach Agnes this way. Obviously, a bright, knowledgeable person to gain this significant position at *The Star*, Toronto's acclaimed newspaper.

"Yes, it's me, Simon Nesbitt," he replied to her cheerful inquiry.

"I said I'd call you back. Just keeping my promise, Agnes. So where are you located?" When she told him Burlington, he realized only a half hour drive for her, so he offered the invitation.

"Sure, I can call you Aggie," he replied to her request. "And I love your attitude as a 'kick-ass' reporter," he laughed. It felt good. "Makes sense to keep those initials! Take your time. We'll put the steaks on when you get here. Just my kids and my best friends, husband, and wife, both lawyers and their young boys. We're the last house on 'Hackberry Road' west side, and park in the driveway, loads of room."

She asked about confidentiality.

"We have nothing to hide. And besides, I've my attorneys with me," he bantered as he clicked off.

Simon headed outside, noticed the twins engaged in volley badminton with young Bryan and Gordie. Since the net was up by the south fence, he hollered a wave.

Esther and Hamish, sunk into poufy lawn chairs by the circular firepit, each held a beer can, and relaxed under the amber canopy. shaped like a triangular sail. The dogs stretched out where they found shade, Charity under a tree, while Kent and Prudence chose the protection of the overhead covering.

"We're expecting Agnes, the reporter from *The Star,* to join us. She'll be here in about half an hour. Anything *not* to tell her Hamish?" Simon cracked open a can of beer for himself, took another deck chair and faced his friends.

"Why did you ask her out here?" Hamish frowned, forehead lines above his dark sunglasses and Esther nodded, loosening her bun.

"*Why*? Well, why not? She wants background on the business of this dude who's implicated in the arrest of Carlos' nephew. We control the narrative, hence the info she puts out to protect our reputation, wouldn't you agree? Besides, she seems smart, quirky, a woman I might want to know better, and I'm more comfortable doing this on my turf. Anything wrong with that?"

Hamish and Esther agreed to the logic of the first part. The latter statement left them feeling flat. Esther adjusted the waist ties of her crisp white 50s-style shirt exposing a touch of tanned midriff. Not exactly *Audrey Hepburn*, but it'll do.

"I've got some baked-potatoes on the grill now," said Hamish. "They'll be ready by the time she gets here."

"And I've put my kale and chickpea salad in the other cabana fridge," said Esther.

"You guys are the best, I must say! The kids can't hear me from here. I feel quite low right now. With Marjorie gone, Carlos gone, I feel empty." Simon felt enough comfort to admit these feelings to his close friends. "Maybe this Agnes, oh, she asked to be called Aggie, will lighten the mood. She's the ex of Bradley Sharpe, the animator. Apparently, he's gay. I'm not gossiping or divulging secrets here. She claims it's open. Nice to know they're still amiable."

Hamish and Esther looked at each other as Simon, suddenly restless, got up and went off to say a proper hello to the young boys.

"Looks like we've got the story, darling," Esther cooed as she leaned over, removed her husband's sunglasses, and kissed him on his cupid fleshy lips. "I'm so lucky I've got you, and our life," she purred. "To us wild creatures," she toasted themselves with her beer.

Forty minutes later, all kids bouncing in the pool playing *Marco Polo,* the adults fussed setting the outdoor dinner table now that a new person was about to join them.

Aggie peered through the gate, then, given the luxurious surroundings, entered tentatively. She upped her confidence level fast since she was a *name* in the media industry. She believed she garnered respect from all social circles. In she strolled and when she spotted Simon, she dropped her satchel onto a chair and shook hands with him, her rings pressing into his large palm. Within seconds he excused himself to run to Fiona who suddenly called for his help on some floating device. He offered his apologies and shouted over his shoulder to make herself at home, he'd be right back.

Soon Hamish stood at her side. She took his hand in greeting, and brazenly said,

"Well, hello there! Aren't you a fine gentleman!" With her most friendly grin, she added, "I'm Aggie Sharpe, journalist. I guess Simon mentioned I'd be here." With a raised eyebrow and in a faux conspiratorial tone, she inclined her head towards him and added, "Do you think I should give my ex, Bradley, your phone number?"

"*Excuse me?*" Hamish uttered as he removed his sunglasses to glare at Agnes. "I'm Hamish Deakin, attorney. For the Nesbitt's." And in a dropped, terse voice added, "And that's my *wife* over there playing with our kids!"

"Oh, sorry!" Aggie feigned regret. In a faux under-the-breath way, she asked, "You're not *out*? I just thought in this day and age..." she trailed with a giggle.

"Aren't you *assuming* a bit much, and for a reporter?" Hamish detested this type of rudeness and vulgar exposure. "But then, I suppose that's your job," he said through gritted teeth.

"It's just that we're a *community,* aren't we? It takes one to know one." She looped her thumbs into the belt of her jean skirt and cocked her head at Hamish, her purple bangs swept to one side revealing a section of shaved head on the other.

"We? What's with this 'we' business? You're implying that I'm gay, and disclosing you're a lesbian? Is there no decorum to your approach? Or is that in the rule book for reporters?"

Simon returned with Kent at his heels, and both sensed dissention in the air, conflict between these two people, strangers to one another.

"Something wrong, guys?"

"Your Ms. Sharpe, here," said Hamish with an angry flourish of his arm in Aggie's direction, "is definitely making an ass out of herself. Remember that word *assume*? Making an ass out of you and me?"

"Yeah, we've all heard that before – the assume," laughed Aggie. "I meant no harm, Hamish. I told Simon, didn't I Simon, that my ex plays for the other team? Allow me to clarify, *gentlemen*: Bradley's on the men's team now, and I'm on the *women's* team," she laughed it off, pride over her face and with her arm swing exposed clusters of silver bands on her wrists and fingers, nicely finished with black gloss nails. These two dudes didn't scare her into any kind of submission.

Hamish excused himself abruptly and moved on to the food preparations.

Simon felt slammed in the head, his spirit deflated. Could things get even worse? A clever and cool gal he hoped to get close to, prefers women. No chance for him. *Fuck this anyway.*

"Well, I'm glad we've cleared that up, Aggie, because I was actually thinking of asking you out to dinner," Simon added, in an attempt to appear nonchalant, hide another turbulent disappointment.

"Well, hey, there's no reason you *can't* take me to dinner. We're just not going to have a romance, Simon. But we could be good friends." As she turned her head to reach for her bag, Simon noticed a small snake tattoo on the back of her neck. He sucked in his breath and realized this woman was not his type anyway. He changed his attitude while Aggie checked her phone.

"Alright, speaking of dinner," he called over to his barbeque man, "Hamish, how are we with the steaks? Let's eat! Esther, would you mind grabbing some wine from the cellar? Your choice. I 'll get the kids settled at the low table."

Simon tried to resume control at his home and of his aching heart. No one would know his pain, his acute suffering, at losing the comforting, efficient, beautiful Marjorie...and his warm, dear Carlos. He felt he needed to count his blessings. He had his parents, and kids, and his best friends. But his heart, and his mind were in battle. He wasn't much for angels, but he thought of that iconic cartoon, and ironically, replicated by the illustrious Bradley Sharpe, himself, of the good angel and the devil warring each other from one shoulder to the other. The power struggle and lack of peace drove the holder insane. He felt it. He tasted it. He wanted to run and hide. But he was a man, a dad, a son, a friend. They needed him. He had to keep it together. Nervous breakdowns had to be put on hold. Indefinitely.

After dinner, when the evening grew dark, the young-sters and teens disappeared indoors to watch a *Netflix* film and microwave popcorn. With drapes pulled, they would be good for another couple of hours, inside. The adults continued to sit around the firepit on the far patio and as the sun vanished, they continued their drinking. The air, still warm, gave no hint of autumn.

They switched to stronger drinks - gin tonics, brandy, so the guests decided they would leave their cars at Simon's and cab it home. No one, though, felt any hurry to leave. The subject turned to sex.

Erotically stimulated by the team of Esther and Hamish, Aggie chose to tease this small group. Despite her earlier decla-ration of sexual preference, she laid it on.

"I'll bet you guys didn't realize I'm even more fluid than you thought. I'm *pansexual.*

"Is that because you were married, Aggie?" asked Simon, uncomfortable with this conversation.

"I don't know, myself," she sipped her gin cocktail. Then she revealed more confessions. She slurred:

"I just know my sexual attractions are not based on *gender.* I like me some *dipstick,* but I'm also open to *lady bits.* And who can blame me if it comes my way? It's freedom, the flag of our times, Kids!" She saluted with her drink.

Esther burst out laughing. "What a mouth!" she said. And to Hamish, "Should we invite Aggie to join our group, darling?"

"What group is *that,* Esther?" Aggie sobered up enough to express interest.

Hamish jumped in, "It's private, Esther sweetheart, you know that. There are others to consider." He mustered some semblance of graciousness but was pissed with this vulgar, little creature.

Simon gulped a large one, somewhat shocked at the words which came from his friends. Yet, these raw words aroused him, and stirred his own sexual juices. Just the distracted relief he needed to overcome this Marjorie and Carlos pain. He covered the rise in his shorts and placed his drink over his lap. *What would she say next, this Aggie?*

It's not what she said, but what she did which held everyone's attention. She set her glass on the side table and popped open the domes of her jean shirt. She had managed to contain a significant cleavage which now burst from a violet, lacey push-up bra. As she flashed her bosom, she announced, "My offer, lady and gentlemen. Any takers?" The edges of her red mouth curled with glee.

Reminiscent of the *Joker*, thought Hamish, unimpressed.

Ruffled as hell, Simon got up and walked to the pool's edge. He yanked off his top, pulled down his shorts and dove in naked. He swam to the far, deep end, stretched his arms and torso and moved vigorously.

Hamish gave Aggie a look of disdain, got up and walked to the edge of the pool. "Mind if I join you?" he asked his best friend.

Simon waved him forward.

Hamish wasted no time. He removed his designer tee, dropped his pants, and dove into paradise. He swam beyond the floodlights to the dark corner where Simon awaited him.

For Hamish, being this close to Simon in the flesh, induced a feeling of pure heaven. He let the welcoming, warm water flood his senses more than any drink. He touched his beloved's body.

First a rub on the broad shoulders, then a stroke to the back of his neck. Slowly. With deliberate hesitation, his hand movements massaged downwards to Simon's narrow hip bones and tight groin.

Simon melted as Hamish's hand curled over his hardened shaft. Hamish's other palm cupped Si's muscular rump.

"Oh!" Guttural groans from both men, as they relished their intense manly pleasure.

Back at the firepit, lost in their own world, the women paid them no notice. They shared a recliner and explored each other's lip gloss and bras.

However, the men recalled, back in the day, how awesome this felt. For Hamish, such closeness spoke to fulfillment of an aching desire, and illusions of romance, even *love*. For Simon, it meant friendship, comfort, and the almighty release. They climaxed within minutes and ducked under to embrace fully, body to body, chest hair touching, thighs entangled, and scrotums gently bouncing. Hamish's elegant fingers massaged Simon's long back as those tiny restorative fishes are said to do and he applied extra pressure to Simon's rectum and sacrum for relaxation.

Their secret bonded these men forever, and provided, on occasion, a much-needed emotional surrender to their manhood. As they came up for air, Simon exhaled and whispered to Hamish, "Remember Marvin Gaye's *Sexual Healing*?" As Hamish nodded, Simon added, "thanks, buddy."

They swam a bit more to distraction, then stepped out in the dark with Hamish's white limbs caught by the moonlight, and Simon's naturally bronzed body dripping. Both men, equal in height, tried to hurry, yet moved gingerly across the concrete. With shoulders bent forward and with the instinctive gesture of privacy, they covered their naked anatomy with their hands, and headed to the cabana for towels.

Hamish experienced a rush of dopamine. *No wonder young people call a great sensation, 'dope.'*

The women, still fixated on each other, remained oblivious to their surroundings.

Chapter 44

"Lord knows there's enough problems in the world."

On Friday, Simon brought his dear Fiona for her scheduled tests to the *Toronto Hospital for Sick Kids*. Staff collected her and reassured dad she'd be in great hands.

This world-class downtown hospital vibrated with activity. Visitors and patients mixed with lanyard-uniformed staff in whites and blues, while green-clad volunteers scurried in various directions. Quick but polite pedestrian traffic gave way to wheelchaired youth and kids.

Simon met Hazel in the Orange Café. They took a corner nook. His wild hope—the fantasy of Marjorie visiting her sister at work— quickly dissolved. After engaging in some innocuous conversation, he focused on the main reason for his being there. Fiona.

Simply a lovely comfort to Simon, Hazel elevated his mood and soothed his nerves. She never lacked for an amusing anecdote, occasionally a racy one - a few laughs to relax anyone in her presence. Simon saw why she made an excellent nurse. He felt good with Hazel. Her cocoa eyes radiated cheer and glistened goodwill.

"Dr. Lim will do a thorough testing of Fiona's blood-work. She'll explore genetic aspects to rule out anemia as well as breast cancer genes," Hazel explained. "Rest assured Fiona's workup will be tops. This place lives up to its reputation."

Simon nodded, and his frown vanished.

"I'm so grateful to you, Hazel, and to your connections. Thank you. And give my love to Marjorie. Tell her we're all thinking of her happiness."

It seemed a little over the top after he spoke those words, but he hoped Hazel would understand. Just being here in this hospital with his darling daughter placed him into a highly emotional state. As for Marjorie—she mattered to him— like family.

Hazel returned to her ward, and Simon wandered the gift shop to tame a tightness in his larynx.

Back in Naples, Simon's mother occupied herself from worries over him and Fiona. Now past the memorials, and over the shock of Marjorie's sudden departure, Virginia picked today to shop with Frieda. She'd get her a *make-over*.

Of course, she wouldn't present it that way. Just a refreshing, much needed distraction, and uplift for them both. She knew she could arrange a priority appointment at *Belle's Boutique* in Bronte.

Frieda was game. She loved being with Ginny. On the way there, the discussion was light, but informative.

"Don't you must make appointment, first?" Frieda asked, curious how rapidly things happened in Ginny's world.

"I hate to pull rank, and don't do it often, but our business holdings *own* the salon, and some other properties, so the manager tries to accommodate us. Sabrina knows me well enough, Darlin', and I try to be considerate of their schedules, but from time to time, she cuts me some slack."

"Slack? *Was?*"

"Oh, that just means, they *adjust* their appointments to fit us in."

Ginny parked in *her* spot. They entered, discreetly, by the back door, not to offend the regulars.

Well- schooled in advance by Virginia, the stylist Sabrina met Frieda graciously, offered coffee and discussed how the grey in Frieda's hair might be concealed with a black toner. Ginny sat in an adjoining chair to watch. Sabrina shaped the cut into a pixie, 50s throwback, a look which suited Frieda's thin, tall frame. The darker shade enhanced her olive complexion. Ginny was pleased. Then, they moved to the makeup station and Cheryl, the expert, finished Frieda's bluish grey eyes with subtle eyeliner and mascara, passing on the false lashes. Plucked eyebrows, shimmering glow on the cheeks, and a matte, bold-cherry lipstick brought forth a *beauty*. Both Ginny and Frieda loved the new look: natural, and elegant.

Frieda's heart pounded. *Is this really me?* She examined her image in the large salon mirror. She fought back tears not to ruin her makeup. The gratitude she felt towards Virginia overwhelmed her. She could barely whisper her thank you.

Off they strolled down the street to *Dora's Fashions*, another of the Nesbitt businesses. Ginny found shopping for Frieda's new clothes just as exciting. She wanted to select a variety of styles for casual but smart wear.

Virginia felt Frieda could be the daughter she never had. She missed Simon's Peggy so much after she died, here seemed an opportunity to fuss over an adult, family female. Even though

Frieda wasn't *exactly* family. Maybe she could somehow be a part of them, anyway. Like those *honorary* relatives.

Frieda tried on pant suits, skirts, dresses, nice pulled-together looks that enhanced her slim figure. A royal blue blazer and cream trousers with a fuchsia print top was the outfit she wore out of the store. And *Dora's* even carried a small supply of shoes. Ginny had suggested a pair of black, patent-leather Cuban heels. They were perfect. Out they went with packages of extras in their hands as they headed to the parking lot.

"Let's go to *Luigi's* for lunch," suggested Ginny.

Soon they found themselves seated at a high table in this elegant restaurant at the Valentino Mall.

The server brought white wine. Later, he placed arugula salads, followed by crispy triangles of mozzarella pizzas in front of them. A perfect light lunch.

"I feel like you are fairy Godmother, Ginny," Frieda held back tears again. "Nobody for years treat me like I am real person. Only Doctor Ranger in Vancouver."

"Bless your heart, Darlin'. I feel you were sent to me by God. I am not religious, but something in the universe, *God-like*, brought you to me. I just *know* it," she whispered. "And I'm happy to be that person for you, Frieda. Lord knows there's enough problems in the world. How lovely it is to be a part of something uplifting. Well, not to get overly sentimental, which reminds me this afternoon we'll shop for lingerie and hmmm, how about a touch of jewelry like some silver dangling earrings?" Ginny sparkled with genuine warmth helping Frieda with her new *look*. "Maybe we'll go to the Naples Mall and get ourselves a manicure there as well."

"I feel you are new *Mutti* to me, *danke, danke.*"

Her gratitude spoken through sad eyes. No joy. Hidden fear.

Virginia tingled a moment sharing Frida's pleasure. But her empathy sensed a different vibe. *This young woman is overwhelmed.* She noted not everyone takes to *so-called* 'do-gooders'. She'd stop the shopping now, move slower, curb some of her enthusiasm. Work on Frieda's comfort level.

"It's okay, Sugar. Actually, I'd rather you meet my small family today. You'll like my husband" she boasted, "the old fella, still handsome, and such a loyal, good man. I'll take you to my place for a visit. And I hope I'm not being too pushy," Ginny apologized as she finished the final drop of her wine spritzer, and set it down, "because I especially want you to meet my son. He's in his late forties and is *single!*" Ginny's *thought bubble*, which she ached to share, revealed the noble, sculpted face of her Simon.

"Single? I thought you have grandchildren?"

"Yes, of course, I told you about them, but their dad, my son, Simon, is a widower. His wife died over six years ago. I really think it's time for him to meet someone new."

Once she spoke those words, Virginia felt the world tilt. *Things are changing. Simon will have to move on from Peggy, finally. Frieda could be the one.*

Frieda, the self-admitted *former drug addict,* swallowed hard and did not feel wonderful with the idea of meeting Ginny's family, especially her single son. But she knew her manners as Virginia's kindness swept her into a Cinderella fantasy. She nodded in acquiescence, rather dumbfounded, forced a meek smile, and found herself reluctantly agreeing. However, the years of self-loathing were not as easy to brush away.

All she really wanted to do now was cry. And find her father.

Chapter 45

"There's someone I want you to meet."

The drive from *Sick Kids* out of Toronto brought start and stop snarled traffic. Simon thought about his massive relief when the professionals said Fiona appeared in good health. A few days wait for results on the genetic issue. The medics encouraged her to eat her greens and instructed dad not to worry.

Wearing headphones, Fiona chatted to her bestie, Sophie. Dad would drop her there. It was Friday, after all, and the girls had plans. Nothing of concern to parents - just back-to-school gossip and dinner at Sophie's, and maybe a sleep-over.

Simon played his music. *Crazy romantic guy*, he admonished himself as he inserted the disc of Welsh bass-baritone singer Bryn Terfel. 'If Ever I Would Leave You' sang Terfel. This title piece, a heartbreaker, Simon loved best. He indulged himself. He allowed thoughts of Marjorie in the moonlight float through his senses. *But I wouldn't leave her, she left me. She left me! Yet, I agreed to it, didn't stop her.*

A call from his mother broke the reverie.

"Hi Mom. What's up?"

"How did things go at the hospital, Darlin'?"

"Well, as you might expect, we have to wait a few days for more results...the genetic testing...good to get out of there. I had a chance to have coffee with Hazel."

"I was wondering if you could stop by my place. Are you taking Fiona home?"

"Dropping her at Sophie's. Why?"

"There's someone I want you to meet. Please say yes."

"Is dad still out with Darius? Did they go to the golf practice range?"

"You're not answering my question, Sugar."

"Mom, I'm beat. I'd just like to drop Fi at Sophie's and go home."

"Oh, please Darlin', you won't regret it. Afterwards, you can nap here until your dad and Darius return."

A woman hard to deny, and he, being an *only child*, felt such responsibility. *When she needs attention, I should comply.*

"Just give me time to stop at home and feed the dogs, Mom, and I'll be over."

Meet someone...always sounds like a set-up, mused Simon, unimpressed.

Satisfied with Simon's answer, Virginia left her bedroom and returned to the living room where her guest waited for her on the pale, plump sofa.

As she heard Ginny approach, Frieda closed the coffee table art book.

"My son just called me from his car," fibbed Ginny. He's heading back from the hospital and after he drops my granddaughter at her friend's place, he plans to swing by and pay us a visit."

Frieda held Portia in her lap, had stroked her beautiful fur. Suddenly, the pet leapt off and scooted to the kitchen. Frieda assumed this lovely creature sensed the tightness in her stomach. She stood. Now she *has* to meet Ginny's son. *Too soon.*

"Is your granddaughter *alles gut?*" Frieda asked, with effort to keep her thoughts in the present moment.

"Of course, we're all praying for that result, dear." She paused. "You know, Darlin', I just can't stop looking at you. You're such a beautiful woman! I'm so delighted we shared this day together. I can't wait for you to meet my Simon. You'll like him. He is a good man even if I do say so myself, as his mom," she laughed, her eyes revealing happy crease lines. "Let me get started on some herbal tea for us."

Frieda reached for her hand. "You are the good person, Ginny. I am such lucky woman to know you." Overcome with a myriad of emotion, grateful but fearful, Frieda's voice cracked.

Sensing her vulnerability, Virginia pulled Frieda into her *mother's bosom*, and held her. After this close comforting gesture, she slipped into her sleek kitchen to fill the kettle.

Still standing, Frieda turned to admire the panoramic view. *Genau wie das Leben in meinen Traumen. Just like life in my dreams.* The perspective stretched to the skyscrapers of Toronto. She remembered her mother's life, years in the sky as a flight attendant. Soft clouds floated at eye level.

Setting out her favourite cups and saucers—painted strawberries on green vines, actually *made in Germany*, so right for the occasion, Virginia rationalized how she'd present Frieda to Simon. Meeting someone from KOH *mission?* Wouldn't go over well. Not that Simon held a snobbish attitude or looked down on troubled people. Realistically, he'd prefer *to date* someone accomplished and in a good place in life. Maybe she could alter the information for the time being until he saw how lovely a person Frieda was? Ginny knew herself a poor liar, Simon would have it figured out in a second. She *could* say they ran into each other there since Frieda, a newcomer to Naples, wanted general information after she relocated.

Ginny just *knew* in her heart that Frieda belonged to their family. *This has to work out.* She'd say Frieda did translations at Vancouver's UBC and worked with disenfranchised kids as a volunteer. That would fit her profile and skill set.

As they sipped the tea at the dining room table, Frieda admired Ginny's dishes, almost like those her own mother treasured. Virginia agreed they were precious, a gift from her husband during his earlier work travels to Europe.

The glass table where they sat was hidden from the sightline of the front hallway. Soon they heard Simon let himself in, and caught his greeting, "Hi Mom, I'm here!' before he turned the corner towards the dining area.

He stopped. His eyes fell on the two women.

Chapter 46

"So, what did you learn about yourself?"

S tretched out on her tummy, Fiona kicked her legs, swung them around and formed a yoga sit. She and Sophie *chillin'* in Sophie's periwinkle-blue bedroom— Fiona on the bench at the foot of the bed, while Sophie leaned against her cushioned headboard— celebrity magazines scattered across the bedspread.

"I'm going to *call* him. Whaddya think, Soph?" Fiona sounded determined.

"I think you should. No matter if he's got a girlfriend, you're just being *nice*, right?"

"Here goes then." Fiona scrolled her contact list, found Ed, and tapped both call and speaker buttons.

"He's not here right now, Fiona." Beryl's icy voice had Fiona off the bench and pacing.

"Oh, yeah, um, he wanted me to let him know how my hospital checkup went today. Is he okay?" Fiona made huge eyes at Sophie. "Why is he not answering his phone?"

"He's busy at the moment. I'll let him know you called. Bye."

"She hung up, Soph! At least she said bye. But why is she answering his phone?"

"You said he seemed really depressed, Fi. Maybe he went to lie down and asked her to field his calls."

"I don't know. That seems fishy. Wanna go to the lake? Let's go to the Lighthouse. I need to walk this off."

The girls grabbed their shoulder bags, sunglasses and told Sophie's mom where they were heading, and they'd be back in an hour.

Once outdoors, Fiona suggested they first stop by her place, "These sandals are not great for walking. Let's check in on Pru and the other two, and I can switch into my runners."

As they trailed down the slope of Alfredo Avenue, the leafy road soothed their mood. Fiona felt a gentle breeze lift her sundress, and Sophie relaxed in her green cotton shorts, her brown ponytail swinging. They rounded the corner onto Hackberry Road, *her corner*, Fiona liked to call it, because her house and family property took up the entire half block on the right-hand side of the street. The opposite side held a row of tall cedars parallel to a paved walkway for the public. Both sidewalks led straight to the lake.

"OMG, Soph, there's Ed's car in the driveway! What's he doing here?"

The girls ran the rest of the way, beyond the house and spotted Ed with Darius and the dogs out back of the yard. Suddenly, a commotion. Dogs running and barking. The boys got up, at least Ed did, and he and Fiona hugged grandly, spontaneously, like long-lost relatives. Sophie fist-bumped with Darius and sunk into a chaise.

"I just called you!" Excited, Fiona held Ed at arm's length and focused on his soulful eyes.

"Oh, sorry, Fiona. I forgot my cell in the kitchen when I dashed out."

"Well, Beryl answered it." Fiona found a guilty pleasure in

this announcement knowing it could tick anyone off. "She said you were busy, Ed, and hung up. I've been worried about you."

"I've been worried about *you*!" Ed emphasized. "But Berri has no business answering my phone. I'll have to speak to her. She wasn't even *there* when I left. She probably went to visit mom. I wanted to come *here*, where dad spent so much time, visit the dogs... and Darius, of course," he added, an afterthought recovery.

Lately, Ed couldn't hide his emotions. His face revealed expressive worry lines, and his darting eyeballs hinted at confusion.

Yet, Fiona saw only handsomeness in those big brown eyes and Ed's afternoon jaw shadow caused her insides to somersault.

"Com' on, let's sit down," she said, picking up her baby, Prudence, with one hand and leading Ed with the other. She enjoyed 'mothering' them both.

"Well, Dad's at Gran's," said Fiona letting Pru snuggle under her chin. "I'm staying at Sophie's tonight, right, Soph? And you, Darie, did you and Gramps have a good day?"

"We did, yeah. But actually, he seemed kind of tired." Darius tried not to look too disappointed and changed the subject. "So, what did you learn about yourself?"

"They were concerned about some blood disease or disorder, at first."

"Isn't that the same thing?" asked Ed scratching behind Kent's ear.

"Well, not really, a *disease* would be blood cancer, a leukemia, something like that. A *disorder* they told me was a genetic mutation like sickle cell anemia. That's what they're still exploring," Fiona explained.

"Sickle cell anemia?" Ed piped in, "that's common, or not *common* as such, but a genetic disorder considered *particular* to Black people."

"Well, yeah, and you have to have two Black parents. I don't even have *one*, so I don't know why they are going down *that* road," Fiona looked baffled.

"Hey," Darius burst through, "maybe we're adopted Fi? Maybe Dad's not our dad!"

"Right, Dopey! Just look at our colouring...red hair, freckles..." Fiona shoulder punched her sweet twin.

"So, guys, what should we do? Sophie asked.

"Let's grab the leashes and go down to the docks," Darius suggested.

"And take photos on the rocks?" Fiona teased.

"We could sis. You're the expert at that."

"Ed. How do you feel? Got time to join us?" Fiona crooked her head at him for encouragement.

He didn't need any. "I'm in." He beamed at Fiona.

His look stirred her soul. "Great. I'll just run inside and throw some snacks into a knapsack. Bananas, cheese pieces, crackers, water. Okay?"

"Sounds totally good to me," grinned Ed. With his spirits lifted, he floated... seemed like a drug high. A sensation he needed... badly.

Before long, the four young people and three dogs left for their late summer adventure down to the Lighthouse where the rocks, and the Pavilion awaited them.

The breeze picked up.

As did their mindless laughter.

Chapter 47

"Something felt current…"

A genuine warm and wide smile borne from outright friendly curiosity lit his face. He moved towards them into the late afternoon sunlight. His eyes sparkled as he focused on his mother's guest. He reached to kiss his mom's cheek and extended his hand to greet the young woman. At the same time, she nodded her head and said, "So pleasure to meet with you, Simon. Your mother is kind lady."

Something felt current. This woman's glance …was she a model he saw in a magazine?

After Ginny's introductions, Simon waved off tea but went to help himself to a beer from his mom's fridge. He returned to the living room where the women now sat. Simon took the wing chair. He shook his head. He grinned, rubbed his stubbled chin.

"Have we *met* before, Frieda?" he squinted a side glance. Then he answered his own question, "I don't think so. I would have remembered your charming accent." He raised his beer can, swallowed the cool amber, yet still focused on her. "You do look familiar though."

"Doesn't she, *just?*" chimed Virginia, tickled. "I thought that too, Darlin', when we ran into each other."

Ginny elaborated on how the women were new to one another but hit it off straight away. Then both mother and son, together, created enthusiasm, talked about lovely Naples and how Frieda should enjoy living here.

Frieda excused herself to use the washroom and Ginny pointed out the first one down the long hallway. Portia, the curious kitty, followed her, then leaped in front to lead the way.

"So, what's *really* going on here, Mom?" Simon asked in a quiet voice as he leaned in towards his mother. "Is this a set-up? I mean she's a good-looking woman but who really *knows* her and I'm personally a bit fed up with women these days. That journalist Aggie was one weird chick Mom, a menace."

"Oh, Darlin', it doesn't hurt to meet new people. It's part of the excitement of life. She's pretty, isn't she? Forget that journalist, hussy. But you think you *know* Frieda from someplace?"

"She just looks so *familiar*, her eyes; I've seen her eyes before...somewhere..."

"Maybe you two could get together. You could show her around Naples. Take her to dinner at *Paradis Patio* perhaps?"

A trigger!

The restaurant's name ignited a visceral reaction in Simon. His feelings exploded into some sort of bizarre anxiety. He belched; his face contorted.

"What's *wrong*, Darlin'?" Lines of concern etched themselves across Ginny's forehead seeing her son so visibly upset.

Simon hard- stared at his mother as though caught in a memory trance. "I *remember* her. I know now! Mom, where did you say you found her?"

"Let's not get into this now, dear. She'll be out of the bathroom soon. Can we talk later?

"The day of Carlos' death. After Albina's, I met Hamish at *Orsino's* and on my way home, I stopped at the red light, Lakeshore and Mariner, right there alongside *Paradis Patio*.

"Well?" his mother looked more confused than her son.

"It's her! She was the *homeless* person on the corner."

"Homeless?" Ginny whispered. "Lower your voice. What are you *saying*, dear?"

"At first, she was turned away and I thought she was a tall, bony guy. Her clothes were worn, a sloppy mess. Then, she faced my direction, and I realized this person was a woman, and I pitied her. I remember looking at her eyes. They seemed vacant. I felt ashamed for staring. She looked at me but looked right through me, Mom. How could this be the *same* person? I'm losing it, here." Portia returned and pounced onto Simon's trousers.

"Beautiful apartment, Ginny. The washroom is like spa, so many we have in Germany." Frieda returned to the main room, her eyes animated. With her lipstick touched up, her mouth glistened. Afternoon sunlight highlighted her cheek bones better than a makeup brush.

She appeared radiant. She encountered a spiritual moment — one of beauty and affluence as though she had broken through the portals of despair into the life she was *born* to live.

The three of them, Simon on his feet, a gentleman's gesture, appeared as a portraiture frozen in time. Seconds from another world. Then, the awareness of reality, stirred heartache. Frieda hastily quashed the fantasy and adjusted her mood with a shy smile.

"Darlin', why don't you show Frieda to the library, see if there are a few books she'd like to take," Virginia directed Simon. She sensed this sudden awkwardness in the room needed to be dispelled. "We've many European ones, Frieda. I'll just tidy up here and give dad a call, see if he and Darius are on their way. She scooped up the cat. "Com' on Portia, let's see what cookin' in your bowl."

"Com' on Frieda," Simon echoed. "Mom means the library in her penthouse *here*, not down the street."

Simon led the way into the library-den through another hallway of the condominium. The windows offered a different view, northside, of spruce trees, reaching high, other condos in the distance, and the marina far below.

The tall walnut shelves held a sliding-ladder. He felt her thrill as she sucked in her breath at the multitude of book spines. He saw her stroke the leather loveseat, watched her eyes expand as she admired the Persian gold and turquoise carpets which graced the floor she stepped on.

As Simon stood back while Frieda explored the books, he noted her long legs, and her square shoulders, a shape which seemed familiar. Her slim hips and long arms with thin wrists, fascinated him. He even walked to the window pretending to look out but instead noticed Frieda's ear lobes, a shape that seemed *right* for her. He felt a weird attachment. She could not possibly be that woman from the corner, could she? Maybe she had a double somewhere and didn't know it. A twin, perhaps. One hears of such stories.

"Oh, I think I heard dad's voice. You stay for a while. Choose something, Frieda. I'll see you in a few minutes. Going to check how my son is too."

"*Danke,* Simon." Frieda felt in no hurry to meet another new person and make small talk. The need to hide her real background from others in this Naples' life produced throbbing headaches.

She appreciated the wall hangings, and especially one of a handsome older gentleman who reminded her of the young Captain in the *Sound of Music* film. She guessed this must be Virginia's husband. He looked a bit like the man with her outside the funeral home the other day.

"Dad." Simon greeted his father in the front room with a gentle shoulder slap. "Where's Darius? In the kitchen with mom?"

"No, Si, he asked me to drop him at home. Hope that's alright? We were both somewhat tired after our expedition today, and he wanted to play some of his video games and hang out with the dogs. We figured you'd be home soon." Quinn slipped off his shoes and took his moccasins from the front closet.

"Sure, Dad. I guess I'll get going in a bit."

He lowered his voice. "Mom wanted me to drop by to meet her new *friend*. I think she's trying to hook us up." Simon made a face. "New *friend* is in our library at the moment."

Father and son turned to the black, steel-framed windows, their favourite posture when standing in the main room: the view they never tired of, still so green, barely hints of autumn's yellow in the trees below. Quinn asked about Fiona and the hospital experience as Ginny came to check if Quinn wanted a cocktail.

At the same time, Frieda returned to the living room.

"*Hallo*" she addressed the family members, now three all together, with a child-like enthusiasm. "I found *zwei Bucher* I would like so much to borrow!" She held them up, and then froze by the look on the face of the older man, Simon's father.

When Quinn heard this accented voice say '*Hallo*', he spun around in shock. Heat surged up his spine. Adrenaline turned his knees to water. That intimate tone flooded him with repressed memories and guilt.

"Ingrid?" he stared at the young woman. Trembling, his heart thumping, he fell into the nearest armchair, flushed, confused. *It cannot be her.* A flow of nausea washed over him. His complexion took on a sudden pallor.

The almost *heart seizure* which invaded Quinn arose from the unexpected encounter with his past: an impact of overwhelming remorse, shame, and unbridled truth.

Virginia rushed to his side and took his hand. Both she and Simon asked simultaneously, "Who's Ingrid?" They looked to Quinn, and to Frieda and to each other for answers.

Stiff as a statue and depleted of colour herself, Frieda replied in disbelief to these people...

"Ingrid *war* my *Mutti,* my mother."

Now Virginia and Simon saw Frieda in a new way. They saw her slim hips and wide squared shoulders, much like those of the husband and father hunched over in the chair.

Frieda dropped the books she was holding onto the sofa. A guttural sob escaped from her body. Boldly as she could, she asked the old man,

"Are you my father I search for my whole life?"

Stunned into silence, Ginny and Simon watched Frieda approach Quinn. She stood before him, looked down at him and stated, "Nobody used my *Mutti's* middle name. She was Francine at work. She told me only my real father called her Ingrid. She told me one night when she had too much drink. I forgot that. I thought maybe my father must be priest. But you, Mister, you look at me and you see my mother stands in front of you, and you call me by her private name. Maybe my search is now over."

Frieda fell to her knees in front of Quinn's chair and put her head in his lap.

"Forgive me child, forgive me Virginia, forgive me Simon, forgive me Ingrid. I cannot hold this secret any longer." Quinn placed his hand gently on Frieda's head as though offering her absolution, freeing her from any blame or guilt of *his* former behaviour.

"What is going on here?" Simon called out in anguish. "Mom, Dad! Jesus Murphy, what is this weird scene, for chrissake? Somebody better explain."

Frieda rose to her feet sobbing. She covered her face with her hands, tried to speak. "I wreck your family. Sorry, so sorry, but I *was* looking for my *Vater* my whole life. "

"Dad, do you even *know* this girl?" Simon's agitation tightened his jaw. "Mom, did you know this? I guess you didn't, did you.? Was Frieda here supposed to be my new *girlfriend*? Is she my sister, now? What the FUCK is going on?"

"Language!" Virginia corrected her son.

"There are no kids here, Mother, except maybe *this one* Dad brought into the world!" Simon felt instant regret with his last comment but didn't let on.

Ginny faced her husband. "Look at me, Quinn," she ordered. "Stand up!"

Shaking, he rose to his feet. He met his wife's eyes.

Virginia swung back her arm and with all her might slapped Quinn's face.

"You cheatin' bastard!" she shouted at him. "And how many other kids are out there without a father, eh?"

"It wasn't like that," stammered her husband. He winced, held his hand to his burning cheek.

"Dad, I'm shocked. I'm shocked because you never owned up to it. You had a child out there by another woman." Simon put his arm around his mother and held her.

"I didn't know about a child. Ingrid didn't tell me." Quinn attempted self-defence. "I told you, Simon, not to put me on a pedestal. I'm a human being with flaws, like everybody else. What was the point of telling you Virginia, and you Simon, about an affair I had forty years ago when I was young and stupid?"

"How long did it last?" Ginny pressed on.

"You're the only woman I have ever loved," he pleaded to Virginia.

"Stop with the clichés, Dad! Isn't that what all cheaters say?" Simon felt as his own anger increased, it lessened the heartache of this earthquake. He hurled a few more insults at his father to kill the pain.

By now, the new, beautiful, and improved Frieda sat on the sofa, curled into herself, and rocked with quiet sobs while this family of three continued their arguing and fighting.

Sometime later, Ginny looked to Frieda and stated, "You, young lady are in our family now. You belong to us, and we are not about to dump you. You hear? You are no longer going to pay for other peoples' mistakes. Except one thing. You can't date Simon, of course."

Realizing somewhat foolishly that now he lost his status as an 'only child' Simon took Frieda's hand and said, "Sister. I'm sorry, and I'm not sorry. We'll talk later."

To his parents he said, "What am I supposed to tell my kids now? Eh?"

Virginia, in a tough mode since slapping her husband, had an unexpected edge of a mother's mature wisdom in her voice,

"Don't worry about it Darlin', those kids could probably tell *you* a thing or two! Don't underestimate them and what's going on in their world."

"With all due respect, Mom," said Simon, "you don't know the half of it."

"What's that supposed to mean?" Ginny walked to look directly into her son's face.

Without flinching, Simon locked eyes with his mom and said, "There's a reason why Marjorie left."

"Which is?"

"Sorry, I'd didn't mean to get into that," Simon hoped he hadn't pushed this too far since he promised Margie he'd keep her secret.

"Well, it's too late now, Darlin' to stand on ceremony," said Ginny. "You don't get to say something...significant and then drop it, back out."

"We'll talk later, Mom. Please. I've got to get home. Is there somewhere I can drop Frieda on my way?" Simon worked on his composure.

"Yes, not far from here. She'll tell you herself. But I just have one thing else to say to all of you here. My husband, like all humans, is flawed. I'm angry with him now. But I forgive his mistakes," she turned abruptly to face Frieda, "and I do not mean *you* are a mistake, Frieda. My husband has loved and cherished me for many years and has given me a wonderful life. For that I am grateful. His mistake was in having sex with another woman, and consequently leaving behind a child without a father. We could have done more for you when you were a young girl, Frieda. And now, Quinn and I need to be alone. Take Frieda to her place,

Simon. Frieda, I will call you soon. Here, take your books and give me a hug."

After embracing them both, Virginia ushered the young people out of the condo.

"Quinn. Are you okay, Darlin'? I'm sorry I hit you. This information today was painful. You see my shock because I never expected your disloyalty, I had such faith in you. Forgive me for expecting you to be a saint." She held his head close to her chest. "I know you love me. And I love you, my dearest husband."

Quinn sobbed in her arms. He felt like he was dying. The shame of being found out was too much.

"Hush, my love. We are together," Virginia stroked and held her man, all hers forever.

"And tomorrow, you will go and change your WILL to include your daughter."

Chapter 48

"The moment encapsuled timelessness."

E duardo *needed* this distraction. The teens created fun. They took selfies in the park's Gazebo. The laughing girls stood on the benches, and posed, hands on swaying hips. Darius held the dogs' leashes. A lightness spread over Ed, masked his depression.

How he *craved* Fiona's company. *It's like she grew up overnight,* he convinced himself. Unbeknownst to her, this special girl offered him a *lifeline.*

Fiona jumped to the grass and Ed caught her. A lock of his dark hair fell over his brow. His muscular arms supported her with ease. A bit awkward. The drop wasn't high. She didn't need help, but he couldn't help himself. Any excuse to touch her electrified him. He imagined this charge as reciprocal.

Kent pulled to chase some squirrels taking Darius and Sophie off for a short run with Charity in tow, over the grounds, beyond the play area, down to the water's edge. They tossed Prudence's leash for Ed to manage.

"Fiona," Ed hunted for a thread of conversation to interest her. "When do you and Darius turn seventeen?"

"October tenth. Why?"

"Just wondering if you guys are planning a party."

"Oh, would you come, if we had one?" She teased, and realized he still held her waist.

Ed blushed. "I might be a bit old for your crowd."

"Gosh, Ed, you're family! Age has nothing to do with it."

"Fiona," he stammered, "I probably shouldn't say this, but I am crushing on you. Can you tell?" He gave her the puppy-dog eyes which could melt any female.

"Ed, you *can* kiss me." On cue, Prudence yelped to be noticed.

Gently, Ed touched the soft lips of her glowing face with his full mouth, barely tapping them. Despite his racing heart, he managed restraint. She felt the scratch of his chin brush hers. Her stomach knotted as did his.

Then he raised her delicate, white hand and like a gentleman who stepped forth from a chivalrous *nether* world, with head bowed, Eduardo kissed it. He watched Fiona's hair tumble from a twisted bun break loose with an abundance of springing copper coils. Fiona's coral sundress exposed a pale bustier of a *décolletage* gown. Her eyes glittered like newly polished sapphires, focused on him, the man who would love her.

The giant oak trees surrounding them transformed into a brilliant forest with a shaft of sunlight piercing through the leaves onto their sacred spot. The roof of the pavilion took on the power of a castle's turret. The moment encapsuled timelessness. A storybook dream fulfilled.

This physical contact lifted them to a new level of experience. They *both* felt it. In a flash, they saw the connection shift their lives, their futures. They would have to answer to others, *her* father, *his* girlfriend, and other nosy people who would state their opinions of them. They knew they wanted to be together. End of story. Beginning of daydream.

And that's how secrets start. With a lack of freedom, the two young people would now have to relegate their dream-like state to schemes and elaborate plans to meet privately. They would have to risk their reputations, if caught. They would have to be accountable to their respective family members.

And they just didn't give a damn.

Simon made little conversation as he drove Frieda to her apartment. Her building, close by, left him grateful it took barely minutes to get there. Mostly, he apologized to cover the 'sins' of his father. He rambled on, senselessly. He internalized the shame. Worse, he wanted her out of his sight. Brought up to have manners - thanks to his mother - he managed to behave as a gentleman. Still, life was, at times, a fuck-up!

As he pulled his Mercedes into his driveway, Simon thought how nice that Ed is here... perhaps planning how he could take over his dad's work. Though, he thought it odd there was no Darius in sight, no dogs, nor Ed either. Only Ed's VW car. He tried Ed's phone which went directly to voice-mail.

Simon was just exhausted from the day's events: the hospital, his mom's, meeting his new 'so-called' *sister,* simply too much for one day. Darius *had* to be out walking the dogs and probably Ed was with him. Of course, Fiona would be at Sophie's.

Free at last, he crashed on the living room couch. He longed for a nap. The accumulation of events of the past seven days, and all the bloody, 'bless-their-hearts' kind people left him trembling and feeling as though his guts had been scooped out like the flesh of a cantaloupe. Even, God, *they say*, rested after seven days. *Meu Deus!* as Carlos would utter. 'My God!'

As he drifted off, Simon's thoughts of being hollowed out like a melon shifted to Marjorie. Such a pro in their kitchen. He loved the simple but smart way she did *everything*. Why did he take her for granted? Why didn't he declare his overwhelming affection for her? *Because it would have been improper.* He was the frigging employer, not her lover. *Ah, there's the rub,* as Shakespeare would have it. The boss is not supposed to be screwing the employee. But love. What about *love*? Love, love, love...he wanted it. With Margie.

Simon slept until the young people returned from the lake. Then he listened to their stories, but just the ones they wanted to tell him. *He* had something to share, too. Better to wait until... what *would* be the right moment?

Fiona looked flushed, Sophie cheerful, and Darius content, but Ed seemed uneasy. The dogs wagged their tails. Everyone talked at once. A vibrancy in the air. Each of them had something to tell but something to withhold.

Simon turned on the stereo and played an old Led Zeppelin rock album, a classic.

'Whole Lotta Love' blasted heavy amplified guitar chords to the ceiling beams.

"Yeah, Dad!" Darius shouted.

The group began dancing together, but alone, as lost figures in a Dionysian frenzy of madness. The end of a crazy week, they let loose in the security of home: a dad, his kids, close friends, and beloved dogs. They indulged in a quarter hour of safe insanity. Then, all collapsed on pieces of furniture, and the floor, sprawled, and spent.

Chapter 49

"He read somewhere you get the life you deserve."

September brought more changes to the Nesbitt family.

Most importantly, Fiona's health showed good promise for the future. Simon breathed tremendous relief to learn she did *not* inherit the BRCA2 cancer gene from her mom, after all. However, a mystery remained of a single *trait* of sickle-cell anemia, but not the disease itself. No immediate danger. Physicians recommended that Simon keep a healthy lifestyle for Fiona to boost her red blood cells.

Pursuing the trend of 2015, Virginia took on a *search* for ancestors. She scanned *Facebook* pages where people exchanged family histories as a hobby. She ordered a kit, then sent the *Ancestry* saliva test to see what interesting relatives might surface. If she liked the process, she would encourage Frieda to take one too.

Ginny *thrived* as a stepmother to Frieda Reichert. And she was right about the teens who were tickled to discover they had an aunt, grandpa's daughter from the past. Now, Ginny imagined Frieda's future and wondered who she might find from their circle of friends as a love match for her. Meanwhile, Frieda still lived in her apartment, but not for long! The senior Nesbitt's hunted for a townhouse, nearby, and loved this quest.

With a new sister in his life, Simon took the challenge of excusing his father's prior indiscretions to his kids. He felt his dad's embarrassment. However, just as his mom said, the twins — modern, resilient youth — found excitement in this information and met their new European aunt with delight, wonder, and acceptance.

Simon continued to pine for Marjorie. The longer she remained gone from his life, the more he longed for her to be back in his home. He allowed his wishful thoughts to gnaw him into headaches. To cope, he swam several times a day in the indoor pool. Since the kids were back at school, and no one in the house, often he swam naked and indulged in his Margie fantasies of her being a mermaid swimming alongside him.

But mermaids weren't real, and Marjorie was the most real woman he knew. He blew it with her. He should have *insisted* she stay in his house, and he should have helped her deal with this unexpected baby situation. But he had worried how the kids would handle it. His mother was right: the kids know stuff anyway, and there was a down-to-earth *wisdom* to them.

He read somewhere you get the life you deserve, and he chewed on that idea. Did he even *deserve* Marjorie for letting her go? Like some Biblical Hagar-figure kicked out because she was *with child.* There are times, in doing the *right thing,* we do the wrong thing, Simon thought. But for now, he would just have to live with the cliché of *one day at a time.* The kids were healthy, good, and his parents united in spite of skeletons from the past. His mother was one helluva *broad,* an expression she used herself when she quoted the late singer Frank Sinatra, someone she had, incidentally, met in Vegas when she was young. She didn't ruffle easily. No surprise his dad loved her so much. Simon knew his mother 'kicked ass'. And he felt Marjorie showed the same grit. His gain, and his loss.

Chapter 50

"Would you care to have *dinner* with me?"

Three weeks into the high school semester, by appointment, Mr. Nesbitt appeared in the office of Vice-Principal, Daphne Jorgensen. The receptionist, slivered hair colour of shiny beets, offered him a seat, an ingratiating smile, and backed out closing the office door.

With both his kids in graduate year, Simon wanted to spell out he'd be available for any concerns the new Vice-Principal might have, especially due to the twins' differences: his daughter known as a high achiever, although he played it down, and his son, sensitive, with academic challenges.

Ms. Jorgensen imagined the son was probably on the *spectrum,* frequent in this decade. *What's in the water, these days?* she mused facetiously, but also thought of her own boy, Nils. Yet, Mr. Nesbitt did not reveal any *diagnosis, per se.*

After a few benign pleasantries in the conversation, they focused on Fiona.

"She's auditioning for..." speaking together, stating the obvious, "the school play." They laughed. Thoughts alike.

"Yes," said Daphne, "I noticed her name on the sign-up sheet. I'm producing the musical *Grease.* I guess Fiona told you."

Simon nodded. "Yes, indeed. She told me. Fiona loves to dance and sing. Talents she, fortunately, inherited from my late wife, a professional opera singer," he stated as a matter-of-fact, and allowed himself a proud smile.

A jolt in this friendly conversation. Daphne offered a quick, professional return.

"I'm sorry Mr. Nesbitt. Being new here, I've not yet dialed in to students' *personal* backgrounds. Condolences. Your children lost a mother and you a wife." Then she gave a wistful nod of her head.

"Six years now. Cancer." Simon added.

Always an awkward moment, Daphne noted, though prevailed.

"But you are *rightfully* proud of Fiona to use her talents. She seems a lovely girl, as well, from what I've observed during rounds in the halls and the atrium. She appears happy, surrounded by a group of bright, *good* kids."

Simon's face and body relaxed at these positive comments. He studied Ms. Jorgensen's pleasant demeanour, found her reassuring. Now he prepared to hear updates on his son from this woman in charge.

Daphne's mind spun: *how should she handle this 'drop in her lap' opportunity?*

After some discussion about Darius and the resource classes he'd continue to attend, she went for it!

No venture, no gain. Not like she was some demure ingenue. And he, apparently a few years younger, not an obstacle as far as *she* was concerned. Simply a gift she could handle.

Her bottomless glass desk worked in her favour. To attract Mr. Nesbitt's attention to her assets, Daphne crossed one leg over her knee which displayed her thighs. The hem of her black, tight skirt skimmed her silky flesh. Fully exposed, her long legs ended in glossy-nude stilettos. Ever so slightly, she swung her top leg. And, since she had yet to meet such an attractive *eligible* gentleman, swept up by subdued erotic desire and a need for practicality, Daphne positioned herself — cheetah style — to pounce.

Inhaling deeply, leaning in on her elbows, hands clasped, elegant fingers entwined, Ms. Jorgensen ventured. She drew his name out slowly: "Mr. Nesbitt."

Her solid blue eyes, a match for her cornflower blazer, radiated confidence as they pinned him. Those eyes held a promise of excitement. In fact, with pupils dilated, Ms. Jorgensen appeared in a hypnotic state.

"Call me Simon, please," he interjected, his gap-tooth grin cheerful, his voice calm.

"Would you care to have *dinner* with me?" she offered in a singsong way, followed by an angelic beam. Not missing a beat. Not breaking eye-contact.

At a loss for words Simon echoed her suggestion, "Dinner?" and gained time to think. Caught off-guard. *Was she asking him out?*

"Are we still talking business, Ms. Jorgensen, or is this a social invitation?" Grateful for his quick recovery, Simon double blinked with amusement.

Daphne lowered her head slightly. Not exactly batting her eyelashes, still her piercing look to Simon aimed playful intention.

"I think it's safe to say my intent would be more of the latter, Simon, but that wouldn't preclude the former, necessarily. And please, address *me* by my Christian name, Daphne."

"You're a forthright woman, Daphne. I find it refreshing and a bit intimidating," Simon confessed, a mischievous glint from his own deep amber eyes.

"How about I take *you* to dinner, if you'll allow me to be the gentleman I was raised to be?"

Sexist! she thought, *but so damn good-looking with that tan and those white teeth.*

Aggressive woman! he thought, *but I must begin somewhere in this dating business.*

Flirting, right in the office, Daphne, ecstatic, but self-composed, detected her own fragrance of *Good Girl* spritz kicking in on this seduction. Her voice softened.

She purred, "Why don't you pass me your phone, Simon, and I'll enter my private number into your contacts? You can text me the details when you have them." She paused to admire his overall appearance. She noted his casual, tidy look: how the white cotton, button-down shirt accentuated his broad shoulders and upper arms; the clean straight-leg blue jeans, and cool tan loafers, *sans* socks. Nice!

Intrigued by this burst of office romance, Simon reached up and handed over his mobile to Daphne.

They agreed he would text or call with specifics, and this Saturday evening would be their date. As they parted, their handshake lingered. They absorbed the warmth of each other's palms, no trace of clamminess. Both grateful and buzzed.

What a winner this Mr. Nesbitt! She couldn't believe her luck. And she would certainly pay greater attention to his kids, now. Although, she hoped Nils would not screw things up for her again. At least he'd be at his dad's for the weekend.

Chapter 51

"From all appearances, he was available."

anilla-honey aroma floated upwards as Daphne Jorgensen pulled the ivory tap to add hot water to her bath. She slid back and surrendered to her foam creation: mixing scented bodywash. *The things you find on YouTube.* A whiff of almond oil also tickled her nostrils. She raised a leg, admired her slim ankle, inspected her toes for polish chips, and noted some needed repairs.

The big date tonight with *Mr. Nesbitt.* Such fun to think of Simon as *Mr.* Like a *Jane Austen* gentleman! Her own *Mr. Darcy.*

Who knew she'd date a student's dad? She didn't consider this against regulations, but even so, she'd keep this juicy tidbit to herself. No sharing with secretaries, sweet as they may be. Often deferential, they complimented her blonde hair, her stylish outfits; these gals did some serious *kissing up,* offered favours, even brought cafeteria lunch. *Probably because I'm new,* she reasoned. Everybody *loves* a new person...until they don't. Art Department Head, labelled her a 'bit of fresh air.' The unspoken statement: *as a staff, we're so bored.* Well, the staff wouldn't be bored for long. She'd get Mister art teacher to design publicity posters for the school show. Oh, she'd have *everyone* engaged, plus her door open to advise and lend fresh ideas. But her *love life*? She'd keep those proverbial *cards* close to her chest. A gal has to have *some* secrets!

Earlier in the afternoon of her date with Simon, Daphne went to exercise. She loved working-out at the YMCA. She appreciated those grand windows, several stories high; this elevation transported her to a Norwegian cruise ship.

The cycle machines overlooked a broad parking lot bordered by tall oaks and cedars. Being at eye-level to a bright sky where strands of white cotton clouds stretched and melded into each other, one could easily imagine being surrounded by a pale blue ocean.

The walking-track on the upper level remained Daphne's favourite part of this gym. She wore headphones, not only to listen to music, but also to stamp out the thumping from the young males who practiced their basketball dribbling skills in the courts below. Yet, she thought Nils should be doing this, too. Playing ball with those guys. Most, brown-skinned eager teens with side-shaved haircuts, their enthusiastic darting movements indicated dreams of being pro players someday. Nils would feel shy around them, and their sleek confidence as athletes. But she'd deal with that soon. Get him involved. *Who knew having just one child would be so much work?*

Now *Simon*. How would she get him into bed? *Naughty girl*, she scolded herself. But she'd make it happen. From all appearances, he was available, and she was *not* about to waste tonight's opportunity. Women must take control of their lives, take things *in hand*. She giggled at her own implication.

She remembered some pills her ex, Lars, took to boost passion. Shared with her. *What the heck were they? Probably valium to chill out anxiety.* Perhaps she'd slip one into his drink when they'd return to her place. Of course, he had to think it was *his* idea to make love, she being so desirable, hot, even. *Oh woman, thy name is Vanity,* she happily misquoted Shakespeare. Super nervous but so excited about her seduction plan for tonight, Daphne convinced herself this night would be memorable.

"I'm going for a shower then, guys," said Simon. "So, all plans in place?"

Early evening this first Saturday of October, the air still warm, all three sat on the front deck: Fiona on the swing chair, Darius took the top step, cushion under his bum. And Simon in the oversized rocker. The lake spread before them, gleamed in stillness. The sun aiming westward, still high in Naples, would take a while before it sank beyond the mountain of the city next door.

"Yup, Dad," said Fiona.

"Do you want a ride to Sophie's before I leave?"

"No, thanks, Pops. But I'll take Pru with me for the sleepover. We'll walk the three blocks. It'll still be light out." She brushed Pru's tiny body curled in her lap.

"And you Darius?"

"Grandma wants to pick me up at six, she said not to eat because she and Gramps have something special planned. I was hoping to hang with Jamie though.

"Sounds like we're all in for a good time. You can call Jamie, Dare. Maybe see him first. Work that out with Grandma, okay?

"I won't be home late, so Kent and Charity should be fine till I get back. We can all meet here for breakfast tomorrow. Maybe invite Aunt Frieda?"

"Sure, Dad. But why won't you tell us who you're dating?" Darius grinned.

"Simply because it's too soon to make a big deal of it. Things don't always work out as one hopes."

"Did you find somebody on-line?" Darius impishly pressed.

"No. And none of your business, mister. For the record, haven't gone that route yet."

After a moment.

"Okay, I'm off to make myself presentable."

"Are you nervous, Dad?" Fiona asked, eyes gentle.

Simon paused, gazed, felt a gut stab, "Yeah, honey. I guess I am... a bit."

"Don't worry, Dad. You're gorgeous and sweet. Any woman should be so lucky to date you," she comforted.

He kissed her cheek.

"She's right, Dad," Darius added. He felt good to offer his dad a spot of confidence. Nice little twist for him.

Simon ruffled Darius' hair, realized a cut due soon.

"*Ahh, the best kids ya 'are! See ya all, later,*" Simon tried his fake-Irish accent. To the kids, the phrase came off as a *Johnny Depp Pirate* imitation. They mocked their adorable dad a few times more before he disappeared.

After dad slipped back inside, the twins sat closer. Darius joined Fiona on the swing. They figured dad wouldn't hear their chat with a shower running and his TV always set to the news.

"So, Fi, *Siserama,* do you think Hamish set dad up?"

"Maybe." She lingered the thought. "He *knows* people. Hard to say. Maybe Esther did. Somebody from her work?"

"I guess we'll hear about it tomorrow," Darius chuckled, "if it doesn't go well. He probably doesn't want to jinx anything, just now."

"Well, for his sake, Darie, let's hope it goes great. We want to see dad happy again, right?"

"Yeah, Fi. Hey, changing the subject, why do you think Hamish and Esther are always sleeping over at Gavin and Samuel's? "

"Never thought much about it; *does* sound a bit juvenile, I suppose. Dad says they're huge card players. They probably play late and don't wanna drive home."

"Know what *I* think?" playing coy, Darius pulled a blade of grass from a planter, slid it into his mouth.

"So, spill!" Fiona urged, twirled a coil of her fiery hair, then shoulder punched her bro. Pru wriggled.

"Ready for this?"

Fiona's eyes brightened. "Alright, what's your theory, smart guy?"

"I think they're *fuck buddies!*"

"WHAT???" Darius, are you *crazy?*"

Pru, all ears now, looked from one twin to the other.

"They probably smoke weed and screw each other," he added, gleefully.

"For goodness sake," said Fiona, "What do *you* know about this? And where are you getting these wild ideas? Who are you hanging with these days?" She whispered, "And keep it down. Dad's room is directly above us."

"Chill, Sis. I'm not some baby. Everybody in this family thinks they have to hide stuff from me. You know, yourself, that I'm only two minutes younger than you. – two minutes, Fi!"

"Okay, Darie, you're not a baby, nobody's saying that, but where are these ideas coming from?"

"Remember when you couldn't make the *Gay-Straight Alliance* meeting because you had an audition?"

"Yeah, I had a voice audition...so what?"

"A lotta *what happened* at that meeting! Oh, and here comes Kent. We don't want him telling dad," Darius snickered. "Those two are *psychic* buddies."

Kent sniffed by, his tail wagging, and parked himself on the step cushion, vacated by Darius. Now in front of the twins, Kent discretely was all ears too.

"By the way, where's Charity, Dare?"

"Probably napping in the sun around back."

He continued his story from school.

"Well, nothing happened at the meeting, but after, Jamie and I talked. He said Nils Jorgensen put his *peen* into Claire Moore's *vag*".

"What are you *saying*? Fiona shout whispered. "You're talking about the new VP's kid. He's in my art class. And why this baby language?" Fiona grew highly uncomfortable with this conversation.

"I know you'd say it's *vulgar* if I used the *real* words," Darius' excused himself as he relished sharing this gossip with his sis.

Fiona's stomach backflipped. She thought of her own recent ways with Ed.

Chapter 52

"I'm here of my own will."

Fiona needed her bestie, Sophie, to cover. Friends *helped* one another. Sophie fit in the *best friend* role since first grade. Fiona would make it worth her while if Sophie backed her when she'd meet Ed. Sophie only had to name it. Fiona's clout at school spoke volumes — an arena where she felt most confident. Talk of school president even in the air this final year. Sophie just might enjoy being a campaign manager!

Undeniably scrupulous, Fiona had to swallow the bitter taste of anxiety which escalated with each deception. Frequently, her delicate skin burst into angry little hives. A dead giveaway she was up to something non-kosher.

This evening she drew black eyeliner on her lids. She fixed her red hair behind her ears, pulling tendrils forward to drop like ruby earrings which framed her high pink cheekbones. The description *sexy* propelled her preparations.

Her magnetic draw to Ed superseded even conscience woes. She indulged her fantasies. She dismissed the teenager label and admired her own softness *as a woman*. Her breasts, lifted in an ivory, wire bra, full and high, were also now considered healthy! Cause for celebration! And her obsession with Ed felt *normal*. She adored his dark stubble, his deep voice, and his yummy but sensitive teddy-bear brown eyes. The slant of his shoulders and strong arms - *such* a refreshing change from lanky, high school boys.

Bouncing and colliding like balls in an arcade game, her hormones set the tone offering excitement, more life! She sensed freedom and joy on a mission tonight to lose her virginity and win her chosen man, Eduardo Delgado.

Beryl, Ed's *non-steady* girlfriend, postponed her fall semester at Saunders College and left for *out-west* with Albina. They used Albina's 'widow's life insurance' money. Together, they inhaled the stunning view offered by *Canada Via Rail* across the country to British Columbia. Their goal: to track down Berri's mother. Or so they said...

Savagely depressed, of late, Eduardo landed the house to himself. *Peace at last.*

Ed parked on a quiet side street, his VW hidden by lofty oaks just beyond the corner of Hackberry Road.

Fiona hurried down the block, flutters in her belly and jumped in on *her* side. She exhaled in a slow stream. Ed waited. Then she turned, tasted the sun on Ed's cheek with a sweet lip tap. Next, she rubbed off his smudge, and laughed.

They drove to his place as often as they managed an escape excuse for her. Laced with intense emotion, Ed's feelings for Fiona felt totally different from his relationship with Beryl. They talked a lot more. And they grew closer.

Tonight, they retreated to his basement, secluded from main level windows and possible prying eyes. The outdated 'rec room' felt cozy and private. The worn, beige couch, large and comfy, welcomed them to stretch out together side by side.

Ed played John Mayer's painful love songs which flamed a silent fire between the lovers in *The Edge of Desire*.

"I could probably go to jail for this, Fiona," Ed whispered in her ear as he slid his hand under her soft green blouse and felt her smooth warm back. Her rust crinkled skirt flounced up around her thighs.

"Why?" she teased. "I'm here of my own will."

"My beautiful Princess, you're underage, and I'm almost twenty-three. Off with my head!"

What did age matter when passion flamed? Romeo & Juliet just thirteen and fourteen, when sacred palms touched- as the story goes. But Fiona and Eduardo overlooked this Shakespearean cautionary tale, even though the fictional lovers at least matched in age. In modern times, Eduardo, considered an adult, would break the law defiling a child.

"I 've got condoms, my sweetheart," Ed murmured. "Do I have your *consent*, tonight?" He nuzzled her neck.

"My father would kill me! But I am yours, my love. I give myself to you."

Ed's depression sublimated into renewed sexual energy. His imagination grew unrestrained. Reality dissolved. He imagined them hovered in a cellar, secluded from the present world, he with his flaming red-haired beauty, locked in a dungeon together.

The only freedom for these two passionate romantics subsisted in making love over and over, no one to stop them. Condoms long forgotten. They kissed and they cried out in soul-exhausting collapse.

Virginity now a thing of the past. Ed forgot there could be bloodshed. Fiona even admitted to stabs of pain.

On emotional overload, Ed suffered as he loved... to an extreme. To this end, he took risks. He tossed aside his mother's crocheted coverlet from the sofa, now bloodstained. He washed Fiona with warm towels as gently as he could and grabbed a pair of his mom's undies which his old lady wouldn't miss. *She probably dished out a few to ole Geoffrey, herself,* a thought to justify his erratic panty theft.

To his credit, Ed treasured Fiona. But he also possessed her. He took her loss of virginity as a sign she *belonged* to him. By contrast, Beryl was not a virgin when they got together. Fiona was his baby, his woman, his own; he would take care of her. His guilt felt assuaged with such firm thoughts. He held her tight and continued to whisper sweet nothings. She embraced and caressed him with a poignant tenderness.

Chapter 53

"A little homage to our folks."

About this time, in Toronto, Hazel and Fuyun cozied up on their chocolate, leather sofa and jotted ideas into a spiral notebook for their upcoming nuptials.

"City Hall or bust?" offered Fuyun, pen held in the air. Her silky black hair fell loosely over her bare shoulders as her almond eyes turned and teased her lover.

Hazel encircled her waist, pulled her in close, nibbled Fu's shoulder and said, "What about the Community Church, Babe? My parents would have loved it if we added a bit of the *divine* to the ceremony, ain't that right, Margie?"

Both lovers gazed with sweet, concealed envy at Marjorie's baby bump and waited for her opinion.

"Hey, guys! Let the spirit move you! Would be nice. A little *homage* to our folks."

"Great. Then let's put *book the minister* on the list," said Hazel, tickled pink, as her drop zebra earrings vibrated her delight. "Then our community's Minister Tallulah will be perfect for our ceremony!"

"When did you say was your fertility session?" asked Marjorie.

"Second week in October," said Fuyun. My mom is setting it up for us.

Fuyun' s mom, of course, the paediatrician extraordinaire who requested a DNA on the deceased Carlos Delgado, as they all remembered. But no longer mentioned.

"That's great! Well, I'll let you sweethearts continue your list while I have a bit of a lie down." Marjorie rubbed her belly and left for the guest bedroom, which was now hers, at least for the time being.

Turned on her side, a light blanket pulled to her shoulders, Marjorie reflected on the six years she lived at Simon's. The second week of October would mark the twins' birthday. They would turn seventeen. Hard to believe. They became her *babies* after Peggy passed. She ached for them, and for their father. With a child inside her and no living father to greet him...or *her,* she sniffed up a tear.

Happy for her sis and Fuyun, Marjorie found solace her baby might have a cousin by next year. She drifted off as thoughts turned to the handsome man in the laundry room...probably gay...she sighed...this was the *Village,* after all.

Chapter 54

"This could be a long night..."

S imon parked in the brick driveway of Daphne's white gabled back-split. This block's small homes, nestled together, spoke to the charm of nostalgia. However, recently refurbished to high-end standards, they ran costly, as did Daphne's rental.

He removed his aviators, pressed the doorbell, waited, and glanced around. He admired the potted, purple plants on the wooden porch, still thriving, positioned amid small wicker chairs. Pretty, he thought, and memories flashed back to his dear late groundskeeper who would instantly be able to name the plants.

Simon swallowed his tic-tac just as Daphne opened the door and faced him with a glamorous grin.

"Greetings, Mr. Nesbitt," she said playfully, "lovely to see you're on time. Do come in. Looking even more handsome than I remember."

He enjoyed her disarming humour and played along.

"Good evening, Ms. Jorgensen, although it's still bright out. And you look positively bewitching." His eyes dropped to the circle cut-out of peek-a-boo cleavage on her leopard-print dress.

Man-eater, he snorted within, *and I'm the prey.*

Daphne led him down the narrow hallway towards the gleaming kitchen island.

Simon appreciated her *Pippa-like derriere* as he followed her to what he hoped wouldn't be the slaughter.

She directed him to a black barstool near the west window. The slim view exposed a wild English yard, tall things entangled. The sun, still bright, slipped through the blind slats and cast stripes across Daphne's creamy face. A glow flashed a cat-like slant over her eyes. Her Fuchsia lipstick shone, as she took charge.

"White or red?" she offered. Her granite counter, back splashed by grey subway tiles, held a silver rack of wine bottles.

"White would be refreshing," Simon replied. "Thanks."

She turned, removed the *Chablis* from the stainless-steel fridge, and poured small amounts into a pair of thin, stem-ware glasses. Then, she raised hers.

"Cheers, Simon, welcome to my home."

He is hot!

She stared at him through that thought. She loved what she saw.

Feeling her direct gaze on him, Simon raised his glass and gulped more than he expected. Unaccustomed to overt flirtation, he managed his discomfort, knew it disingenuous not to respond in kind. *I don't like this, but I'll try to play along.* He looked at her, standing in front of him. *Maybe... Man, she's overpowering.*

"Well, look at you!" Daphne leaned over the island. "We didn't even call each other."

"What do you mean?" Simon's face a mask of concern. *Wench has lost it.* "I *did* call you."

Oh, innocent puppy. Daphne rolled her eyes as Simon glanced down.

"Simon," Daphne threw her head back and laughed, loosening a strand of her blonde hair. "You and I are matched! Can't you see?" She pursed her lips, made a pretend scolding face. "Your brown suede sports coat, and my animal-print dress are colour co-ordinated. And we didn't even plan this, my dear!"

"Okay, I get your drift." His shoulders relaxed, the wine a welcome stream down his throat. *This could be a long night.* With a woman of surprises, he needed to stay sharp, ill-prepared as he was for *dating.*

They drank their wine, nibbled on her water crackers, brie, and mini sliced cucumbers, then moved on to the restaurant, minutes away, in downtown, Naples.

In their Penthouse, Virginia buckled her low platform heels. As she raised a leg, she noticed Quinn admiring her ankles. Still a joy to see his appreciation, even at this age.

"I like the sensuous look on your face, Darlin'," she cooed.

"Of course. Always my Beauty...but I have a deeper thought and a question I'd like to ask you, my love."

"Shoot, Handsome!" she giggled, then crossed her other leg over her knee.

"Have you *never* had sex with another while married to me?"

Even weeks after the *Frieda showdown,* Ginny noticed how Quinn's guilt lingered.

"Nope, not ever, Darlin'. You were my one and only. I never cheated on you."

Quinn looked happy and miserable at the same time. "Well, I feel lucky, but ashamed I couldn't match your standards," he confessed.

"Don't worry too much," she released a husky laugh. "When we were *going steady* back in the day, I panicked and gave in to a couple of flings."

"You didn't! You wicked hussy! How is it I didn't know?" Quinn brightened.

"Well, actually, now that you ask, there were two in competition with you."

"What? Who? I'll kill them!"

"Too late. They're already dead!" Ginny enjoyed this bit of tease.

"Remember one Henry Watkins? He wanted me to handle him, *flute* style. I'm sure you get my drift – we're old enough to be corny, Darlin' -no need for vulgarity."

"*OMG*, as the kids say. Did you? No, don't answer. I don't want to know!"

"Oh, he was just a blow-hard, nothing to brag about...I begged off. I heard he fell off his tractor and literally broke his neck, poor fella. Probably had too much drink."

"And the other guy?"

"Well, you remember Mr. Wilbur Chad Henderson, don't you? When you came to Kentucky? Such a wonderful rider. We rode the woods together and did a bit of nuzzling and not just with the horses, either. Down in the meadow Virginia came pretty close to losing her virginity," she howled at her own play on words. "But relax. I didn't.

"Even though Will was definitely competition, you were a stranger from Canada with this cute accent, even a bit Scottish like your dad, with your red beard, and French flare from your mother, I was smitten. And, you had such a great body. Still do, Sugar," Ginny chuckled in her throaty way.

"Thank you, my love. I don't deserve you. I love you forever. So, what became of Wilbur?"

"He died of strep throat. Maybe a disease from some brothel. There was talk he visited such haunts often. Wilbur was rumoured to be well-endowed...and required many women to keep him satisfied.

"And now, Darlin'," said Ginny as she stood up and hugged her husband, "let's get our grandson and take him to the *Red Lobster* for dinner. He'll be waitin' for us by now."

And with a lip peck to each other, cheerful to be alive and together, they left the condo.

Chapter 55

"My pleasure, indeed, Daphne."

They entered *Vesuvius Steakhouse* — a fine-dining, Italian restaurant in downtown Naples, and were met by Stefano, owner, and *Maître d'*. He greeted Mister Nesbitt and his lady with flourish and poise, as expected of a person in charge.

Stefano led the couple towards their corner table and made small talk with Simon as Daphne paused to view the stucco mural, stunningly spread across the main wall. It featured an Italian hillside village, populated with miniature homes of rust-coloured rooftops and multiple winding stone steps. In the distance, a magnificent mountain framed the scene.

Well- familiar with Stefano and his restaurant, Simon noted how pleased they were with the success of his business – perfect for Naples – and for investors, *Nesbitt Holdings*.

Once seated at their elegant table, spread with cream-coloured linen, Daphne welcomed the ambiance, the dark-wood floors, plus the thick candle posts acting as burning torches. The room appeared both grand, yet intimate. Attractive back-lit wine shelves and vintage plates of grapevines enhanced the authentic Italian décor.

They both exhaled.

"First time here?" asked Simon. He wet his lips with a sip from his water glass.

"Of course! As you know, new to town. Just lovely here, Simon. Thank you."

"My pleasure, indeed, Daphne."

Italian instrumental music streamed romantic international pieces.

The dining room, already three quarters full, with guest conversations and laughter plus the clinking of silverware, offered a congenial atmosphere.

Waiter, Flavio, brought Simon and Daphne orange Prosecco aperitif cocktails *on the house*, and left them leather-bound menus.

They raised their glasses, to cheers. Then Simon looked down to scan the fare.

Daphne sipped her drink and studied his face.

She *adored* his face. His chin shadow, masculine, but neat. His tight auburn hair, his thick eyebrows, those warm, alluring eyes — cinnamon sparkles. She took in his lips, full and soft. When he laughed, she found his tooth-gap smile added boyish charm to his character. And those few freckles on his high cheeks bones gave a tenderness to his overall appearance. Not least, Daphne loved his dark, long eyelashes! *Why is it men come natu-rally to such enhancements?* To top it off, Simon smelled like fresh shower soap, with a lingering earthy base of musk after-shave. She swooned, alright, and she hoped he sensed it.

To conceal a stab of nervous energy, Daphne now busied herself, too, exploring the menu. She expressed a desire for the 'seafood sensations'. Happy to concur, Simon ordered shrimp starters. The main course would be the finest steak cuts of sirloin. A bottle of expensive *Brovia* Red with its wild berry and leather aromas appeared shortly. Once the wine was poured, they were on.

"Here's an official welcome to Naples, Daphne," Simon toasted with a raised goblet.

"Thank you, Simon, sweet of you." Daphne dropped her eyelashes in a faux bashful gesture, then with a raised chin, she looked him straight in the eye as they tapped their gold-rimmed stemware.

"Let's hear about your background, Daphne, and how you landed here." He held out the breadbasket for her to choose, took a chewy piece for himself, before setting it down next to the glow of a small flickering candle.

They worked their dinner forks through the fresh taste of lettuce greenery and tiny tomatoes in the salad, olives, and thin purple onion rings. Minutes earlier they had pitched their seafood tines of king shrimps into a piquant red sauce which excited their palates.

Glad to receive optimism from Simon to talk about herself, Daphne reveled in the opportunity to spin her positive image to this lovely man.

"I was born and raised in Toronto, big city gal..." she began and laughed at her own words, slightly self-conscious.

"Go on," Simon encouraged. Easy to speak and listen as they nibbled through salads with the scent of steak trailing in from the famous kitchen close to their table.

"I'm from a Lithuanian father, and a German mother. My dad, Victor Valaitis was an engineer; my mother, Erika Schmidt, a tailor, an exceptionally good one at that. We grew up in Toronto, the Ossington/ College area, downtown. My brother, Arnold, and I. He's a couple of years younger, studied at OCA, now an art designer for homes and offices. Not married, but he goes through tons of girlfriends, many of them models and actors.

"Are your parents still alive?" Simon ventured.

"Yes, they are, thanks...retired."

"Mine are still with us too, I'm glad to say. Feel so blessed."

Daphne felt Simon's kindness palpable. A rare gift. She also noticed he listened with his eyes. She found his generous attention highly attractive. Her gaze lingered on him, and his cute distinctive ears.

"Tell me a bit about your marriage, your career moves, and your son, of course, if you feel up to it. I'm a good listener, so I'm told," laughed Simon.

"Well... I studied at McMaster University for my undergrad, and later got my teaching qualifications from the University of Toronto. When I did my undergrad, I shared a rented house in west Hamilton with a few girls."

"That must have been fun," said Simon with a twinkle and his gap-tooth grin made a shy appearance. "One usually makes lifetime friends. Did you?" He sipped from his glass and held a steady comfortable look.

"Oh, I sure did," Daphne replied looking down, moving her fork around the plate. Then she looked up and said, "We drank too much in those days." *Let's not get into this.*

And roommates are not always what they're cracked up to be.

She changed the subject. "I met my ex, Lars, at Mac. We're still friendly, not close, but cordial, I guess you could say." *Better watch how I manage this history. Do not want to come across as a bitch.* Daphne needed to play her cards right.

Another cheerful waiter, Giovanni, brought their steaks to the table with his *Buon Appetito!* Eagerly, they each cut into the tender and juicy meat, bringing their forks to their mouths, and nodded together making murmuring sounds of deliciousness. They savoured the flavour. This main course exploded as a shared experience of sheer delight.

As he chewed, as she did too, they did not speak.

Simon allowed his mind to drift. He thought her red lipstick suited her and he wondered how it never smeared as she spoke, drank, even as she ate her food. *Marvellous creatures, women.* Pleased to be in the company of this bright and sexy woman, his body stirred in many ways. He swallowed ice water. His eyes penetrated hers. He yearned for something. He wanted to enter several of her warm orifices. But he minded his manners. His Southern mother taught him to be a gentleman. He shook off the distraction. Continued the conversation.

"So, if you and your ex are friends," he ventured, "do you feel like telling me why you split up? If it's not too personal. Actually, why don't you tell me how you guys met?"

"Sure, that's easy enough," said Daphne. "Lars and I met a few times in the pub at Mac. But we really got to know each other through the university's theatre program."

"How is that? Were you both theatre students?" Simon's curiosity piqued.

"No, I was interested in show production during my undergrad years. And Lars, he was a visiting professor from Copenhagen."

"In theatre?"

"No, he pursued research in microbiology, biotechnology. Already a grad and prof from Aalborg University in Copenhagen when I met him. You know, he worked with environment, food stuffs, that sort of thing. He had a passion for theatre, too. I'd say his career and hobbies are pretty standard Danish choices."

"Good passions to have," Simon punctuated, finishing a roasted asparagus spear.

"So. we both found ourselves working on an Ibsen play, and the rest is history, as they say." Suddenly feeling a bit uncomfortable, Daphne brought her napkin to her lips.

"I'm really glad Lars did not convince me to become a *vegan* yet, at least for tonight's dinner. That was simply delicious, Simon."

"We'll pass our compliments to the chef. You're most welcome, Daphne."

Simon gave her a smile and a breather, then continued...

"Incidentally, I studied at Mac too. Business. I guess we were in different years." Then, he decided not to pursue *this line* because he felt she was the older one. Could be awkward. He changed the subject.

"Ready for dessert, now, Daphne?" He raised his eyebrow.

Daphne's mind: *You're it.*

Simon's mind: *You're it.*

They both burst out laughing - a pair of mind-readers. The unspoken corny dessert joke. The effects of great food and wine had kicked in.

"Well, I guess I'll *settle* for a tiramisu," Daphne faked disappointment.

"Excellent choice! I'll join you in a piece of that heavenly melt-in-your-mouth whipped chocolate lightness. An excellent 'pick me up.' Did you know that's what it means?"

"I'm not surprised because it's coffee-based, but a good one to remember."

In both their minds, their *date* was moving along super well.

Chapter 56

"The screen did not show a music video…"

T he bar in Port Credit where Lars planned to meet his *Tinder* date, jam-packed! Typical Saturday night at *Skipper's Landing*. He scanned the joint, waited, figured she backed out. It happens. He sighed, relieved. He didn't want Nils alone in the condo for long. After all, this was his *dad* weekend.

Lars stroked his salt and pepper goatee. He'd stick around for a beer. He could have stayed in his neighbourhood, *Square One*, Mississauga. Yet, he hesitated to date close to home. Although one *could* disappear in the crowd since Mississauga City stretched far. Still, Lars preferred the charm of *Port Credit Bay*, as well as its less threatening exposure. He squeezed into a spot at the bar. Soon he snagged a bartender's attention: his advantage being a Scandinavian of six feet five — a height Lars attributed to some Dutch genes, too. He adjusted his wire-rims and peered at the high screen. A re-run of European soccer on display. Our *football*, he mused.

Someone tapped him on the shoulder.

"Small world," he laughed and shook the firm grasp of a colleague from the university. "You here alone?" Lars shouted.

The prof, also bearded, admitted to just looking. People chattered, rhythms pulsated through indistinguishable lyrics. The noisy atmosphere limited conversation. The men smiled at each other, nodded, and raised their glasses. Then, they turned to stare at the screen, above, as several efficient baristas of mixed genders rapidly wiped the bar and served countless thirsty customers.

Nils liked this time to himself. He sat in the second bedroom— his dad's office, in front of a large Samsung computer screen. His back to the open door, Nils wore oversized head-phones. He chilled with a beer from his dad's fridge, and a small piece of *ice* he managed to score on Friday from a dude in the woods behind his school. *This meth, powerful. Sick of being a loser.*

He *Googled* names of people from his classes. Played some tunes. Thought he lucked out to hit on Claire from science, a nerdy girl, glad for attention. But he *really* wanted that Fiona from art class. Her beautiful red curls and tiny waist bewitched him. She seemed friendly enough when he sided up to her to view her sketch: a white horse head, with pointed ears and long-lashed eyes, perfect nostrils with a thin braid down its nose. And man, how he would have loved to mount *her* — the artist. A bit more meth and he'd work it. He'd get her. For sure. Time on his side. Still early in the semester, and he *was* the new guy, VP's son. Score one there!

Nils did not hear his father come in, nor did he expect him this soon.

Lars tossed his keys on the coffee table. His sparse living room appeared tidy: *Scandi* burnt-orange sofa and teak-wood side tables.

He noticed Nils' backpack open on the kitchen floor and wondered if his boy had the essay in the office, working on a thesis revision for Monday. Maybe he'd supervise and help his kid with a boost of ideas rather than having him slave over it alone.

Lars went to his guest toilet first, then down the hall to the home office. At the threshold, he stopped. Stunned by the sight ahead, he called his son's name.

Preoccupied, track pants pulled to his knees, Nils only heard grunts, as he feverishly jerked on his exposed woody. The screen did not show a music video. It exploded with porn: a naked male with a grip on a small female butt.

Lars moved to Nils, lifted his headphones, and in his Danish tongue, voice gentle, stated as he switched off the screen, "Son, we must talk. This is not healthy."

Nils, glassy-eyed, hung his head. A chunk of his fair hair hid his reddened face. He grabbed at his pants, flung himself around in the chair, and flew from the office. He screamed as he locked himself in the master bathroom.

Lars called for him to come back. Said it would be okay. They could talk about it. He wouldn't tell mom. He rapped on the bathroom door.

"I hate you," Nils yelled, high-pitched. "I hate you both!" He pounded his fists on the inside of the locked door. He hollered obscenities which made no sense whatsoever.

Lars listened to his son's savage outbursts and recoiled.

A sensitive man, Lars felt shattered, once again.

Why? Why? Why?

Chapter 57

"*She* was his Ipanema girl..."

On the drive home, Daphne suggested Simon stay for the *proverbial* nightcap. To which he agreed. The elegant dinner and conversation relaxed them both. Simon shared his dog anecdotes. He told Daphne these endearing creatures kept their noses so attuned to family business, he and the kids occasionally resorted to French phrases to throw them off the scent, *as it were*. Daphne laughed at Simon's joke.

She admitted keeping a cat once. Siamese. She described the time she returned home after work and caught Tessie swinging from the drapes, claws ripping the silk fabric. Tess had also displayed temperamental favouritisms and hissed at any date she brought home for coffee. Her parents agreed to take over. Tessie didn't get on with Nils either, so he wasn't sad to see her go.

Simon reached across and took Daphne's hand.

"You probably needed to get your Tessie a scratching post," he chuckled.

"And you're right, I'm sure. But as a first-time cat-owner, I was hopeless! I didn't realize all the junk they needed to stay happy."

Daphne felt it a sweet gesture for Simon to hold her hand. She sensed a tenderness in his movements, and in his funny stories. Yet, her heart pounded. Anxiety now.

Was it sheer excitement which tightened her chest? *Obviously, a good sign.* She felt he liked her. His touch, warm and inviting, held more significance than any handshake.

Inside, Daphne tapped the pot lights to lower the dimmer. She set a sensual mood. She plumped the violet toss cushions on her L shaped, grey sofa.

She handed Simon a small liqueur, suggested he chill, loosen his tie, remove his shoes, and stretch his legs on the extended section of the couch. She pressed on her music player and slid in a classic disc of gentle *Bossa Nova* Brazilian music: earthy, light samba jazz sounds, both romantic and sexy. *The Girl from Ipanema* began playing to soft percussion, and saxophone accompaniment of Stan Getz as Astrid Gilberto sang of strolling by the sea.

Simon shed his jacket, tossed it to the long end of the couch, kept his mobile. He texted Darius. Reassuring news. The guys were into a blockbuster movie; Jamie might crash in Darius' room. Kent and Charity dozed at their feet. All good. And Simon knew Fiona and Pru would be fine at Sophie's.

Now he sipped his drink, then closed his eyes as the music created a swaying breeze. He smelled beach waves. He imagined himself a surfer. His belly gyrated. The drink. Odd sensations. Yet, grateful for Daphne's music choice. Nothing rowdy. He melted in this atmosphere as his hostess took a quiet exit up to her bedroom.

Leaning his head back, Simon soaked in the wonderful melody, and thought about Marjorie. *She* was his Ipanema girl. She'd love this sound. With her light-brown skin, born to be a nature girl of some sort, he mused. Such a natural beauty, with her wild hair, and fit body. He pictured her shapely, tanned legs in a bikini. He imagined holding her hand, strolling the soft sands of *Rio de Janeiro* beach with her. He sipped more of his drink.

Memories washed over him of women he loved and lost. Peggy forever. Marjorie alive and well but gone from his life. He missed her in such a deep way. The brandy intensified his emotions. Now wistful, he also felt good. *Must find what's this drink?*

Like a nymph, Daphne, her blonde hair brushed loose to her shoulders, her alabaster skin with a hint of pink cheeks, appeared before him. A short, silken-black garment with thin straps hung from her slim frame. Cut low in front, full cleavage exposure, it flounced at the top of her taut, milky-white thighs. She stood still, as though on display, and held a small brandy snifter in her hand.

"May I?" She indicated his lap. However, she took what she wanted, did not wait for his answer. She flashed a black lace thong, when she raised her right leg and extended it across his groin. She brought her left leg up to push a bare foot on the yielding sofa. Calculated slow moves on her part. Careful not to startle.

Daphne saw Simon as pretty much wasted. She hoped he'd hang on for another forty-five minutes.

Simon's thoughts, now jumbled, allowed him to relax. Daphne presented herself as one gorgeous woman. Not really his type though. Pushy.

Confused, Simon realized she sat on him, pressed on his crotch. Without intention he felt strong phallic pressure. He couldn't believe it, but knew his wang had a mind of its own. In fact, it grew like a root-plant bursting through soil.

He'd had plenty of hard-ons in his life, but this one was a fuckin' earthquake. His brain not catching up to the physical action in his pants.

"To us" she said, and they both took another sip, understanding the customary phrase is followed by a drink. He wasn't drunk; nor was she. But they both slid into a weird state of being. Self-control had left the room. Anything was possible.

"Did you put LSD into this brandy, Daphne?" he lowered his dark eyebrows, but kept his expression friendly and light. He wanted to laugh but thought it might be offensive.

"Don't be silly, Simon. Where would I get shit like that? Tell me, are you feeling *good*?

"I am, woman. I am."

His reply sound. His voice deep and content which Daphne interpreted as agreeable and *fuckable*.

She took both their glasses and set them out of the way on the side table, just a twist to her right. She kept her place on his lap. With hands free, Daphne held Simon's face, his beautiful manly stubble, while his arms encircled her slim waist as she leaned in. Both aware of the background music which added to the sexual atmosphere, they joined their open mouths. She explored the soft thickness of his tongue and sucked, gently but greedily, on his lips, and he slurped all the juices her mouth had to offer. She kissed the right side of his neck, losing herself in pleasure.

"Whoa!" carefully he pulled away from her kisses. "Don't leave any hickeys," he slurred. "I've got kids to face in the morning. Won't go over well – teenagers." Then he realized he didn't need to say that. This wench— their *vice-principal*— after all, not just a blind date.

He moved his large hands to her creamy breasts which were practically in his face anyway and scooped them from the satin fabric. He covered one with his mouth, teased it with his tongue, then moved to the other's rosy areola. Suddenly, he stopped. A shot of clarity and a twang of conscience hit his earlier, fuzzier thoughts.

"I should get going, Daphne."

She wouldn't hear of it. She moved her hand to his fly, opened and reached inside to feel his granite flesh.

"We cannot *waste* this, Simon," she whispered. Her husky tone held irony and desperation.

The Siren had him. He wanted it. But he didn't want *this*. Not tonight. Not ready for this. Not now. He couldn't help his erection. Sober enough, embarrassed to say no. Yet she brought his sexual organ forward, and deftly stroked him. She whispered as she nibbled on it, "Stay, Simon. I don't bite. I aim to finish what I start."

Empowered, she knew he was helpless.

But she lied.

She heard his groans and pulled him from her mouth into her wet, honey pot. Where he, unwillingly, but naturally, exploded. After a bit, he shuddered, angry.

"Daphne, why did you pull this crap? Get off me. Please."

Shaken, embarrassed, and of course, physically exposed, he needed to cover this mess. Daphne passed him a box of tissues to wipe up.

"I've not had sexual intercourse with another woman since my wife died. I have stained her memory, Daphne. I was *not* ready."

"Oh, Simon, grow up! You were as ready as any man could be."

"I apologize for my hard-on. Not planned. Let me get myself together and get out of here. I don't feel good or relieved having sex with you tonight. Oh, shit. We didn't even use a condom."

"Not to worry. I won't be getting pregnant."

"Not just that..." Simon drifted in thought.

"Nasty implication, Simon. You won't get an STD from me."

What a dick! Daphne now cursed to herself about Simon's attitude. She slid from his lap, humiliated.

Wobbly, Simon sobered up enough to grab the rest of his clothes and get to his car. And he thanked whatever God would hear him, for the short drive home, only possible through those short back streets away from traffic, or he'd really be screwed.

Ashamed, humiliated, he felt less of a man. *Sonofabitch.* He cursed himself. *How did I let this happen? Sex, with a damn orgasm. I did not want to fuck Daphne. My kids' vice-principal. Insane!*

It was years since Simon felt ugly about himself. That brief time when he was a kid, with Hamish. Later he understood common boy play. Boarding school stuff. When Simon was sure of his own sexual orientation, Hamish became his best friend.

Never in his male mind did the words *consent, rape,* or *sexual victim* cross his thoughts as applied to himself. Not before tonight, not even now. *How could a man feel overpowered by a woman?* Visceral feelings registered in his gut as great shame. Was he angry with Daphne, or himself? He wasn't even sure. These emotions ripped at his chest and stifled his breathing, his conscience wild with remorse. He pulled over, shoved open the car door and vomited into the ditch of a laneway. After he spat the bile, Simon hammered the steering wheel several times with his fist and shouted hoarsely into the dispassionate night: *Fuck Me!*

He parked in the garage, tapped the house code, and entered through the mud room. Barely in the house, just out of his shoes, he saw Kent padding towards him. *Man's true best friend.* Simon ruffled Kent's ears, took a water-bottle from the fridge, and the two of them headed downstairs to the home office.

Simon turned on his Chris Botti and Yo-Yo Ma album and melted into the soft leather chair which Marjorie sat in that Sunday morning when they had their talk about her business.

Over the instrumentals, the rich voice of Josh Grogan sang lyrics about why I let you go, and Simon's heart ached from missing Marjorie. Although he loved Peggy forever, he no longer felt apologetic to want Margie.

Maybe it's the familiarity, the sense of family we shared. You just can't forge that from fornicating with someone new. Not that it was my plan for tonight.

In total frustration, over the sweet cello strings, Simon called out, "Come back to me, Marjorie!" His emotional pain echoed in the stillness of the night.

Kent's ears perked up. He knew that name well. He turned to Simon.

Man, and his gentle beast stared at one another.

Both sad, missing her.

PART TWO

150 Years Earlier

ANCESTORS

Chapter 58

"Just one beat. A turn of her head."

Washington, D.C. 1865

Sarah-Jane's eyes glitter. She thrills at her surroundings. What an opportunity! Her seventeenth birthday, April fourteenth, and she is at the theatre in the state's capitol.

Mama and Papa so generous and kind to bring her to this special event. Her emerald-green taffeta gown rustles when she shifts in the red plush seat. As nonstop laughter peals from the audience, the noisy atmosphere seems perfect for her celebration.

Our American Cousin is in performance: a play well-known for its hilarious plot of Asa, a common, honest American fellow who sails to England to claim an unexpected estate. The poor chap struggles to understand the ways of a British household. His rustic American habits shock the servants as Asa *showers* fully clothed.

Sarah-Jane watches her Mama flutter her fan close to her face. Mama conceals her chortling which lacks a lady-like image.

Papa gives full manly guffaw to his amusement. Sarah-Jane feels so grown up in this company, father, Colonel Benjamin Thomas Hill, and mother, Mrs. Grace Hill. But another guest of great renown is in the audience this evening. The Honorable President of America: Mr. Abraham Lincoln.

The three Hill family members sit in the first balcony. A level higher, decorated in Union flags, with heavy gold side drapery, an ample four-seater box overlooks the stage. Seated there are the President, Mrs. Lincoln and their guests, a young couple.

"Mama, I think Mr. President saw me looking at him," says Sarah-Jane during intermission. The play is now between Acts II and III.

"Well, I am not surprised, daughter," the Colonel puffs with pride. "Given your natural beauty, and those gleaming chestnut curls, I reckon you capture many a gentleman's attention. You stand out in a crowd, Darlin'."

Mrs. Hill nods, "Your father is correct, child. Such an honor to be noticed by this fine man. And Mrs. Lincoln appears fashionable herself this evening. They and their guests seem to be enjoying the play. Wonderful to see them relaxed. Lord, this *war* finally over, and their personal suffering with the loss of young Willie. God bless them."

Lady Grace shakes her head in sympathy for the horror of losing a child. Everyone knows of this tragedy: the third son of the Lincoln's who died right here in this town, at the White House, three years ago. Just eleven years of age. Typhoid fever. And the President's long-lasting depression well-noted in the press. What suffering to endure. However, this evening proves to be healing those painful memories.

"Darlin'," the Colonel looks to Sarah-Jane, "I am going to have our seat neighbor, Mr. Burgess, here, keep an eye on you while I escort mother to powder her nose. I do believe we still have time before the third act."

Sarah-Jane blushes. "It's all right, father. I do not need a chaperone," she whispers. But of course, she knows better, considering her gender and conventions of the era.

She smiles at Mr. Burgess. He acknowledges with a tip of his head, keeps his hands folded over his bulging belly. With her parents down in the lobby, Sarah-Jane thinks her own sentimental thoughts.

Her beloved only brother, Hudson, twenty-two years of age, stayed behind in Louisville with his regiment. No doubt he is fortunate, thinks Sarah-Jane, to visit with his sweetheart, Amelia, this Easter Weekend. She does not begrudge him any happiness whatsoever. And here she is, in the *Ford Theatre*, in the same building with such a supreme figure as the President.

She glances at him again during this intermission. She notices his head turned in profile as he speaks to the young officer sharing the private box. She notes Mr. Lincoln's deep sunken eyes and his full beard. Oddly, on this Good Friday, for Sarah-Jane, the President recalls the lord Christ in his suffering. He seems to embrace pain throughout his entire body. She looks away before his gaze might catch her staring.

She feels lucky to be born a white girl. Although President Lincoln shows himself to be an extraordinarily humane and kind President in his perseverance to abolish slavery, Sarah-Jane feels it would still be a long time for Black people to feel safe. She heard many slaves had already escaped to places like Canada, which seemed like a world away. But their relatives left behind could suffer at the hands of the prejudiced plantation owners. She does not understand much about the individual battles which took place over the last four years of the Civil War, sheltered as she lives in their Kentucky Manor, but she heard bits and pieces from Hudson and her father of Confederate sympathizers who still linger everywhere, behind the next tree, as it were. Some even in plain sight. She shuddered when she heard they would stop at nothing to preserve their ideals. She's even heard the word *traitors* bandied about recently.

The overhead gaslights flicker. Gentle violin strings encourage patrons to re-claim their seats. Sarah-Jane's parents return, and Act III begins in lively fashion.

An extravagant interior set of the English estate appears, evidence of the Trenchard aristocracy. In this drawing room, conversations take place among several dissenting characters.

Asa has now endeared himself to some new relatives; yet true to English farce, mistaken ideas arise. Along with emerging confusion, busybodies take center stage: an insufferable woman tries to manipulate circumstances to her benefit: Mrs. Mountchessington. Earlier, she had advised her daughter, Augusta, to be *attentive* to this *wealthy savage.*

Meanwhile, Asa discovers a cousin, Mary Meredith - a sweet, but poor dairymaid, a granddaughter of that late, old curmudgeon Mark Trenchard who had disinherited his family, and made for America.

Thus, upon Trenchard's demise, Asa, unexpectedly finds himself the sole beneficiary of this much lusted-after estate.

Despite her lower social status, Mary proves to be a charming young woman. And dear Asa, a true gentleman, regardless of others' haughty opinions, *lies* to Mary about her grandfather.

He tells her that grandfather changed his mind about the disin-heritance and burned his will.

In fact, Asa himself burnt the will. He convinces Mary of her *rights* and reveals his love for her. She accepts him. However, Mrs. Mountchessington wants Asa to propose to her Augusta, and takes on a haughty attitude.

A climax of humor spills from Asa. He bursts through the woman's rudeness aimed at him. He bellows:

"Don't know the manners of good society, eh? Well, I guess I know enough to turn you inside out old gal – **you sockdolo-gizing old mantrap!***"*

The house ROARS! What a punchline! An unrestrained explosion of boisterous laughter, oh, so loud, *blasts* throughout the entire theatre.

Eager to catch Mr. Lincoln's reaction to this nonsense, Sarah-Jane hopes for a smile on his serious face, wishes to see him joyful, at last.

Just one beat. A turn of her head. Heat flushes her entire body. She sees Mr. Lincoln slumped in his seat.

A man stands over him. He tosses a gun. She recognizes a famous actor. *Was this part of some theatrical distraction?* Rapidly, this man draws a blade from his boot, and stabs the soldier who lunges at him. Mrs. Lincoln's gaping mouth indicates her unheard screams. The young lady at her side collapses.

Sarah-Jane's eyes bulge riveted in disbelief. She watches in horror with the rest of the audience as actor JB Wilks leaps from the viewing box onto the set. He injures his leg, yet manages to right himself, flee upstage, and disappear behind the flats.

After a hushed confusion, the full house mumbles in shock. Sarah-Jane's father wraps his arms around her, and her weeping mother grips her hand with both her own.

The house lights come up and producer Laura Keene announces President Lincoln has been shot by JB Booth, alias JB Wilks, a well-known actor. Of course, the play is suspended. And the *Ford Theatre* remains closed for a hundred years.

Despite the tragedy wherein the President dies the next day, and John Wilkes Booth, the once dashing, now *notorious* actor, Confederate sympathizer, is caught and shot within ten days in Maryland, the Hill family, itself, flourishes.

Colonel Benjamin Hill's son Hudson marries Amelia who gives birth to Nathan, who with *his* spouse Rose Adams, fathers Abraham Adams Hill –the father of Virginia Divera Hill, and granddad of Simon Ignatius Nesbitt.

A clear historical path of noble ancestry on Ginny's *father's* side.

Only two years after she witnesses the assassination of the great Emancipator, the architect of the Thirteenth Amendment, gentle Sarah-Jane thanks God, as President Lincoln often stated in his speeches: the populace was not to thank *him*, but to thank God.

Sarah-Jane enters the novitiate of the Dominican Sisters of St. Catherine of Sienna in Springfield, Kentucky. She lives until age ninety-two.

She holds her great, great-grand niece, three-year-old Virginia, on her lap before she dies in 1940, and speaks softly to her about love for humanity, and for people of all colors and races. She feels Virginia is a special, caring little girl.

Virginia's only sibling, a brother, becomes a monk. And Virginia names her only child, Simon, after her brother Ignatius.

NAPLES, ONTARIO

1865

Maternal Ancestry

Chapter 59

"She stuns herself by agreeing to be his wife."

The tiny boy escapes his mama's arms. His mama reaches for his suspenders but loses her grip. Her small son dashes towards the magnetic, Reverend Ebenezer Roberts whose tremulous deep voice, like an utterance from God Himself, beckons all to rally round, and pray.

'Pray', bellows the Reverend, as he dabs his broad, brown forehead with a white linen cloth, 'for our tremendous loss. But we shall overcome', he consoles. And soon the child reaches the top of the chapel's aisle and hugs the knees of his preacher father.

On cue, the vibrato of a violin string and the mellow hammer of old piano keys, invite the choir, donned in purple robes, to sing the Negro spiritual, 'Swing Low, Sweet Chariot' as the Reverend lifts his son into his arms, and holds him tight. He nods to his wife to remain in her pew.

Throughout the humid, crowded chapel, along with the singers, the brightly dressed congregation, in colorful straw hats murmur 'Amen Lawd'. The scent of Easter Lilies and florals of sweet fragrance permeate the small wooden interior and waft up to the rafters, towards the Lord's heaven. This *African Methodist-Episcopal* holy place with its A-shaped roof stands on the *Lakeshore Pass* in Naples, just next to the fishing river of Sixteen Mile Creek.

Their noble Emancipator, Abraham Lincoln, shot to death, but never to be forgotten. News of his assassination spreads quickly from Toronto's *The Globe* newspaper.

Reformist newspaper-founder George Brown, known for his anti-slavery sentiments sends word through his horse couriers to all areas outside the big city. Newspaper issues update all day with reports on tracking the evil scoundrel responsible for the American President's demise.

* * *

Thirty years forward, the Reverend's beloved child, Chikelu, a light-skinned Negro raised in Naples at his father's side as a pastor's aid, faces tragedy.

His parents and several parishioners succumb to a raging influenza spread from new European immigrants. Subsequently, at thirty-three years of age, Chikelu decides to search for his American ancestors in Virginia, and Kentucky. As a youth, he learned how his father made it to Naples, Ontario through the *underground railroad*, a connection of safe, meeting-places for runaway slaves.

He still finds it hard to stomach how his father had arrived in a wooden, cargo box shipped to the neighboring village of

Bronte Woods, Ontario. The suffering and horror of this escape from the grips of slavery weigh on Chikelu Roberts' mind.

A decent fellow like his father, Chikelu feels ready to contribute to his new community in some significant way.

After a long train ride to his destination, Chikelu finds work in a printer's shop, and a room upstairs to let. The proprietor, a white man, Mr. Timothy Watson provides opportunity for Chikelu to wash floors and clean the machines. Watson soon notices Chikelu's skin glisten with effort and determination. A progressive thinker, Watson who believes in rewarding arduous work takes Chikelu under his wing, and invites him to his grand home, which he, himself, had inherited, in Charleston, Virginia.

It is the year 1895, and Watson feels proud to introduce Chikelu, a Black man, to his love Anabel. She had worked as Watson's housekeeper for several years nursing Watson's wife, Wilma, throughout her illness until her death. Watson and this mulatto girl Anabel became a new family when Anabel gave birth to their daughter, Caroline, now a saucy beauty of fifteen years.

With her thick hair, plaited down her back tinged a foxy red, and a spray of freckles glowing on her smooth cheeks, Caroline appears as a vision of freshness.

Chikelu's heart flutters upon their first meeting, and never lets up. He reckons amongst all the pain and degradation his ancestors had experienced, there are still kind strangers in the world.

Watson's daughter, Caroline, feels like a dream as she returns Chikelu's earnest smiles, and they continue in witty conversation. Watson allows the courtship but knows spies still exist who might create trouble; small gangs of Secessionists leave him worried.

Yet life continues in a positive vein: the young couple marry in 1898. Caroline gives birth in the big house the following year to twin sons, Timmy, and Carly Roberts. Watson and Anabel thrill to the honor of becoming grandparents. And all their hearts simply burst when a year later, little princess Justine with a mass of black fluffy hair arrives as a good omen for the new century 1900, on the fifth of February.

The children love horses and learn to ride. Life seems ideal until the children grow to be teenagers as the First World War breaks out in Europe. Everyone is conflicted where or how to help the cause.

First, America supplies Great Britain with war materials; then in the summer of 1918 American President Woodrow Wilson sends 10,000 men a day to the Western Front.

Timmy and Carly Roberts are drafted. However, they do not see war. The twins perish, not in combat, but before they make it to France. They become statistics in suffering the fatality of the Spanish Influenza outbreak of 1918.

On learning this news, old grandfather Watson suffers a heart attack and remains an invalid for months. Anabel falls into depression and speaks rarely, to anyone. The deceased twins' parents, Chikelu and Caroline, find themselves overwhelmed with grief, and smother their daughter Justine with their sorrow.

Justine's own pain ages her, drives her to ride and ride to feel the wind blow away her anguish over the loss of her beloved brothers. That same year she finds herself consoled by their farm neighbor, old man Portman, a widower.

From loneliness, Portman invites Justine to drink tea with him and soon proposes marriage. She stuns herself by accepting to be his wife. A place to hide. Besides, she values his kindness.

Yet, Justine Roberts Portman becomes a widow within six months of her wedding. Her new husband falls to his death from his own trusty mare. During a trip to the *Hill Estate Farms* to acquire a new pony for the maid's child, old man Portman slips and cracks his skull.

Ready to console the young widow, one young gentleman, Abraham Adams Hill, offers deep sympathy. An attorney investor with a large property in Kentucky, Abraham is on a visit to his parents. The sudden attraction of these two young people is electrifying. They know they are meant for each other.

Thus, the beautiful Justine with sun-kissed skin, and the large-boned discerning Abraham unite. They bring Virginia Divera Adams Hill and her brother Ignatius Jonas Adams Hill into the world.

Ignatius enters a monastery, and Ginny marries a French/Scottish Canadian, Quinn Nesbitt. Their only child, a son, born in Naples, Ontario, they name Simon Ignatius Nesbitt.

PART THREE - MODERN TIMES

Naples, Ontario

Fall- 2015

Chapter 60

"He didn't expect this scene."

Fiona couldn't breathe. Her teeth chattered. She gulped air.

"Ed, Ed, I don't feel well..."

Eduardo sprayed the blood-stained blanket with his mother's bleach. Fiona's whining irritated him. Pressure he didn't need. Couldn't handle.

"It's okay, you'll be okay," he yelled from the laundry corner of the basement. "You're just getting a panic attack. Let me finish this, Fiona, and I'll drive you home."

"I *can't* go home," she shrieked. "Not like this. And I'm supposed to be at Sophie's."

She rocked back and forth, moaning. Her painful genitalia shocked her into reality. Remorseful - her virginity lost at barely seventeen. Her morals compromised. They never even *bothered* with the condoms

Blinded by sunburst, she had run and slammed into a concrete boulder.

Dazed by shame and overwhelmed with fear, Fiona yanked her disheveled hair and cried, "Mommy, Mommy. Margie."

Shocked by Fiona's startling, infantile behavior, Ed perspired. He wiped sweat from his forehead with the back of his hand; it had dripped down his nose. He fought his own tension, stuffed the bulky evidence into the washing machine and switched it on.

He *had* to keep his shit together. *What were they thinking? All that thrusting. Who knew she would bleed?* Not exactly the romantic mood he'd planned.

"You *know* your mother can't help you, Fiona! Are you hallucinating?"

"I want my dad," she cried. "No, I don't want my dad! He'd kill me!"

"What are you jabbering about Fi? Eduardo sat beside her, now, put his arm around her shoulder and pulled her in tight. "It's *me* he'd kill, not you. Let's try and stay calm. We love each other, don't we?"

Ed turned her chin to face him, saw her mascara smudged over her freckles. Their eye contact felt weird. Definitely not the same Fiona as earlier. He looked away. His head ached. He didn't expect this *scene*. Regret, self-hate strangled his throat, choked the spit out of him. His thoughts nauseated him.

I had none of this crap with Beryl. Serves me right, hitting on an underage girl - the boss's daughter. So much for the 'you're family now' crap.

She answered his question - the one about love - which had already evaporated from his mind.

"I don't know, Ed. I just know this doesn't feel *right*, anymore. I'm sorry we did this, and I can't breathe well."

"You're only hyperventilating..."

"Shut up, Ed! You're not helping," she wailed, and pulled away from him.

"I thought we *loved* each other, or we would never have done this." His justification to appease himself— his sexual activity with a minor— fell flat. Bitterness burned his tongue, as he suggested a solution, an escape.

"Please don't tell your father. We'll make this right. I'll get you a 'morning after' pill."

"What's that?"

"You don't *know*?" He was shocked... *in this day and age...*

"No! I've never done this before," she sobbed, vocally now, and rocked with greater intensity, wailing. "It hurts down there too."

Ed found Fiona's behaviour unnerving. He never imagined this from her. He pulled at his own hair.

"Agh, agh," he screeched. "Shut the fuck up!" He put his hands over his ears and ran upstairs. He needed to get away from her childish behaviour - so different from just a while ago. His own nerves raw, he needed to think.

Fiona located her purse, found her phone, and called her dad.

Simon answered the call display. "What is it honey? It's late," he mumbled.

"I need you, Daddy. Help me. I'm sorry."

Simon sobered up fast. "Where the hell are you? Aren't you at Sophie's?"

"No, I'm with Ed at his place. I'm sorry, Daddy. I'm so sorry."

"Stay there. I've been drinking. I'll get a cab and be over to get you. It's okay baby girl. I'm coming."

He sobered up even more while sensitive Kent ran back and forth in this emotional conundrum.

Simon reached a driver from his company's cab service. He asked to be picked up at home immediately, stated no questions nor conversation beyond greetings and provided the Jordan Street address.

On his way to the Delgado home, Simon tried to phone his son. No answer on Darius' phone. He called Jamie's house. When the father answered, Simon faked a normal voice, claimed he was checking because he thought the boys were supposed to be at his place. The dad said they were at Jamie's and safe. Charity there too. Simon thanked him and apologized for the disturbance and misunderstanding.

At the Delgado address, Simon asked the driver to wait.

He hammered on the door.

Ed opened.

He looks spookily calm, thought Simon.

"Where's my daughter, Ed? Is she here? She called me."

"Yes, sir. She's in the kitchen. She worried it was late."

Simon pushed his way past Ed and moved towards the kitchen where he saw his Fiona curled on a chair, shivering, a blanket draped over her shoulders.

"Honey, what happened? Simon crouched down to her level. "Why are you here and not at Sophie's? What's going on?"

"If I could explain..." interjected Ed.

"I want to hear it from my daughter," Simon snapped.

"Did something happen to you, Fiona? Did Ed hurt you?" Simon glared at Ed as he said this in a state of shock that he should even *make* such a statement about this young man they all admired.

"I'm sorry, Mr. Nesbitt. We were intimate and Fiona got frightened."

Simon stood tall and eyeballed Eduardo.

"Intimate? *Intimate?* What the hell is that supposed to mean? How *intimate?*

"Daddy, it's okay. I'll explain later. Please just take me home. Please Daddy. No more questions. I can't breathe."

"Alright, I've got the cab waiting outside. Ed, you better get your story straight because if you assaulted my daughter, I *will* have you charged for molesting a minor. Do you understand me?" A lion's roar to protect his young, and with clenched teeth, Simon startled at his own fierceness.

"Yes, sir. I never meant to hurt her. We were just cuddling."

"What's that noise?" Simon turned towards sounds rising from the basement.

"Oh, it's just the washing machine. I have my laundry in." Ed muttered, eyes lowered.

Simon gave Eduardo a doubtful look, then gathered Fiona in his arms, picked up the blanket which slipped from her shoulders, took her purse, and walked her out to the waiting cab.

Watching them leave, now alone with his crushed fantasies, guilty thoughts, and his soul-sucking depression, Eduardo acted on impulse.

He ran back to the kitchen, and with violent strength whipped open the utensil drawer. At the clang of stainless steel, he grabbed a carving knife and plunged the sharp blade into his upper chest. He just missed his throat. He collapsed to the floor.

Shocked by the instant clarity of pain, he crawled to his phone which had dropped from his pocket. He pushed *emergency* for 911. *Papai help me* ...floated through his mind. A call to his beloved, deceased father. Then he fainted. Red bubbles mixed with saliva escaped through his nostrils and drooling mouth.

Chapter 61

"But she's single and we need
to find her a partner."

"**S**ugar, you awake?" Quinn's restlessness prompted Virginia to check. He grunted his reply.

"Can we talk then?" she kept a hushed tone.

"What time is it?" he murmured into her neck. "Don't turn on lights, Babe. Just check your phone. On nightstand, eh?"

"Yes, Darlin' – it's ...four-thirty."

"Why aren't you sleeping?"

"Why aren't *you*?" Ginny whispered back. Not waiting for his answer, she continued, "I guess we both have lots on our minds." Then she turned her body left and placed an arm across her man's mid-section.

"I'm getting up," said Quinn. "Washroom." And gently removed her arm.

While he was gone, Ginny turned on the nightlight. Her tap stirred the crystal drops of the silk lampshade. She sipped from her water tumbler.

This family has been through so much lately, but we are survivors. She sighed, then smiled inside. She couldn't help but *love* that girl Frieda *even if* she did arrive to them by way of Quinn's ancient infidelity. *Meant to be.*

Glad the search for Frieda's birthfather finally ended, and in such a surprising way, Ginny now saw her as a real part of this family, forever.

But she's single and we need to find her a partner. New thoughts sparked new ideas. She'd find Frieda the *right* person. Introduce her to people.

Their recent purchase of the multi-tiered townhouse for Frieda brought them all great delight. A new construction. Set on a cliff, high, among treetops. The spacious third-floor deck offered a far-reaching, water-front view. On a clear day, one could spot the horizon's scribbled wavy outline of small towns in New York State. As well, Ginny loved how Naples named this road *Via Chiara Lane.* And only a five-minute stroll from their Forest Street condo, and about a twelve-minute walk to Simon's.

Ginny appreciated the European flavour of these names. She didn't think there were Italians in *her* heritage, but she considered what fun it might be to get one of those DNA tests, check out *what was* in her bloodline. So popular now-a-days, television ads urging folks to trace their roots, discover their genetic families. She knew of the test where you spit saliva into a tube, and send it to *Ireland*, of all interesting places. She just might try it. For fun.

"Wonder how Simon's date went with that mystery woman, Sugar," she said to Quinn as he made his way back to bed.

He moved his body in a dignified manner, posture straight, even at night — his way to fend off feeling *elderly.*

Quinn ignored the gossip. He noticed the duvet flipped back. He paused, reached for his wife's nightdress, raised it above her waist, turned her hip over with his one hand and firmly slapped her exposed, plump butt-cheeks with his other palm.

"Sexy woman," he growled, "stop waking me up when I don't have a hard on – making me crazy, you wench!" Then, he switched off the lamp. And dropped to his side.

From the darkness, in a raunchy tone, Ginny offered, "Can I *help* with that issue?"

"Be my guest!"

Then he added for good measure: "You gorgeous piece of ass!"

With such encouragement, Virginia slipped her nightie over her head and disappeared into the lower regions of her man's anatomy. Her fleshy breasts brushed his inner thighs, as she aimed to please, her lips moist, tongue wet, fine-tuned.

She heard him moaning in ecstasy.

"You're still the hottest wildcat on the planet." This just before he released his juices into her mouth and left some drippings on the lavender-scented silk sheets.

Then he was silent. He pulled his wife's soft, bare frame to stretch fully onto his flat belly, while their arms, legs, even their unwaxed, groin hair, entwined together.

The young kids had nothing on them, he thought. *There's real erotica in our familiarity.*

Miss Portia, not one to be ignored, meowed, and leapt onto the bed. She insinuated herself in there somewhere between her two humans, and curled up, while the grown-ups slept naked in each other's embrace until sunrise.

Chapter 62

"It was bloody tough to get him here."

I t was almost midnight when Lars *texted* Daphne. He avoided a direct call because of her 'date'. He checked her availability, first. Desperate to speak with her about Nils, Lars left this message:

We're OK now! At Credit Valley Emerg. Nils took illegal substance, freaked out. Will be admitted soon to psyche ward.

Daphne texted back: *Phone me!*

Shortly afterwards, with their son transferred to a bed and sedated, Lars called his ex-wife.

"I'm fucking drained, Daphne," he exhaled. "It was bloody tough to get him here. I drove him myself, didn't want EMS to put physical restraints on him, freak him out any more than he already was. Man! What a struggle. I had to slap his face. God, how I didn't want to do that, Daphne. Managed to get a couple of diazepam into him. Had some in the medicine cabinet. Just needed him to settle down a bit."

"Now, that he's admitted," cried Daphne, "what happens *now*?" Panic set in as she pictured her position at school.

"I think he'll be okay in the long run. They'll keep him maybe a couple of weeks."

Daphne burst out with a sob.

Ever the peacemaker, Lars tried to distract her from her fears, so he asked Daphne about herself.

"How was your evening?" He stepped outside so they could speak freely. Some insects buzzed overhead, drawn to the floodlights of the hospital's back patio. "Your date?"

"Oh, for Christ's sake, Lars, it started out simply fine, but it got out of control – I mean the sex part. He wasn't into it and is pissed at me. Shit. What a miserable night."

"That's too bad, Daphne. Looks like it's been a rough night for all of us. My *Tinder* stood me up. I didn't stay out long, just so you know. Came home to Nils, a mess. He's on a 'youth suicide watch' now."

"Oh God, well, if he's admitted and sedated, why don't you go home and get some rest?" suggested Daphne, now slurring, barely able to keep her own eyes open.

"Ya, I think I will do that. Let's meet tomorrow at the hospital." Even late at night, the constant traffic noise in the area made it difficult to listen on a cell phone.

"How did this happen to *our* kid, Lars?" She couldn't let it go.

"We're not the first parents this happened to, Daphne. It happens with teens."

"Oh, but why us?"

Then Daphne decided to end their conversation, "I think I will take a leave from my job ASAP, until Nils gets better. This is not good for my reputation as VP."

She neglected to mention how she drugged her date for sex, a gentleman with a big name in town, with connections, and with teenage twins at her school. She wanted to just fucking disappear.

Her son's medical breakdown appeared as the perfect excuse for an escape.

"But let's talk tomorrow," she finished.

Lars left the hospital feeling worried, lonely, and disturbed how everything turned out. As he drove back to his apartment, it was already past one a.m.

He wept before falling asleep.

About the same time in Naples, Simon, weary and dishevelled, sat in the taxicab with his daughter on their way home from the Delgado place. Simon leaned into the padding to allow room for Fiona to rest her head on her dad's shoulder.

An emergency vehicle with lights flashing and spinning, screamed past them, whizzing in the opposite direction. Followed behind, the piercing siren of a fire engine.

Involved with their own issues, father and daughter startled, slightly. The streets usually quiet this time of night, but, they mused, perhaps some elder suffered a heart attack.

They never imagined the EMS vehicles rushed to the address they had just left.

They spoke in hushed tones, although the driver wore earbuds minding his own business.

"Why were you there, Fiona? Why were you at Ed's? And why was he doing laundry late on a Saturday night with you there?"

"We were interested in each other."

"What do you mean, *interested*? Were you there to help with his laundry? With his mother away, is that why he was doing it on a Saturday night?"

"No, Dad. Com' on! You don't believe *that,* do you? Why don't you just get it over with instead of pretending? Obviously, we had a crush on each other and wanted to spend time together. I'm sorry I lied about being at Sophie's."

"But Fiona, honey, you're barely seventeen, and he's an adult. Did he touch you? "

"No, Dad, no. Not like you think" She hated this lying to her father. But she couldn't get Eduardo into any more trouble.

"Well, what happened, honey, to make you get so upset, cry, and call me?"

"I just got scared being out so late and lying to you. Then I was worried about Prudence because I left her alone in my room. With snacks and water. At least I'm glad I litterbox trained her. She's such a tiny little gem."

Fiona wiped a tear thinking of her precious little Pru.

"And again, Daddy, I hate lying. I care about Ed. He's been through a rough time with his dad dying and his mother taking off with that Beryl and leaving him by himself in the house. He's sad, and I wanted to cheer him up. Then I realized how late it was and I'd be in trouble." She searched for a tissue in her purse feeling worse than before.

"You sure that's all it was, Fiona?"

Fiona couldn't see her father's raised eyebrow in the darkness.

Finally, they were at home. Safe.

For now.

Chapter 63

"All these people, related, who don't even know it."

S aturday evenings often proved to be busy times for doctors and nurses. So, Marjorie delighted in this quality home time with Hazel and Fuyun. Lovely to spend the first weekend of October together.

They began with Scrabble. Fun for a while. Fuyun playfully insisted on the validity of her own word choices. But an hour and a half in, they shut it down. They all wanted to just sit back and chat as girls. Nobody *drinking* tonight either. Babies on their minds!

"He's really moving these days," Margie stroked her belly.

"Why you thinking this baby's a *he* all the time?" Fuyun asked as she loosened the pins from her top bun and let her black hair flow.

"You're right, Fu...it's just my default thought during pregnancy. Maybe this munchkin in here is a girl," said Margie as she adjusted a lumbar cushion behind her back. "Still, I'm glad I didn't want to know the gender. It's more exciting this way."

"Well, we take what we get, too," said Fuyun, the one receiving the IVF hormone injections to conceive a baby with Hazel.

"We sure will, Boo," Hazel leaned into Fuyun and smacked a noisy kiss on her smooth, olive cheek. "How lucky we are to live in these times of medical advancement!"

"And respect for gays to raise a family," nodded Fuyun. "But you so energetic with shot in my bum, Baby," winced Fuyun, with a cute smile to her partner and a playful slap on her arm.

"Imagine that latest news about the doctor who used his own sperm on infertile patients." Margie piped in. "Science fiction come to life! That sounds so gossipy and Frankensteinish, don't you think? All these people, related, who don't even know it."

"Well, *Sistah*, for you that answer will be clear in just a few months. What's your heart say about *your* baby-daddy?"

"I'm trying not to guess, Haze. I do know whose I *wish* it were..." Margie sighed as she raised her pomegranate juice glass.

"You not telling us?" Fuyun narrowed her eyes. "Why not share with us, your family, what you hope for your child."

"I wish this child were Simon's," Marjorie blurted out. "There! I've said it."

Hazel and Fuyun looked at each other, then stared at Margie.

"Did you and Simon have something going on, *after all*, and didn't tell me?" Hazel's dark-coffee eyes shone, and her matching eyebrows shot up.

"Of course, not. You know better than to ask me that, Hazel! Only in my fantasies. Let's change the subject. Tell me more, girls... about your sperm donor."

Chapter 64

"He began a short letter, but it grew a life of its own."

S imon put his shaky daughter to bed. Then, he prepared to pull an all-nighter. The house still, he made coffee. He knew what he *must* do. For his heart's peace, he needed to get real. He had to *act*. Alone. Even his supportive mother couldn't rescue him on this one. Maybe this idea *might* just heal his painful soul.

Seated at his desk, he watched a melon moon linger in a dismal sky. Feeling like a lone wolf seeking his mate, Simon's urge to howl consumed him. He sipped his coffee, set it down.

A window left ajar allowed a breeze and a taste of wet earth from the lake's edge. An owl's hoot underscored his solitude. Years since he suffered such a palpable attack of loneliness. Added worries over Fiona, his humiliation by Daphne, all gnawed his gut.

But this fresh idea arose and curled above him like the gauzy vapour of a genie. Could this magic *actually* work?

With renewed hope, he reached into his desk drawer, and took out the buttery stationery saved for special correspondence. He would *hand-write* a letter. He'd ask her to return. To him. This would take *balls* on his part. He wasn't sure how she'd react.

Being a closet poet, Simon first scribbled a few thoughts to himself:

Without her...I ache
Without me...she thrives
What glow of love will it take?
To finally couple our lives.

Then he began a short letter which grew like untamed vines. He summoned his energy, spilled some tears. The process took hours. He wrote in rough, first. After copying onto the beautiful paper, exhausted, he slipped it back into his desk drawer and left it to mail for the next day.

Simon crawled upstairs to his bedroom with thoughts of installing an elevator in the future. He crashed until the rising sun appeared. He had neglected to draw the drapes. With one eye open, he reached the bedside button to automate closure and slept another few hours.

* * *

Stored inside the desk, Simon's letter released his heartfelt thoughts to Marjorie:

October 4, 2015

Dear Marjorie,
    No... I want to say dearest Margie.
    I have never truly declared myself to you, revealed my feelings. Now, I find the courage to do this. Why now, you might ask? And you would have every right to

wonder. But first I must admit to you that my love for my late wife, everybody's beloved Peggy - and I know you would agree with this - that kind and beautiful person, taken too soon, left me both scarred and scared.

Scared to try anew with anyone else. Scared a new love might be snatched from me... by the whims of fate. Scared of disloyalty to my late wife. However, the scars in my heart have been healing! My heart has felt lighter, with more space to allow a new love to enter. But I felt trapped in the classic 'denial' phase.

I had lately been considering 'dating' and recently had some casual evenings at the gentle urging of the ladies in question, and these experiences only drew my thoughts back to you. You, Margie. I stopped thinking of you long ago as 'just the housekeeper'. There's not a 'just' to it anyway because your presence in this home was invaluable.

No, I take some of that back...'just' actually fits your being here.... just your aura, your smile, your good sense, your scent. Just your warmth and beauty meant everything to me. Forgive me for spilling out my heart to you here.

And furthermore, allow me to apologize, dearest Margie, for my wild and uncouth anger that morning in my office when you told me about your pregnancy. I was a boor who jumped to lascivious conclusions. You were and are a free woman. Your personal actions were and are none of my business.

But here's the catch. You were my business, the business of my heart. I could not admit to myself that I had fallen in love with you. I was inflamed with jealousy when you told me you were having a baby. I had wished it were mine! That's true. I wanted it to be mine. And maybe, it still can? Be mine?

[Simon winced at that part. Too much like a valentine? But left it in.]

Yes. Now I have said it. I am in love with you. Please don't think me a fool who doesn't know what he wants when I say I want you back in this, our house.

Remember that song by Sinead O'Connor? 'Nothing Compares to You?'

That's true about you. That day when Carlos collapsed, you returned to HR, and you brought not only your dinner talents but the warmth of your presence for us all. You felt like a salve, a healing balm. I noticed your gentle touch to Darius, how it soothed him from embarrassment at a comment he made about death and awakening.

That evening as we sat together in the moonlight, I swear I felt both our hearts pounding. I had a magical sexy dream of you that night. Thank you for entering my dream, Margie.

It doesn't matter to me who the father of your child is...what matters is having you here with me, and the kids. I want a chance to hold you in my arms properly, and make love to you, belly, and all, and express my long-suppressed devotion to you. I confess I admired the passion which flashed in your eyes when you told me you were determined to keep your baby! I applaud your decision. And am humbled by it.

You might be thinking have I even considered your side of things? What would be your feelings towards me? I cannot take you for granted, I know. But when you were still here, I felt electricity between us, as well as a deep closeness from the years you spent here — a connection on both our sides.

But you were my so-called 'employee' so neither you nor I ever crossed the line. We were decent people trying to do the decent thing. Am I wrong?

If so, please tell me, and put me out of my misery, darling Margie. I hope I am not being too much here, but you know me best, that I'm a romantic. Forgive me.

I honour you. And I will honour your feelings, whatever they may be. God help me, I pray they might be in the affirmative. If you should say you return my love, dearest woman, I will never let you down. Allow me to prove myself to you.

With my heart's sincerity and fervor,
I remain,
Yours,
Simon

Chapter 65

"Fiona, we're going to talk about last night."

When she awoke, Fiona stumbled into her dad's crumpled bed and cuddled beside him - his baby girl - even at sixteen.

The dogs barked in their distinctive tones as Darius, given a lift home from Jamie's family, slipped off his runners, and bounced up the stairs. He moved straight towards his dad's bedroom and burst through the door.

"Why aren't you guys up? The dogs need breakfast. I fed Charity at Jamie's."

"We had a rough night, son," Simon coughed out, clearing his throat.

Suddenly both kids remembered their dad had some big date last night.

"How did your date go?" Fiona raised herself on her elbow, looked at her dad's darkened, whiskered face. "I forgot to ask."

"Fi, you look crappy, what's going on? You both seem worn out." Darius leaned against the footboard of his dad's bed.

"We'll sort it out this morning," Simon ventured, his tone gravely. "Please feed our dear beasts now, son. I'm going for a shower. You feeling okay honey?" He asked Fiona gently and caught her discreet nod.

"Com' on Dare. I'll go downstairs with you. Just let me grab my hoodie. I have a little shiver. Let dad have his space."

After his shower, Simon arrived in the kitchen, saw his twins scoop cereal from their bowls at the island. The dogs, now fed, lounged, hopeful eyes peeled for any sign which might suggest a *walk*.

"You guys play alone for a while," Simon directed as he opened the lower part of the white verandah door to let the dogs roam safely in the fenced yard.

"Thanks for making coffee, sweetheart," Simon turned to his girl as he poured himself a mug.

He sat with them, legs resting on the lower rims of the stool. He felt like hell. Too much upheaval in such a short time.

"My date didn't work out. That's all I want to say about that. Sorry guys, no juicy info. Fiona, we're going to talk about last night."

Darius looked from dad to his sister, "What happened last night?" green eyes large and curious.

Fiona curled into her stomach. "Do we *have* to? "

"We do, my dear girl," Simon broached tenderly. "You were at Ed's home, not where you said you'd be, at Sophie's, and you called me in distress. WHAT was going on?"

"Holy shit, Fi...really?" from Darius, as he brushed a lock of his red hair back from his face.

"Did you *know* about this, Darius?" from Simon.

"No, Dad. Honestly."

His hand shot up like swearing in court.

As the conversation continued between Simon and his teens at *HR* this Sunday morning, Frieda, still in her apartment, but passionately excited to move soon to her new townhouse, dressed in the black *Nike* jacket and athletic pull-on pants Virginia bought her. She planned a drop-in visit to her *brother's* home. *How nice to have a brother,* she thought. Simon had given her keys and entry code — whatever she might need. She would walk, not jog, avoid a sweat. She tightened the boot laces of her old, black combats, and thought how she loved the kids, and the dogs. Her life now so improved, her heart so full. And she...just so grateful for these unbelievable blessings.

Less than a twenty-minute walk to Hackberry Road, Frieda chose the fresh, lakeside paths, rather than the streets. Wonderful waves splashed the boulders and dissolved over pebbles at the shoreline. She found the Naples' cathedral leafy trees always so amazing.

Finally *living*, she appreciated her good fortune. She found her father, plus gained a brother, niece, and nephew to her now incredible life. And, not least, she lucked out with the kindest stepmother in Mama Ginny.

Not wanting to press his vulnerable daughter too hard, Simon accepted her explanation of Ed being lonely. Ed's offer to pick her up and take her to his house for company seemed plausible. Best friend, Sophie, covered for this change in plans.

They talked too late, Fiona told her father, and she was worried about getting into trouble and that's why she called him. Simon took her at her word and made her promise not to pull this type of covert meeting with an older guy again.

Still shaken from her experience, but relieved the story was out, Fiona hoped the truth would *never* surface.

And Darius changed the subject to talk about the video games he played with Jamie.

Simon's phone binged text mode: he read a message from Dr. Jim Schroeder to drop by on his free morning for some guy time. *Was he around?*

Less than twenty minutes later, Schroeder arrived, bro-slapped his buddy *Igster* on the back. They sat in the family room, stretched out, with more coffee, while the kids played with the dogs outdoors.

"When do you want to do this baby DNA testing, Iggy?" Schroeder asked. "We still have Carlos' DNA stored."

"Well, it's out of my hands now, Jimbo, since Marjorie is living with her sister," Simon suppressed a telling sigh of disappointment.

"I suppose you know," drawled Jim, extending his long legs, "her sister and her partner, Fuyun, the anesthetist, are trying for a baby. Pat Lim told me her daughter was looking for a male donor and had been hinting at *me*."

"What did you say, man?" Simon leaned in, curious to hear of anything to do with Marjorie's family.

"Not me. Nope, I said. But I recommended Alan Banks from MRI – he's a decent dude."

"So, they're going with him, then?"

"I believe so."

"What's his story? Married? Single?"

"Gay. In a relationship. Hard worker, good guy. Might even take a parental interest if his partner is cool with it."

The mudroom door popped open. The men heard footsteps. Into the family room breezed Frieda, her black, edgy short hair, wind-blown. Through full, closed lips she wore a smile of genuine joy.

Schooled in gentlemanly behaviour, both men rose from their seats. They watched, in surprise, as she approached.

"Ah, my sister, Frieda," said Simon to Schroeder. "How nice!"

"I know you not expecting me, but I had desire to spend time with my new family," Frieda spoke in her best English. She hugged Simon as he reached her.

Dr. Schroeder stepped forward, his long neck leading ahead of his shoulders. He extended his lanky arm, and firmly pressed Frieda's hand.

As she touched his flesh an instant current shot between them; the *recognition* of a shared *darkness* in each other created an immediate connection.

He noticed her thin waist and multiple ear piercings.

She admired his buzzed haircut and dark, arched eyebrows above his glasses, his pale skin, thin moustache, and his long slim torso.

His throaty voice which drawled, "Pleasure" held her fixated.

Schroeder had not displayed such gallantry before, thought Simon, as he watched him lead his half-sister to a seat on the scarlet sofa.

The two of them engaged in conversation while Simon excused himself to take a call from Hamish.

"What's up man?" Simon hoped there wouldn't be any more drama today.

"I received a call from your landscaper's son. He's at Credit Valley Hospital and was allowed to phone one person before they placed him on a secure ward. He called *me*."

"Our Eduardo Delgado? Carlos' boy?"

"That's right, Iggy. He pulled a *suicide* attempt last night! Wanted to reach someone who knows you but was afraid to call you. Why?"

"For Christ sakes! He had Fiona at his place last night. He looked unsettled. I picked her up from there when she called me. Holy shit. What happened?"

"Apparently, he tried to stab himself but managed to contact 911. EMS traced the call and brought him to the *Credit*. He's in the psyche ward."

"Jesus, Mary and Joseph!" whispered Simon. "What a fuck-up! He had my daughter. She was a mess." Simon moved to the garage. "I brought her home. Ed seemed weird, but a suicide attempt, I didn't expect."

"Yeah, nor would I," admitted Hamish. "Maybe he went into a deep depression after Carlos' death, even more than we realized."

"And maybe he developed an *obsession* for Fiona! His mother and girlfriend went out west together for some indefinite time. He was living alone, lately. And, Ham, when we left his place, we saw EMS racing in his direction. They were probably going for *him*."

"Is there anything you want?" Hamish hoped for a free Sunday.

"No, man...thanks. I'll drop by the hospital later, see if anybody'll talk to me, or if I can visit him. Appreciate the notice, Ham. You have a late night? "

"We had our usual romp with Gav and Sam. Esther invited our reporter, Aggie. They hit it off, so now she's in our group."

"Good, then. You put your differences behind you. I had a date with the school's VP, Daphne, and she hit on me big time. I think she even drugged me. Feel like shit today. But Schroeder's here this morning, met Frieda. They're inside talking up a storm."

"Schroeder talking? Must be a *thing* now."

"Yeah, Ham. Better not seem rude. Thanks for the update. Catch ya later, buddy."

Simon didn't wait for Hamish to comment on Daphne. Another problem delayed.

Chapter 66

"Everyone obviously hiding something...."

Simon made his excuses, reminded the kids to complete any homework, and at her suggestion left his new sister in charge, with Dr. Jim hanging about for company.

Before leaving, he slipped into his office, placed his *Marjorie letter* into an envelope and tucked it into his sports coat in case he'd lose his nerve. He hoped to drop it in the post along the way.

Simon explained he needed to visit someone from *Nesbitt Holdings* who was hospitalized in Mississauga. Wasn't a complete fib since the Delgado family was still on the payroll. He hoped it wouldn't be long, but they could always call the grandparents to stop by and *order* lunch. He drove away with a peaceful mind about his family; yet soon his stomach tied itself into knots. Eduardo.

What the fuck was that guy thinking? Why would he be suicidal when Fiona had spent time with him? Knowing Fiona's sweetness, you'd think he'd feel comforted. Suicide attempt? Bloody serious business.

After Simon parked at Credit Valley Hospital, he made inquiries which led him to the nurses' station of the ward he sought. As he identified himself, about to state his purpose regarding Eduardo Delgado, Simon looked beyond the nurse.

His eye caught two people down the hallway, backs to him, turn, and walk in his direction.

Holy shit! A cannonball shot through his gut. His knees weakened; he gripped the counter. Heading towards him a fair-headed gentleman in conversation with a woman. Beside the guy, high heels clicking, traipsed *bloody Daphne*! Daphne from last night's fiasco. Daphne, the *dazzling* Vice-Principal of the kids' school. He had to man-up with composure. Fast. They didn't notice him. He shifted his body towards the attendant, positioned his arm and hand to block his face. But when hairs on the back of his neck, tingled, Simon felt the pair upon him.

Ever the actress, Daphne feigned innocuous pleasantry.

"Hello, Simon! What a surprise to see *you* here."

"Well, I could say the same thing." He pulled back, held composure.

A slant of light from the hallway window, exposed Daphne's heavy eyelids.

"This is my ex-husband, Lars," she revealed.

A perfunctory handshake between the men, a hint of sheep-ish discomfort. Everyone obviously hiding something, not want-ing more exposure.

Simon reached for common ground, "How do you know Ed?" he asked.

"Ed? Ed who?" Daphne dropped her phony expression, her curiosity piqued.

"I'm sorry. None of my business," Simon faltered, realized his error.

"Pardon me," he mumbled to Daphne and her ex-husband and turned back to the attendant.

"Can I help you?" Another nurse addressed the couple. "Are you here for Nils?

"Excuse us Simon," Daphne uttered, as she and Lars shuffled towards the sidewall. They spoke in low tones to the nurse about their son.

Then the lock device snapped open. They passed through large steel and glass doors as the nurse led them into the ward.

So, their son is in here, Simon realized. *What sort of bizarre coincidence is this?*

He had overheard, hadn't paid much attention, a time his kids mentioned the VP's son seemed *off the wall*. Thought it might be some cool way of dressing, being different.

He gathered himself and spoke about Ed to the woman in charge. He would be allowed to visit the patient in his room for fifteen minutes.

Next, Simon cleared the same automatic doors as Daphne and her ex-husband to face his late gardener's son.

With a dry mouth, tight throat, Simon felt light-headed. His shoes squeaked on the tile.

What would he say to this son-of-a-bitch? What would he say to this *sick guy?*

Did you fuck my underage daughter?

Chapter 67

"She pronounced his name *Jeem*."

After Simon left the house, proud in her new role, *Aunt Frieda* checked with the teens regarding their plans. Both tired from long Saturday nights, Fiona, and Darius each expressed a wish to chill in their bedrooms. Pets, music, and naps would fulfill their needs. They wondered did Auntie need *them* for anything?

No, she was good.

So, they vanished upstairs. Followed by their furry devotees.

Jim and Frieda felt it. Their magnetic link. Curious about each other, they wanted to pursue more conversation, share more time together. Did not want this visit to end.

"Shall we take a walk?" proposed the bass-voiced Coroner.

"I think would be lovely. Wait. I fill water in dogs' bowls."

"You have keys, and your phone?" he checked.

"Ready." She pushed open the side door, waved him through, and pulled it tight.

They hit the pedestrian path in moments, admiring the boulders, the bluest of skies, and now, a still lake. As the path narrowed and sloped, he took her hand, and *never let it go*. And she, Frieda Reichert, rose from the shadows of a melancholy life.

Doctor Jim wore a beige windbreaker, Frieda, her zipped, black athletic suit.

They began shy. With a fresh-air sniffle, he pulled a tissue from his pocket. Wiped his nose. She hoped he wasn't catching a cold. She laughed, self-conscious, turning aside.

"Let's head for the Lighthouse," Jim suggested, "and the boardwalk."

"Your hand nice and warm, Jim." She pronounced his name *Jeem*.

"Aim to please, *mi lady*." Thrilled with her comment, he could barely hide it.

"So, tell me about your family background, Frieda. Before you arrived here. In fact, I'd love to hear your ancestral story. Everyone has one. I suspect there's more to you than people know. Will you share with me? Whatever you tell me, I'll keep in confidence." Reassuring words from Halcyon Region's Chief Forensic Pathologist as his interest heightened.

Known as a man of few words, Doctor Schroeder held deep thoughts. To most, his usual mode of discourse seemed curt, sardonic. Now, careful not to overwhelm this seemingly tough, but delicate creature at his side, he moved gently.

Like kids, they kicked at colourful leaves. Then took a bench by a droopy maple, under a canopy of rust and gold shapes. Not in any hurry, they relaxed. Frieda's square shoulders dipped with comfort, and she crossed one knee over the other. She felt *safe* in the company of this unique, intelligent man.

"I could tell you about my grandma," she offered through a sunlight's squint."

"Okay, good place to start," encouraged Jim. "In Germany?"

"*Nein*, no! Must be patient, doctor," she pretend scolded. "Not Germany. Ethiopia."

"Ethiopia?" Jim echoed, fascinated, and not hiding it. "Let me see your face again." He turned her chin directly towards himself. He adjusted his black frame glasses and peered at her, more tenderly than he realized. Her eyes, a deep violet, and her skin, soft glints of gold and ivory.

"How well you know history, Jim? Remember Emperor Haile Selassie?"

"Actually, I do. His original name, Tafari, gave rise to the Rastafarian religion. I did pretty well in school, I'll have you know," he teased.

"During *His* time, my grandmother, young black woman in 1950s, worked in capital city, Addis Ababa, in hospital for mothers and babies."

"An obstetrics hospital?" asked Jim.

"*Ja*, she was secretary. Smart one. She was beautiful, too."

"And I see you take after her..." Jim hoped to score some points here, as Frieda continued, more interested herself in her own background, now free to share it.

"So, my grandma, Kamali Alemu, worked in this clinic. Two white doctors, husband, and wife come from New Zealand to run clinic. The man doctor make pregnant my grandmother. Because he shamed of this secret, he planned for my grandma apartment in Paris. He wanted to save his big name – you know, *reputation*, right?"

Jim nodded.

"He had connections in France. She was twenty-two years old and told her family she wanted to model in Paris, and she found a ...how you say? A backer?"

"Yes, a backer, someone to provide for her." Jim clarified. "Go on..."

"In Paris, Kamali become artist's model when she pregnant and after, too. She happy there. She make friends in the Sorbonne through art program. She took the name of instructor, Evald Reichert, like arrangement, but they not marry. So, Kamali have baby girl, *Francine Ingrid Reichert*, my *Mutti*."

"Fascinating, Freddy. May I call you that? My pet name for you?"

"Is okay, Jim. Like pet cat?" Frieda laughed, her hand over her mouth.

"Why do you cover your mouth, Freddy, my pet?" Jim pried gingerly.

"I embarrassed."

"Listen, let me guess, you are worried about how your teeth look when you laugh?"

Frieda dipped her head. "Why you ask this?" She looked to her lap.

"Before I met you, I heard some of your story from Iggy. Of course, he was quite surprised to discover he had a sister. I learned how you suffered with long-term addictions. It must have been *hell* for you." He raised her hand to his lips and gently kissed her fingers. "This happens with long term drug use," he continued. "But it can be fixed, and I'm sure, as we speak, Ginny is setting up appointments with orthodontists for you."

Given *that* image, they both burst out with a huge laugh, aware of Virginia's well-known stature as an adorable 'fixer' of problems. Now their perfect icebreaker.

"And one more thing," explained Jim, "in *my* line of work, I see everything! Not easily shocked." And he changed the subject and the mood.

"Let's get up and walk some more. And you continue your story."

"Okay, but what about your story, Doctor Jim?"

He stretched his arms and long legs and helped Frieda up as a gallant gesture. Over a small hill and some cobbles, they shuffled ahead through the grass and some brilliant cranberry leaves.

"Two times divorced, no kids." Jim offered as his profile.

"Sorry" said Frieda. "You unhappy?"

"No, not at all. Things just didn't work out. I take life as it comes. I spend a lot of time at my work, examining the reason people die. Maybe add something to the scientific world while I'm at it," he drawled.

They reached the boardwalk. Sunbeams glammed up the lake like a pro's skating rink. Jim held Frieda's hand tighter, as they made their way to the white and red tower at the end of the walkway. He watched a woman ahead allow her toddler dash around, could easily fall in, and it worried him. He felt there should be side barriers. He didn't like to examine deceased children. A softness in him he kept to himself. Not many people knew of his little brother who died of a brain tumour at age four. Children were sacred.

And just as quickly, the child stumbled over a small boulder. Jim lunged for him and hung on. The mom, on her phone, still unaware, had not yet turned around.

"Hey" he shouted ahead.

The boy screamed, feeling assaulted by a stranger.

The mother ran back.

Jim released the child. "He tripped, lost his balance."

The woman's guilt showed on her face. She managed a thanks, pulled her kid away, her head down, humiliated, as the child howled being squeezed and scolded.

"Let's turn back," suggested Jim. "I mean just to the coffee shop, not home yet."

Frieda put her arm around his thin waist and pulled her own boney hips to match his.

"You good man, Jim. I am happy to walk with you. And café is okay. Let's go."

Chapter 68

"I feel still I am dreaming."

S imon arrived at the hospital prepared to give Eduardo proper shit. But, despite his anger, his distress dissolved. A surge of innate empathy flooded him instead. Overwhelmed, he swallowed hard at the sight of this broken young man. Lying in a bed, chest bandaged, and visibly sedated. He kept his comments short and comforting. Simon would not press this vulnerable guy. He wished Ed a full recovery, followed by an arm squeeze, and some head stroking. He promised to visit again, soon.

Carlos' son, after all. Family.

Leaving the hospital room, Simon told himself: Just one thing. Ed could *not ever* know the information he would still extract from his daughter. And he would get to the truth of what happened at the Delgado house between those two.

* * *

Frieda and Jim agreed to take their coffee as a carry-out from *Second Cup*. This notion would save time. She didn't want to be away too long from Simon's in case the kids needed her. They probably wouldn't call, thinking she had an informal 'date' with Dr. S.

"Maybe we could take walk to my new townhouse – not far from here," offered Frieda. "Mama Ginny and Papa Quinn bought so beautiful place for me. I feel still I am dreaming. I move next week. I need furniture. Maybe you have ideas for me, Jim?"

"I think I can make time for you, Freddy," joked Doctor Jim. "But now finish your story. We left off when your mama was born – your *Mutti*."

Happy to be able to show her new best friend at least the outside of her new home for now, Frieda wanted to focus on Jim until they got there.

"No, your story now, Jim," she urged.

"Well, if you insist..." he uttered, secretly delighted to share any revelations with someone that matters.

"So, you told me, Jim, you at boarding school with Simon. Why boarding? Why not school in city?" She looped her free arm through his. Felt snug, natural.

"I was born and raised in downtown Toronto. My parents travelled a lot for work. My mom was an engineer and dad, an architect. They designed projects together, commercial buildings in Ottawa, and Vancouver. So, boarding school was the place for me."

"Were you much lonely?" She looked up at him. They were crossing the *Sixteen Mile River* bridge — marina now empty of boats for the season. The water view ahead extended from muddy brown to pristine blue and stretched to infinity. The wind picked up, fluffed Frieda's bangs and with forehead exposed, brought a softness to her face.

He stopped their steps. Sipped his coffee.

"Yes, at first. But I got used to loneliness, Freddy. And the upside is I made great, lifelong friends, like your brother Simon and his parents, who had me to the house many weekends. Made me feel like family. You know *who* ..." and they looked at each other and shouted, "Virginia!" They raised their paper cups to this wonderful person.

They turned the corner across from Quinn and Ginny's condo to head south, further towards lakeside. Then Jim wanted to return to Frieda's background.

"So, tell me more about your mom and your grandma Kamali."

"My *Mutti* finished Flight Academy, was flight attendant for airline and my grandma died of stomach cancer. I was about ten years old. We so sad."

"Well, let's back up a bit," said Jim. "Your mom was born in Paris, right?"

"*Ja.*"

"Well, how did your grandma do with her modelling and her Mr. Reichert?"

"Good question, Jim. *Mutti* told me that grandma had best friend at art school. *Fleur*. And Evald was nice, but he killed in motorcycle crash. Leave only small money."

"So, grandma finished raising your mom, Francine? And your mom became what was then called, a Stewardess? And when did you come along?"

"I know *now* she met man from when she flight attendant, in Paris; she tell me *nothing* about him. Only his *Mutti* live in Paris, and he go visit her.

Jim's brain over-coffeed, unyielding. He dug in a bit more.

"Your grandma had a good French friend called *Fleur*? Beautiful name, fairly popular, I understand."

"*Ja*, she come to grandma Kamali's funeral. It was not much. But some people did visits."

"And you were about ten years old when grandma died?"

"*Ja*, why you ask so many details, doctor of deceased people?"

"Deceased? Your English is improving, Freddy. And because you *interes*t me, young lady." He kissed her cheek.

Frieda touched her face where Jim left a kiss, and said, "In Vancouver, *deceased* was word I hear a lot. Thank you for kiss, Jim."

"Of course, how ignorant of me. Just teasing, not trying to patronize."

"And I understand word, *patronize,* too. Why you so *interest* in me, Jim?

"Because you are a genuine person, Freddy. Real. And the kiss...my pleasure. No need to thank me for my delight." Then, he looked down, almost embarrassed.

"I know *genuine* means. You are genuine to me too, Jim." She turned, made eye contact, and felt her tummy flip. In a huge, good way.

But what was that exchange? Our first fight? A silly thought which both considered, but quicky dismissed.

Rather, this verbal exchange suggested an emotional connection of pure acceptance, and warmth. The latter, a rare experience for them both.

They now stood in front of her new house. High-branched golden and green elm leaves hid part of the A-frame rooftop. Wine-colored smaller Japanese maples to the side. Stout brick-red posts connected by black, wrought iron mini fences, stood as guards before the path to the front door.

"Look, only two neighbours, on this side," the introvert in Frieda enthused.

"And a tiny forest on the other," added Jim with cheer. Maybe you'll spot a coyote. Would that worry you?"

"I think not. I like to see nature."

"What a beautiful area. I'm so happy for you, Freddy."

Jim's usual gruffness dissolved around Frieda.

He strode partway down the common car port, excited with this layout as well as the townhouse. "I like this spacious alleyway, too, Freddy; you can see the bay ahead, so transparent."

She trailed him.

"I'll help you with the move." Jim said, over his shoulder. He wanted her to need him.

Now edged at Jim's side, Frieda paused, and gazed into his deep-set hazel eyes.

Then, she reached up on her toes, and whispered in his ear. "Thank you, *danke* dear Jimi," (which she pronounced Jeemee).

She felt valued.

And he sensed it.

Soon they tossed their cups into the city's recyclable container. They took a few phone photos of the house and of the short woodland street, itself: *Via Chiara Lane.*

Then they embraced. Jim spread his arms, like large wings, around Frieda. She wrapped hers about his waist. They enjoyed a tight, full-on hug before turning back.

They believed they could very well be a natural fit for each other. Each felt *seen* by the other. Felt understood. Felt respected. Even felt deeply *wanted.*

Like rare birds who mate for life, Jim, and Frieda, given their dark, eccentric backgrounds, wouldn't have a problem identifying as the loving, *human* version of the Black Vulture species. Together forever.

Chapter 69

"No earthquakes, only life quakes."

"**D**ad! You're back!"

Fiona set her guitar on the sofa and slid across the tiles to greet her father. She cuddled into his arms, her nervous system still fragile from last night.

"Hi baby girl. What are you guys doing?"

"We're composing," Darius filled in from the piano bench.

"A duet?" asked Simon. "Brother and sister thing?"

"That's the idea. Remember those in your day, Dad?"

Simon loosened his tie, "Donnie and Marie Osmond? Or maybe *The Carpenters*?"

"Something like that. We want to give it a shot, right, Fi? We looked up the *Carpenters* on *YouTube*. They were great. We'd like to be like them, even better."

"Wonderful ambition, guys," said their dad, happy to lend support.

After he released his hug on Fiona, Simon looked around for signs of Frieda.

"Where's your auntie? Did she go home?"

"They went for a walk. A long one," said Fiona.

"They?"

"Doctor Jim and Auntie Frieda," bellowed Darius, as he continued tapping piano keys.

"Oh, well that *is* interesting, indeed," Simon reflected to the room, including his pal Kent who tail-wagged his way forward.

The twins returned to their music creativity as Simon trudged upstairs to change. Kent joined him for moral support. Exhausted from lack of sleep and the bloody secrets he'd chalked up - about his date with Daphne, then the Eduardo fiasco, and now Daphne's kid with some issue too. He also needed to know if Fiona and Ed had sex. But how could he press his daughter on such a delicate topic without her freaking out?

To curb overthinking, negative vibes, Simon now evaluated everything *good*. He grinned thinking of Frieda and Jim out together. Seemed intriguing.

Glad he sent the letter to Marjorie. Glad he had the greatest two kids in the world. Pleased he even had a sibling now. Decent buddies, and the best parents. Focus on the bright side. No earthquakes, only *life quakes*. He'd heard that expression somewhere. Maybe Margie will *accept* him, a charming term from the olden days. *But sleep would be the best right now*, he thought. And then his cell chimed.

"What's up, mother dearest?" he teased.

"Just wanted to check on plans for the twins' birthday coming up."

"We'll have a family dinner, Mom. Next year is their biggie. Low key it this year with all that's been happening. By the way, did you know, sis Frieda is on a jaunt with Jim? Apparently, they are hitting it off."

"Well, that's just wonderful, Sugar! *You* sound tired though. You okay?"

"Nothin' a nap wouldn't cure." Simon brushed off his *issues. Why bother his mother with a lot of confusion.*

They said their goodbyes, and in tee shirt and boxers, he crashed on his bed. Kent slipped in beside him.

They had twenty minutes of sweet slumber as soft tunes wafted up from the family room. Small chunks of peace. Grateful for these precious moments.

Chapter 70

"I have something important to tell you."

Returning to Simon's house, Jim, and Frieda, caught in the glow of feeling like a *couple*, chose the same scenic, romantic route back. They dashed through the park-woods rather than stroll the village sidewalks. Their intensified conversation, which focused on discovery of the other, took priority.

"You live in Naples, too, Jimi?" Frieda thought how odd she didn't yet know.

"Well, yes, Freddy. I'm in Bronte Village, just west of here. I like it because it's close to the Halcyon Region Health Centre and Hospital."

"Oh, *ja*, Bronte. Nice area. Mama Ginny take me there for shopping, and hair salon. And you in a house, Jimi?"

"I have a fifteenth-floor condo, also looks to the lake. Great view. I'll take you to see it real soon, Freddy," said Jim, renewed excitement in his voice. "Very modern, all windows." His effort to impress her that being single he didn't live in somebody's basement.

"We so lucky people, Jimi. I can't believe changes in *my* life."

"Why did you and your mother leave Paris?" Jim prodded. They had passed the Aberdeen Museum and were headed towards the water.

"After grandma Kamali die, something happen at Mutti's work and she leave Air France, and we move to Germany. I learn to speak German fast, call my mother *Mutti* like other kids. We lived in Frankfurt. She then work for Lufthansa. But was accident. And you know she die some years later of aneurysm."

Jim, holding her hand, pressed it gently.

"You've been through more than anyone should, Freddy," he consoled. "But I have a necessary question for you about your past.

"Who came to grandma Kamali's funeral again? You were telling me..."

"Her best friend, Fleur, bring man, husband, I think — big guy with red hair. You know I was just kid then, so long ago, Jim, but his name sound funny. That's only why I remember. He called something like *shameless*. Funny name, right, Jimi?"

Still gripping Frieda's hand, his heart pounding, and sensing dampness under his armpits, Jim pulled her quickly towards a vacant table he spotted, just beyond the children's playground. Plenty of parents around, pushing kids on swings or playing catch ball.

"We need to sit down for a minute Freddy," he said, slightly out of breath. He led her to an old wooden picnic table, with attached benches, chipped and stained from years of use.

"You okay, Jimi?" Frieda worried he now seemed unwell, pale. Something wrong with Jim.

"You look like people say somebody see ghost, Jimi. I am scared."

They sat across from each other. Frieda's back to the lake. She focused on Jim's face without distraction, saw his worry lines, and his expressive eyebrows.

He leaned in, held both her hands, which, covered by his large palms, practically disappeared. "I have something important to tell you, Freddy, dear girl."

The wind from the lake shrouded them. Children's laughter diminished to a faded echo.

Now she fought a familiar sense of dread in her gut. *What would Jim say to her?*

Then suddenly, she ducked.

A soccer ball flew at them. Jim raised a long arm to stop it. Fisted it back to the embarrassed lad and offered a hand-wave of understanding dismissal.

"You scare me, more now, Jimi. Did something happen? Did I say something wrong?"

"No. No, no no...you are *everything* that's right and beautiful, Freddy. Let me touch your face, look at you some more."

He cupped her small face, now, and said, slowly, to this innocent woman who'd suffered so much over the years, "You are an heiress."

"What *air is*? What you talking about?" *Heiress* was not a word in Frieda's lexicon.

"Freddy, the good people who came to your grandma Kamali's funeral, who had been her friends, are also *your own grandparents*." He stressed that last word.

She pulled away. Breathless.

"Jim! You must explain. I am so confused!"

"Tell me, first, do you remember Fleur's last name?"

"I think it was Chance, something like that."

"Would you say, she was Fleur La Chance?"

"*Ja, das ist* Fleur! *Ja.* She lovely. Hugged me."

"She's your *other* grandmother. I've *met* her! She and her husband Seamus are the parents of Quinn, your real father. They are the grandparents of Simon, too. Both of you."

Frieda's eyes widened. "*Mon Dieu!* my grandma Kamali would say. *Mon Dieu!*"

"Both your grandmothers, Kamali and Fleur *knew* each other, were friends! How cool, lovely is that? And Seamus Nesbitt, which I guess you thought sounded like *shameless,* your grandfather, is a Scottish- Gaelic name for James, my own name too, but mine is the British version."

"Jim?" Frieda repeated, *dazed*, "is James, too?" She felt disoriented. An out of body experience, heat flushed at her temples.

Her silver earrings jiggled as she shook her head in shock at Jim's news. Not about his name, but rather, Frieda was absolutely astonished by the *greater* statement, and *implication* of just who her own relatives were!

Excited for her, Jim continued.

"Seamus was a wealthy shipbuilder. They built the house Simon lives in today. That's why I said you are an heiress. Like a princess. This is *your* family and birthright. Your time has come. We have to share this information with Simon. And Virginia. And Quinn, of course."

"You kidding, Jimi. How you *know* this is true?" Her voice raised, Frieda shivered from lake chill, and from this unbelievable, bizarre information. Her anxiety increased.

"Because I'm telling you, Freddy, I *met* her - Simon's French grandmother when I visited the house as a teenager. She told me stories about her beautiful apartment in Paris' Left Bank. In the Fifth Arrondissement of the Latin Quarter. She talked a lot about it. She returned there often, especially after her husband died. I'll bet Simon and Quinn know about Kamali, too, or at least heard of her."

Frieda left her seat on the bench and ran around the picnic table to circle Jim's neck. She leaned into him and hung on. Despite her firm grip, Jim turned his head to face her. He moved a leg over the bench to make room for her. She sat and shifted her hips to meet his lap's curved space. She trembled. A ray of sunlight split through the trees which added glow to Frieda's already burning cheeks. She felt giddy and she wanted to crawl inside of Jim's soul where she would feel safest.

Oblivious to their surroundings, they held each other.

"I need your tissue," she cried.

He fumbled in his pocket and withdrew a piece.

"That's a lot of news to absorb. I'm here for you, Freddy, sweetheart."

Frieda melted in his kindness.

And Jim simply loved how she evoked his emotions. Thus far, tender feelings remained hidden to others —his heart's secrets masked by his *tough guy* image.

Playful, they hugged, snuggled into each other's necks. Pheromones trailed. For Jim, she carried the essence of lilacs and vanilla.

For Frieda, he exuded a sexy tang of male sweat, mixed with a whiff of leather.

As they pulled back their shoulders and admired each other, their eyes revealed tender passion. Feelings intensified. Ignited hearts pumped strong. Relatives faded.

Jim tapped her lips with his and suckled them. A tingling sensation descended Frieda's body, slid past her belly to settle in her heated, most private of places. Swollen with longing, she surrendered to the aching moment as a burst of endorphins shot throughout her anatomy stronger than any ingested drug. She felt sexy, seduced, but mostly, she felt loved.

Together Jim and Frieda sealed a bond with their sumptuous kiss. This type of love, seemingly premature to the naked eye, mattered not, since they *recognized* the moment for what it was: *something grand, sensuous*, and real.

Lost in their own romantic, spinning globe, they explored their mouths. Juicy, eager tongues intertwined. Stabs of pleasure pierced their insides and deep yearning offered comfort. Sheer joy.

A *love match* only found in gushy romance novels. They were *home* to each other. Although neither one a person of Faith, this intense attraction seemed a deal-breaker, a *Godsend*! They could almost become *Believers*.

Chapter 71

"The name would suit either gender."

Last month when Marjorie received Simon's handwritten letter, she swooned. She felt girly. She also believed his sincerity. He wanted her, regardless that she's carrying another man's child. He wanted her as *his* woman, as the love in his life, no longer just the housekeeper. This felt good. To be *desired* by Simon.

Yet, Marjorie needed to think this through. She loved Simon but was she *in love* with him now that he declared himself to her? They never had an opportunity to romance one another. They never got to flirt, or date. Now she was having a baby - not even his. This new reality called for further consideration on both their parts. She wasn't a woman who would just come running. She felt strength in her own being, capable to achieve, raise a child, find another position. Had she been taken for granted? A whirlwind of thoughts spun in her head. Yet, she was practical. Simon would have to do *more* than beg her to return to his house. What would it take for him to prove himself? His romantic gesture of a snail-mail love-letter, although sweet, didn't quite cut it with her anymore. She would wait and see.

Earlier, when the girls were at work, Marjorie sat at the dining room table in their cozy condo and flipped open her laptop.

With a mug of black mint tea and her reading glasses balanced on her nose, she replied to Simon by email.

With her left hand she stroked her round belly. She smiled to herself because she had one name ready whether the baby would be a girl or a boy. The name would suit either gender.

She also had another secret.

She looked up through the glass patio doors. Nostalgia swept over her. Today's windy forecast had indeed blown some fall leaves onto the balcony chairs. *Back home,* as she definitely considered Naples, one always expected a magnificent, multi-coloured leafy display surrounding *H.R.*

Margie longed for the freedom of nature. The city of Toronto, exciting as it was to many visitors, just didn't do it for her. But she knew life didn't always hand you your dreams. A struggle often precedes any sort of real happiness.

Of one thing she was sure – she was happy to be expecting a baby. At this stage of her pregnancy, six and a half months in, she didn't care anymore who the father could be, merely curious. She could handle this kid on her own.

But now, here was Simon declaring his love for her. Hadn't this been her dream for years? How had this changed? *Had* it changed? Wasn't she just telling Hazel and Fuyun she wished the baby to be Simon's? She did need a future for her child, but was that reason enough to encourage Simon's affections?

She began a draft copy of her letter, composing thoughts as she typed…then she re-read her email to Simon and hit *send.*

To: SIN@yahoo.com
From: Marjorie Wallace
Date: November 2, 2015
Subject: re: Your Lovely Letter

Hello Simon,

Sorry for my delay in answering. We all needed space to digest so many happenings.

Your letter, breath-taking in its wholeheartedness, is so YOU. Being your housekeeper for six years, don't I know what a wonderful man you are!

You've never been one to pull punches with your candor. And dear man, I am flattered by your words, believe me, my head is spinning.

Yet, I am somewhat surprised by your message. That you say you are *in love* with me.

I wonder...since you feel emotionally ready now to date after Peggy, that if some dates don't work out, am I your 'fall back on' person? You *did* say you had been seeing other women, right?

I miss the kids, **a lot**, & hope they are happy, and eating well – please give them my love and hugs. Would enjoy hearing more details about them when you find the time.

I may *call you,* soon. There's something *more* expanding in my life these days, as well as my bouncing baby...no hints just yet!

Perhaps we can meet as friends and just chat for now, Simon.

With love,
Marjorie xx

Chapter 72

"They would not go to the police…"

D aphne Jorgensen requested family medical leave from the school board and relinquished her position as acting vice-principal. A bit of tough luck. Yet, she had relief —she would no longer have to face the humiliation of seeing Simon's children, or worse, deal with *him*! After all, he treated her like some *rapist* after they returned from their dinner date at *Vesuvius*. *The nerve of him!*

Grateful to avoid the Nesbitt family, Daphne found work with on-line teaching. Eventually, after Nils completed his health program, she would get him some home-tutoring. Better for him to avoid the troublemakers at school.

Daphne was truly glad for Lars who befriended a university colleague at an art exhibit. A professor of Italian Studies, Silvia Cappelli had a teenage boy, too, and offered comfort and understanding when dealing with a distressed youth.

As for the school musical at WCSS, a few staff members stepped up to hold it together. The grateful students continued to show plenty of enthusiasm and displayed savvy singing and dancing skills. Not to mention many teens of this community proved to be blessed with great acting chops!

Alas, a traumatized Fiona dropped out of the school show. She missed her *Period*. Experienced nausea and fatigue. As a best friend, Sophie urged her to take a pregnancy test. "*So easy to do these days, Fi,*" she encouraged.

Shocked by a *positive* result, Fiona knew she had to tell her dad. Soon. Although scared to death of this decision, she trusted in his love to support her.

Through contacting Beryl's father, Simon learned how to reach Albina and Berri. He updated them on Eduardo's health and his hospital stay of several weeks - until his nervous system improved. He played down any suicide attempt. They could find more information themselves, upon return.

Once home, Albina invited Beryl to move into her house while Ed stayed in hospital. The nature of their relationship remained unclear to outsiders. However, Berri did not find her mother during the Vancouver trip. What *was* clear, the romantic relationship between Ed and Berri was over.

Eduardo and Nils became friends through group therapy sessions at the hospital. They soon discovered they had *people* in common. Nils respected Ed and his love for his late father. He decided he would make changes towards his own dad, whom he came to understand as a kind, caring, decent guy.

But what surprised Ed and Nils most, occurred during their private conversations. They realized they had both lusted after the same girl – Fiona Nesbitt. And both agreed neither one of them would be right for her. They might even be out of her league.

When she came to him in tears with her dilemma, Simon held his daughter tightly. He discussed the pros and cons of an abortion with her. His feminist soul, borne from his mother Virginia, spoke to protection of the young woman's body and rights, first, while the pregnancy was still in the embryo phase. He worried his daughter would face disgrace, or stigma should she be forced to have a baby at seventeen, in high school, and unmarried. He offered his parental tenderness so Fiona would not suffer the shame of a teenage pregnancy.

They agreed to a termination and to keep this strictly to themselves. Not even Grandma Ginny would know. It would be their secret.

Upon reflection, Simon found a huge solace when his daughter came to him: she trusted in his protection. He remembered a school chum's agony years ago when the lad's girlfriend tried to induce her own abortion and bled to death. His friend had no knowledge of the pregnancy until it was too late. Such a tragedy.

Besides, Fiona would have a proper lover when she was *ready.* She would have a baby when she was *ready.* With these thoughts, Simon counted his blessings.

They agreed to forgive Eduardo in their hearts because he seemed to lose reality after the death of his beloved father. Yet, his punishment for seducing underage Fiona, even though he imagined himself *in love,* would be never to know of this pregnancy or of her decision to stop it.

With such thoughts, father and daughter decided they would not go to the police but would expect Ed to receive help from the psychiatric therapy given him at the hospital.

Chapter 73

"Who *were* these people?"

O n the ground level foyer of her luxurious condo, and cozy in her cranberry lounge outfit, Virginia collected her daily mail. She greeted the newly hired lobby security— a young Black man —with her upbeat, 'good-afternoon!'

Handsome fella, she thought to herself, noting how crisp and smart the white shirt of his uniform looked against his dark complexion. Her brilliant smile left them both with a warm buzz.

In the elevator to the Penthouse, she shuffled the pieces of mail, not expecting anything special *today*, but there it was — already in her hands. The Ancestry DNA envelope. She had forgotten she even sent for this!

Sitting on the edge of her sofa, the mail torn open, Ginny rocked her body as she texted Quinn. Since he was at the Club, she didn't call. Just: "Come home NOW! The DNA results here."

Portia fluffed her tail, took up and down sofa leaps, noting atmospheric change.

Virginia wept. Joy, sorrow, an unimagined history of relatives, her people.

No disappointment on her part. Just a revelation so unexpected, she ran to the storage closet of souvenirs, and dragged out the ancient photo albums to see what might make sense to her. Who *were* these people? Old black and white photographs. Her father never explained because she never found these albums until after his death. She didn't *know* these people. Would she know them now?

Quinn reached home quickly.

This condo, closer to the Club than their former home on Hackberry Road, made for a shorter walk. The Lakeshore bridge blew windy, but with an upturned collar, cap and scarf, Quinn much enjoyed the fresh-air jaunt to *Twelve Forest Street.*

Now, the DNA results preoccupied him.

He could *hear* her voice in Ginny's high-pitched text, in those few typed words. A bit of acid flushed up his oesophagus. Would the news be pleasant or disturbing? He'd deal with whatever arose. He was her man, and he would protect her forever. A lump thickened in his throat: *my Virginia, my love.*

Quinn found his wife flushed, cheeks pink and with a glass of white wine, still early in the day. This had to be *something.* He shed his outerwear and tossed it on the hallway bench. Went to her.

"Darlin', oh my darlin," Ginny pulled her husband down to the couch and embraced him.

"Did you *know any* of this? Did you?" she insisted. She flipped pages of an album and pointed to old photographs of well-dressed Black people, not servants.

"God, no, Baby!" Quinn replied. "How would *I* know your family's history?"

"Remember, Sugar, your father and my daddy were great friends! Maybe they held secrets?"

"We only dealt with white people, not coloured," Quinn clarified, as fascinated as his wife.

"I knew so much about my daddy's side of the family," Ginny added, "but almost nothing from my *Mama's* side! Seems Mama had Black ancestors! Oh, Quinn, that means I am African American. Imagine that. Like President Obama! I am from a race of people proud and talented." Then Ginny looked into Quinn's blue eyes, and said, "but also oppressed and abused!"

"Alright, sweetheart," Quinn held his woman. "Let's let it all sink in. Let's look through this report and examine the names - see who's who from your father's albums here."

"Do you recall, Darlin', I told you Daddy said when I was three, I sat in the lap of his great aunt who became a nun... she was in her nineties when I met her, and I was too young to remember. Daddy told me how on her seventeenth birthday she sat in the Ford Theatre and witnessed the horrible assassination of President Lincoln. And my daddy was named after him."

"Of course, I remember," Quinn stroked his wife's cheek with tenderness.

"Sarah-Jane. Look this must be her, don't you think?" Ginny pointed to an old sepia print. "Even the white people look brown in these old photos. Their haunted eyes."

"Now check the names on Mama's side. Mama was a Portman?" Ginny looked confused.

"I think it's by marriage," Quinn searched with his finger reading the information.

"Appears Justine Roberts - later Portman, was the great, great granddaughter of Minister Ebenezer Roberts who was a runaway slave. He made it to Ontario and preached at the *African Methodist Episcopal Chapel* on Lakeshore Road, in Naples."

"What??" They cried in unison reading this aloud.

"That's the little building around the corner, Quinn! The Spencer family's antique shop! Used to be an old church for the Black community. How many times we read that plaque on the side of the building, ourselves. Oh, dear lord, he was one of my ancestors - the Black minister." Ginny was almost shrieking with shock and joy.

"Look, my Mama's daddy was Chikelu Roberts, a Black man from Ontario."

"I see your eyes in him," offered Quinn.

"You know, I do too. I also see Simon. A Black Simon in his great granddaddy, Chikelu."

Chapter 74

"More connected to the universe now..."

Initially, the news of his Black ancestry shocked Simon. He pressed his mother to his chest, then held her at arms' length and gazed deeply into Virginia's eyes. As if caught in some motion picture design to transport time, he saw a tunnel of decades swirl by, an unbelievable past which led from himself through centuries of a complex heritage.

Now he checked any mirror searching for signs. Overwhelmed with this information, Simon told his parents he felt special - in a good way – proud, and even hip. Black people had made so many inroads for themselves over the last decades, and even a Black president in Obama, one of his heroes, as Mandela had been.

His heart lifted with thoughts of Black contribution to the world: the extensive music genres, from classical, vocals of soul, jazz, reggae, rap. The *amazing* athletic stars, the creative world of Black actors, writers, and scientists, as well. He was now part of the that club, or lineage. What a fantastical experience to learn about oneself. And the woman he was in love with, coincidently, biracial too, with a Black father, and white mother.

Simon just felt more connected to the universe now. He had *diversity* in his genes.

However, Marjorie's email, slow in coming, brought him down to earth. She wasn't buying his love news. He saw her as a strong woman who wanted to be sure she was loved for herself. Not some *fall back on* person. Although, a bit embarrassed she had come to this conclusion, he got that. He'd meet with her and woo her. Start again as friends, then maybe sweethearts.

Not exactly *thriving* at school, his kids managed to stay on top of assignments and avoid trouble. They kept to their semester schedules, glad to be focused on academics in their final year.

His sister, now coupled with his loveable, idiosyncratic friend, *Jimbo,* proved to be an asset to the family, helped the kids with language courses, in French, and German.

His parents defied old age, still fondling each other, proud of their PDA. In fact, they boldly displayed it like some prize they had all to themselves.

Life was good.
Except for one thing. He wanted his woman.

Chapter 75

"You're not going to believe this!"
"Nor will you!"

O nce the Nesbitt's got used to their exciting family tree, Virginia urged Frieda to send in her own DNA. She wanted Frieda to discover the roots of her white grandfather in New Zealand, the doctor who impregnated Frieda's grandmother Kalani, in Ethiopia, then set her up in Paris. What *more* was there to *that* story? Did he have other children who would have been half- siblings to Frieda's mom? They would be Frieda's relatives, aunts, and uncles. She might even want to meet them. A trip Frieda and Jim might take on holiday to that beautiful part of the world. Ginny would get her on it!

November 14th was a bright, fall Saturday, and Marjorie just couldn't *wait* to share her news with Simon. As the gals were at work, she had the condo to herself. She hinted in her last email that along with her sweet baby, (who was quite the kicker these days) other things were happening, too.

She felt these changes taking place would enhance her life, and bring her closer to Simon and his kids, again. She sure missed them. So, now— she called him.

At this time, Simon sat at his home office desk, overlooking papers for *Nesbitt Holdings*. Fiona cozied herself in the soft swivel chair, feeling close to her daddy, as she read a French novel for school. Curled on the floor in front of the window, Kent and Prudence snoozed by Fiona's blanketed feet.

Out with buddies, Darius, had taken Charity with him for a run.

On this lovely, fall morning, the house remained still. Breathlessly quiet.

Floating musical notes: Simon's cell chimed. Startled the room. They all jumped from their peaceful, resting positions. Simon looked up at his iPhone in its stand and saw Marjorie's name on the display.

"Well, hello dear lady. Lovely surprise to hear from you. Just in the office with Fiona. Okay if I put you on speaker?"

(*Wow. Marjorie almost forgot how warm and sexy Simon's deep voice sounded.*)

"Of course! Hi sweetie" Margie directed to Fiona. "How's school? And Pru?"

Kent and Pru stirred, ears perked at this familiar voice.

"Great, Margie. Happy to hear from you, too!" Fiona made round eyes at her dad.

"So, you're *not* going to believe this, guys," said Marjorie to them, "but I have some big news to share!" She took a sip of her raspberry herbal tea and prepared herself.

"Nor will you!" Simon announced, concealing a chuckle.

"Nor will I *what*?"

"You're not going to believe *my* news, either. So, great timing for sharing! But *ladies first.* Go ahead, Margie. Let's hear it!"

"*Ready* for this?" she teased.

"Well, don't keep us (a glance to Fiona) in suspense much longer. Are you inviting me to guess?"

"Okay, go for it," laughed Margie.

"You're having twins?"

"Ha, ha, an interesting guess, Simon, but no cigar!" She enjoyed the joking.

"Well, go ahead then, we're getting anxious." Simon antsy, even a bit nervous now.

"I'm moving to Naples."

She heard Fiona shout, 'YAY!'

"**What**? Am I hearing you right? Should I spruce up, redecorate the apartment?" Simon locked eyes with Fiona as they both held their breath and raised their eyebrows.

"Oh, dear man, I have to quit leading you in the wrong direction. Hazel and I bought a *house* in Naples! She'll stay in the condo with Fuyun because of their jobs. Oh, and by the way, they are pregnant, too. "

"How wonderful," Simon enthused, and Fiona clapped her hands, "but what's this about a *house*?"

"We bought it together from our parents' inheritance, but only *I* am moving in – with the baby, of course. I'm also planning to have my baby in the Naples hospital. So, I'll be moving as soon as possible."

"Wow, I can't believe this Margie. It's *huge* news!"

"Let me tell you more. I'm so excited about the house. The front verandah has so much old-fashioned charm with thin carved spindle posts in the railing. Just love it. And down the street there's a church with a lovely nursery, day-care centre in the building. It's almost at the corner of Bonita and River Streets, just north of your parents' place. Oh, Simon, just wait till you see it." Her enthusiasm was infectious.

"Marjorie Wallace, you are making me so excited for you, and proud of you!"

"Thanks, Simon. But there's more... I've chosen a name for the baby."

"You know the gender, now?"

"Not yet, but..." she wondered how he'd feel about her decision.

"I decided to choose a *nickname* to suit either a girl or a boy. The formal names would, of course, be gender appropri- ate." She braced herself and continued. "I focused on names to honour Carlos...uhm, regardless of any paternity *speculation*. Which is not an issue. Carlos was a good man, and a friend to me, too. Whatever the future brings, I feel my child will forever be connected to your family, Simon, as I am."

"Well, I'm speechless," Simon admitted. His knees turned weak. "Let's hear it then."

"The baby will be called, *Charlie*. Officially: Carlton, if a boy, Carlotta, if a girl."

At this point, Fiona appeared stunned, the reference to *paternity* cut like a fresh wound. And then some. Marjorie's *implications* confused her.

Upbeat at all costs, Simon raised the perspective with "How lovely, Margie!"

His changing reality was heading in the right direction. This, he felt, was a big deal — Marjorie's sharing openly with him.

He sensed her resolve and happiness. Perhaps, with a bit of luck, he could contribute to keeping it in this positive vein.

"Now tell me *your* news, Simon! I've been hogging all the news-time."

"No rush, it's okay. But you might find it surprising, if anything," Simon spoke in a measured way. "I was actually *shocked*, Margie."

"So, what's up, Simon? Do tell, mister!"

"Mom got her DNA done. It seems, like you, Margie, I'm *biracial*."

"Oh, my goodness, tell me more!" Marjorie practically choked as she gulped a swallow of tea to brace herself.

"Mom's line of relatives on her *mother's* side came from Black slaves in the South. She found albums she hadn't looked at before. Lots more to discuss, at another time, Margie. Mind blowing stuff. And, while I'm at it, are you sitting down for this?"

"Of course, I'm sitting...but still, BIG WOW!"

Simon then delivered his other piece of big news.

"On my *dad's* side of the family, long story, but we discovered dad had an *indiscretion*, you might say, years ago, and I have a *sister*!"

"Oh, I don't believe it." Her voice dropped, then rose. "How do you *know* it's true?"

"*That* I'll tell you when we get together. But it's true, alright. She's in Naples now, has even met Dr. Jim, and the *two of them* have already developed a beautiful intimacy. Hit it off, right away, a natural pair! Her name is Frieda. She's European. And, if my dear mom had not been doing volunteer social work at *KOH,* we'd *never* have met Frieda. The ways of our amazing world. I'm still shaking my head," Simon confessed.

"You're not kidding, Simon. *It is* mind-blowing!! I turn my back, and all this happens! So, when are you taking me on a proper date? We need to share time together and you can fill me in with more details. Can I just say how much I miss you and the gang? Specially the kids, of course!"

"I'll make some dinner reservations at a nice hotel in Toronto, and text you right after. In the meantime, you text me if you come up with other ideas, have other preferences. Oh, also, when you move back to Naples, Margie, and have your baby, if you still want to date me, I'll take you out on all the dates you wish. In fact, I'll even bring my own *babysitter* for Charlie." Simon grinned and gave Fiona a conspiratorial wink.

Fiona left her chair and rushed to sit on daddy's lap. She piped in, "Oh, Margie, I would even be able to *walk* over to your place anytime for babysitting!"

Upon hearing the word *walk,* Kent raised his head and barked. And Prudence circle- danced in front of him. Her vigorously, wagging tail smacked Kent in the mouth.

Happy days returned to Hackberry Road in Naples.

THE END

ACKNOWLEDGMENTS

GRATITUDE is the word which first comes to mind. Feeling grateful to family and friends for their support. I include those folks (several writers) on Instagram who offer encouragement and enthusiasm. These positive vibes, so needed, especially during the last few years living through a pandemic. Example: @marcandangel.com (best source of inspiration & common sense).

Thank you to my sons and their partners. Oliver J. & Elaine Gleeson offered comfort and stability in town. Doctor Joe, and Sandra – supportive from a distance – raising questions to consider in my manuscript. And Tommy, often my 'go-to' son for computer glitches.

Sue Koziey-Kronas, a cousin, an early beta reader, helped me focus my direction. I welcomed her kind and astute advice.

Grandson Obie (Oliver Bram) Gleeson worked on moving my design elements to the correct locations.

Granddaughter Alice J. Gleeson provided me with the watercolour painting (based on my photo) of the house on the front cover. I appreciate her unique technique and time spent.

Thank you to Catana Tully, author of *Split at the Root* for sustained friendship.

Thank you to lifetime friends, Toni McDermott, and Judy Nydegger for the feeling of home.

In addition, I want to acknowledge several traditional novelists who (unbeknownst to them) had a huge impact on my material: Diana Gabaldon, Nancy Horen, Stephen King, Alexander McCall Smith, Alice Munro, Elizabeth Strout.

Thank you to my family doctor: Dr. Renee Graice for keeping me healthy, and for her enthusiasm for me as a writer!

There are many more people who deserve a mention, but lacking space here, I keep them in my heart and prayers.

Special mention: Antanas Valys (cousin); Richard Van Westen (dear friend, Rudy)

ABOUT THE AUTHOR

Sylvia Valevicius is a former secondary school teacher of English and dramatic arts. A graduate of University of Toronto (B.Ed.) and McMaster University, Hamilton, (BA. MA.) Over the years, an occasional actor, known as Joey T. Oliver. Now, Sylvia creates books, reads plenty, and writes book-reviews. (Amazon; Goodreads; and Verdant Isle Production on FB) She enjoys Latin jazz, sacred choral music, dramatic films, fitness-walking, and foreign-language study as a fun hobby. She loves both *Toronto Blue Jays,* and the *Toronto Raptors,* but most of all her *family,* with its variety of cool grandkids.

Social Media sites:
Website: *whoissylvia.net*
Instagram: *@sylviamvalevicius*
Twitter: *@Jtosnest*
Facebook: *Verdant Isle Productions*
Sylvia currently lives in Oakville, Ontario